DIVER

DIVER

A Royal Navy and commercial diver's journey
through life, and around the world

TONY GROOM

SEAFARER BOOKS
SHERIDAN HOUSE

© Tony Groom 2007

Published in the UK by Seafarer Books Ltd
102 Redwald Road • Rendlesham • Suffolk IP12 2TE

Second impression 2008
Third impression 2008

www.seafarerbooks.com

ISBN 978-1-906266-06-6 paperback

A CIP record for this book is available from the British Library

Published in the USA by Sheridan House Inc
145 Palisade Street • Dobbs ferry • NY 10522

www.sheridanhouse.com

ISBN 978-1-57409-269-1 paperback

A CIP record for this book is available from the Library of Congress

Photographs not otherwise credited are copyright of the author,
or from private sources and used with the photographer's permission.

Cartoons on pages 200, 267 and 310–313 by Chris Drake

Editing: Hugh Brazier

Design, typesetting, maps and diagrams
not otherwise credited: Louis Mackay

Text set digitally in Proforma

Dedicated to the diving fraternity in general.

*In particular to Charlie Smithard and Taff Rees, of Fleet Team 3,
who survived the Falklands Conflict but not the coming home.
Both died within a few short months of their return.*

Britain lost 255 men killed in the conflict.

*Since then, unofficial figures from the South Atlantic Medal
Association suggest that at least 264 Falklands veterans
have committed suicide.*

Foreword

Throughout my career in the Royal Navy I have had the privilege and honour to work with a number of Mine Clearance Divers, and each time I have been struck by their supreme levels of professionalism and dedication. Underwater bomb disposal, often in the cold waters and zero visibility of the seas and ports around the UK, is not for the faint-hearted and often requires levels of courage, stamina and sure-footedness that exceed those expected in other military disciplines. Such a hazardous lifestyle creates bonds amongst its proponents that are exceptionally close, along with a unique and highly developed sense of humour (you have been warned!). The demands of commercial saturation diving are no less rigorous. In this book Tony Groom provides a fascinating, no-holds-barred account of his remarkable life and of the world of professional naval and civilian divers. His story is gripping, humbling and highly amusing in equal measure – all the more so for the matter-of-fact manner in which he tells it. From clearing unexploded bombs lodged in ships during the Falklands War, to hair-raising exploits in the oil fields of the North Sea, he shines a light on a calling that demands the coolest of heads and extreme courage. I strongly commend it to anyone with an interest in extraordinary human endeavour or the sea.

Admiral Sir Jonathon Band KCB ADC
First Sea Lord and Chief of Naval Staff

Preface

In my ten years in Her Majesty's Royal Navy, there was never a boring moment. I joined at the tender age of seventeen, and had qualified for basic diver by the age of eighteen. I was then shipped off to sea aboard one of the Navy's smaller minehunters, for what should have been a year's draft. However, my term aboard the *Kirkliston* was cut short. I was accused of being a modern-day Fletcher Christian, cast out as a mutineer, and sent back to diving school.

I didn't know it at the time, but being in effect sacked from my first ship early was a blessing in disguise. To punish me, the Navy saw fit to fly me halfway around the world to an island paradise in the South Pacific, with orders to blow parts of it up. Every boy's (and man's) dream.

Eventually, coming home a tad worldlier, I joined the globe-trotting Fleet Clearance Diving Team in Portsmouth. I decided it was time to advance my skills and take an intensive seven-month course to become a Leading Diver. Then, to put some of my new-found skills into practice, I joined the Portsmouth Bomb and Mine Disposal Team, where I gained a great deal of experience, mostly of blowing things up. We would drive around the country picking up all sorts of ordnance, washed up, fished up, sometimes even dug up.

Having escaped sea for three years, I was on someone's radar for another sea draft. HMS *Bronington* was my next ship. Prince Charles had left when I arrived, but he would come to sea with us every now and then, 'just to get away from it all'. Having survived the year on the *Bronny* without being cast adrift as a mutinous dog, I went back to the Fleet Team.

During all these generally positive experiences, there was never a hint that I would be going to war. Never for one moment did I think I would find myself sitting alongside live unexploded bombs during an air raid.

World War II was long gone. The end of the Cold War was fast approaching. So who would have given a second thought to a tiny piece of news in the bottom corner of the broadsheets?

> **March 19, 1982**. A group of Argentine scrap metal merchants working in South Georgia, in the South Atlantic, is escorted by some Argentinian military personnel. Britain calls Argentina to remove the military personnel without delay. They receive no response.

Hardly anyone took any notice. Even the British government saw nothing to overly concern them. Where was South Georgia anyway? I would soon find out.

My war took longer to get over than I realised. I thought I was fine, but looking back now I see that I wasn't 'all there' for a number of years afterwards. I saw and experienced things I will never forget, things I think about to this day. Things that make me appreciate everything that I have, with my wonderful family and close-knit circle of friends. Some, who were just unlucky, who were simply in the wrong place, never got to have an adult life, a wife, kids, the things we all take for granted.

This book is not meant to be precise. Not every date, time, casualty etc has been exhaustively verified. A large part is about the Falklands conflict and is taken from the diaries I kept on a daily basis. If I heard, for example, whilst aboard a ship that there had been fourteen casualties somewhere, that is what I wrote down. Now some might say I should go back and check every figure. That would mean tampering with my diary and it would take away the realism of what it is like to take in a war as it goes on around you. What you hear on the day of a tragedy is never going to be completely correct. That is the same in civilian life as well as the military, whether it's a train crash or a ship sinking. So

I'm not going to do it. The diaries are published as I wrote them, sometimes under duress, sometimes under tables, but word for word they are what I thought, wrote and knew at the time.

Some names have been changed, for obvious reasons, some haven't.

Everything I have written in this book is true and happened. I've not tried to build any parts or characters up, or shoot them down. I've tried to tell it as I saw it. There is more on my website at **www.deep-sea-diving.com**

Acknowledgements

I would like to thank Jonathan Veale (WriteAway.co.uk) and George East for their constructive criticism, which kept me on the straight and narrow. I am grateful to my parents and my sister for their belief from the beginning. I have been helped by a multitude of 'Bubbleheads' who rallied round, namely Chris Drake (who drew the cartoons), Mark Cheeseman, Chris Christie, Pete Digweed, Mick Fellows, Phil Kearns, Mac McCabe, Grahame Murr, Mick O'Leary and Jan Sewell. Thanks also to my publisher, Patricia Eve, whose enthusiasm possibly eclipsed even mine, and to Hugh Brazier and Louis Mackay – what a team. Sally Attard of the BBC and cameraman Neil Paton planted the seed of an idea which grew into this. And a special mention to Commodore Michael Clapp, who really got the ball rolling to get me published. He had utter belief in getting this story told, and has now helped me win twice – once in a war and once with a pen!

Most importantly, I thank my Marie and Harvey, without whom I would be lost.

Tony Groom
October 2007

Bluff Cove, 1982

Always, you hear them well before you see them. The chopper appeared out of the night with no navigation lights, and landed on the helideck. I thought I'd seen all the helicopters out here, but this one was matt black, with no markings.

This was an opportunity I was not going to miss. We chucked our two hampers aboard, containing the diving sets and explosives, then clambered aboard this 'Special' Sea King. I managed to bag a seat as close to the cockpit as possible as I loved to sit near the front of these choppers and watch the pilots at work. When we left the deck of the *Fearless*, we were off at full speed; looking out to the front of the chopper I could see we were already doing 110 knots.

The pilot dropped the chopper nose down until we were just skimming the waves. We headed southeast for the head of San Carlos Water and were over the beach in less than a minute. The big side door of the chopper was open and the door-gunner had his deck-mounted GPMG (general purpose machine gun) constantly panning around looking for a target. Fast and low was obviously the way to go. There are lots of little brooks that flow down from the mountains of the Falklands, which over millennia have carved natural furrows into the landscape. It seemed to me this 'Special Ops' pilot was doing his utmost to swing the body of the airframe around the spinning rotor and keep the bulk of the aircraft in the lowest of these contours of the terrain. There was a full moon, but I can only guess that the pilot had night-vision gear on, or we would have flown headlong into the first mountain.

When we did approach the first, near-vertical, face, I thought he'd left it too late. At the last minute, he threw the aircraft up onto its tail and into a steep climb up the side of the mountain, at which point you are driven deep into your crude, webbing seat. As we came to the top, there was that gut-wrenching moment

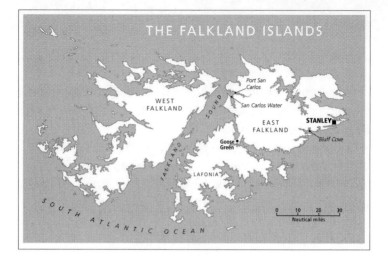

THE FALKLAND ISLANDS

Port San Carlos

WEST FALKLAND

San Carlos Water

SOUND

EAST FALKLAND

STANLEY

Bluff Cove

FALKLAND

Goose Green

LAFONIA

SOUTH ATLANTIC OCEAN

0   10   20   30
Nautical miles

when you are weightless, like cresting a humped-back bridge; the nose went down, the tail rose, and we were racing down the other side. We all seemed to be carrying the same nervous smile, as in 'Wow!' It was a bit like being on a roller coaster. No one was yet screaming, though.

Then things got more exciting. As we came down the other side of the mountain and levelled out, the rain had gone from light drizzle, at take off, to a torrential downpour. Looking into the cockpit, I could see the wipers were thrashing back and forth as fast as they would go. I then saw and heard alarms going off, flashing lights, and then the quick movement of fingers over the controls. All of a sudden, the pilot threw the aircraft up on her tail to stop her as quickly as possible. The airframe vibrated and groaned as the rotors bit into the turbulent air. As our forward motion slowed, we levelled out and there was a very heavy bump. We were on the ground. These boys knew how to fly. They also made it quite apparent that we needed to be on the ground real quick.

Now, I'd looked at the chart previously, and I couldn't believe we were at Bluff Cove already. We weren't. We'd had a major systems failure – or at least a warning of one.

This wasn't fun any more. Only three weeks previously 22 men had been killed cross-decking from HMS *Hermes* to HMS *Intrepid* (18 from the SAS) by what they think was a bird strike. It was a bit like an animal sanctuary down there, a bird paradise.

I couldn't hear the pilots, but they had what looked like a heated debate whilst looking at each other. There was lots of nodding, then shaking of heads and gesticulating. While this was going on I looked across at Mick Fellows. He wasn't that happy either. Then a gloved hand gave us a thumbs up, the revolutions increased, and we were up and on our way again. Now everyone on board was definitely nervous. I could see lads looking around for an oil leak or feeling for any odd vibration. 'If he was now a bit gentler with the controls, it would probably be fine,' I thought. None of it. Straight back to full speed. If anything, he was even more aggressive. I knew we were a bit late now but we'd be even later if he insisted on flying like Luke Skywalker. At some points the ride was really violent, but it was equally clear this guy was good. We then had a second near-catastrophe.

The pilot threw the airframe to the left and right, and then left again. One of the SBS troopers was standing up, leaning on the port forward door, weapon in hand, as nonchalant as you like, when the door popped open. He was half in and half out. The ground was just a blur in the dark as it tore along underneath us, the racing air outside tried its utmost to pluck him from the safety of the fuselage. Rain was now hitting me in the face through the half-open door and the wind buffeted around the inside of the chopper. The Sea King crewman, as quick as you like, leapt forward and unceremoniously grabbed the middle of the trooper's tunic and wrenched him back in. He closed and clipped the door, and wagged his finger at the trooper in a mock telling-off, as if to say, 'Don't lean on the aircraft doors, sonny!' After the initial shock, we all had a nervous giggle. The SBS lad wasn't laughing though; he sat on the aircraft floor with his head between his knees, taking deep breaths and shaking his head. These guys had been heavily involved in all sorts of sneaky stuff from well before the invasion, yet he had nearly died doing a back flip out of a helicopter – before we'd even got to the job. Had he fallen out, we would never have found him. He was fully camouflaged up and looked just like Falklands foliage.

What was meant to be a ten-minute flight turned out to be more like half an hour because of all our unplanned activities. We finally landed, shaken but in one piece, at 20:15. As soon as we touched down the pilot looked back at us and grinned.

'Yeah, that was hilarious,' I thought. To this day, it was the most eventful flight I have ever been on. All this was just to get us there. Next, we had the simple task of undertaking a mine clearance dive, in the dead of night, with one bank still in enemy hands ...

Make like Jacques Cousteau

'Diving is a cold, wet, and dirty business, son. What did you do before you wanted to be a diver?'

'I was a shithouse attendant in Alaska, sir!'

When I joined up at HMS *Raleigh* in November 1975, I was a little over seventeen years old and I was going to be a diver. I'd decided.

Basically, when you join at *Raleigh* you are a seaman first, as in pulling ropes and doing up shackles, but as a baby seaman, there's a lot of cleaning and painting also. Then, if you pass basic training, you go on to learn your trade: Radar Operator, Torpedo and Anti-Submarine (TAS ape), Mine Warfare (Muppet) or others, perhaps even a Bubble Head (Clearance Diver).

My very first day there, our class Petty Officer (PO) said, 'Right, who's the wannabe bubble 'ead, the one who's just come from *Indefatigable?'*

'Me, sir?'

'Right. You know how to march. You're now class leader until you fuck it up. Where's Fuller? You are deputy class leader. March the class off, Groom.'

Dave Fuller and I were best buddies from boarding-school days at the *Indefatigable* (*Indy*) and chance had us join the Navy on the same day, and be in the same class again, only unlike boarding school, this time our roles were reversed. I was class leader and he was deputy. The Navy knew the *Indy* was a nautical boarding school so we already knew the orders to march and the correct way to do it. I didn't really need or want this. In my class of 40, there were some lads who had changed over from the Royal Marines, who I thought would make much more suitable class leaders. There were lots that were in their mid-twenties (old timers), and here I was having to take charge of them all at the age of seventeen.

If you told them you were there to be a diver, as I did, they gave you that knowing smile and asked you to pick a second and third choice. 'Just in case you are disappointed and don't make it.' Well I could understand that for other people, but not for me. I was only going to be a diver, you see. 'But you need to choose something else, just in case,' they kept saying.

What's the point? I'm here to be a diver; nothing else will do. Tears, near-death experiences, hypothermia, hospital, you name it, I couldn't do anything else, because that was what I was in for, that was what I was going to be. Simple as that. Non-negotiable. The others can fail. I'm not going to.

Some had seen Jacques Cousteau on the telly, cave diving or dolphin stroking, and probably thought, 'I'll try it. If not, I'll do something else.' But the reality of jumping into the water in Plymouth Dockyard soon puts you right.

The first time I'd taken an 'aptitude test', to see if I would cut it, was at HMS *Raleigh* about a week after I'd got there. I'd never even gone sports diving, never been under water apart from holding my breath – which I'd done hours of in preparation.

I was a bit worried about the diving part. Would I even like it? That was the least of my worries. Before you even get near a diving set in the Navy they try their level best to put you right off the very idea.

Over the ten weeks you're there doing basic training, I would guess some four or five hundred lads must've thought, 'I'll give diving a go.' Now, they aren't going to give them all a dive, so the first thing they have to do is get the numbers down to a manageable level.

Around 50 went on the same first day as me. The first thing you do is go for a nice long run. When we got back we were already down to 40. Then it was beasting time: sit-ups, press-ups, star jumps, burpies and lots of shouting that seemed to reduce our numbers again. Next, it was time to put you in a diving suit. Mine I remember was a size 5. I am 5 feet 5 inches and then, at the tender age of seventeen, not exactly built like a brick shithouse. But I was fit, thanks largely to a year at boarding school with a merciless PE teacher. When I eventually started the course I was wearing a size 2 dry suit. So this one was more than double my build – there was room for a few guests inside with me.

'Wow! Maybe we're going diving!' The next couple of hours were spent in pairs, doing fast dresses until our fingers bled. To the shout of 'AWKWARD!' each pair had to get into their Avon neck-entry rubber dry suits within two minutes. 'Not fast enough! Get undressed. Try again. And again.' You don't just have to get into the suit through a seemingly impossible-size rubber hole, you must also get your neck rings, neck seal, and neck clamp on both divers, before you are finished. You keep this up until there is a more realistic class size. Then we must be going diving? When I did eventually manage to get into my enormous suit, I looked like I had elephantiasis-legs. There were rolls and rolls of spare rubber down by my ankles. Our numbers were down to around 15–20 already, and it wasn't even lunchtime.

Next we went for what they called a mud run. How it got that name, I'll never know. 'Run' should not be in the title at all.

Mud-drowning, mud-crawling, flailing around in the mud in a gasping manner with no sense of purpose or direction. I know that is too long a description but it would be about right. Another thing that has always bothered me is, why are Navy bases always so near to thick black stinking mud anyway? Is it by design, or just sheer luck?

Running as a group, we came across the mud flats, and luckily for us the tide was right out, leaving a majestic swathe of the black, stinking mess for us to go fall and get stuck in. There was a distant post stuck out on the horizon.

'Right!' said the Chief. 'Run round that post, and back here in ten minutes. Any questions? GO!'

After only ten or fifteen minutes, people to my left and right who, not long ago, were sane, reasonable, normal-thinking young men, were turned into gasping, heaving, black, lumbering wrecks. Some of the aptitudees seemed to be going in one direction only, and that was down. I was making light work of it compared to some and I was going full speed to nowhere. My titanic efforts didn't seem to be appreciated at all by my superiors and they seemed intent on encouraging me on and on to even greater endeavours. I thought my lungs would burst.

There was one lad who was a little too stout for all this strenuous activity – and after getting less than 50 yards into the course he just could not move, or breathe. It was not unlike a climber who cannot go up or down. The thing I discovered over the years was, if you stop, you've had it. The longer you are in one place, the more you sink. If you stop and sink you have to put your weight on one leg to lift the other one out of the mud, to try and stride forwards. If you do this, your standing leg is now stuck, so you have to put weight on the other leg to lift your standing leg, and so on. Exhausting isn't the word for it: it drains you to the very core. In the end they threw him a line and someone had to tie it under his arms and the instructors pulled him unceremoniously over the mud, mostly on his back, but sometimes on his front, to safe terra firma where he lay for an age trying to catch his breath. His face was the colour and shape of a bruised tomato and he kept getting long, black muddy worms out of his nose and sinuses. Somehow, the mud seemed to have even got behind his eyes! The instructors barely looked down at this dying swamp monster at their feet. I never saw him again.

An hour in, and even I was not faring so well now. I had rounded the post – but I was dying. The life would get sucked out of you, you get so hot because your body heat cannot escape the neck and cuff seals. Because you are watertight, you are of course airtight. It's like being a boil-in-the-bag meal, like being poached alive.

My huge suit was in charge of where we went, not me. I had to take about three steps before the boot parts of my suit, which were dragging a way back behind me, started to move. I was actually standing in what would be the knees for a six-footer. You see, the suction of the mud just takes your boots off. Sometimes I would drag myself forward that one more step, so they could see I hadn't given up, and the boot, stuck in the mud behind me, would lose its fragile grip in the suction and come flying at me like a catapulted welly, which is what it was. Just over halfway around, I was constantly getting abuse and being told to give up but, being 'very determined', I was not going to. I was eventually dragged out close to the finish by one of the 'Second Dickies'. I'd not given up, that's what had kept me there. I'd survived. That part anyway. Only one racing snake had managed to complete the mud run.

The Navy's excuse (or reason) for inflicting these mud-flailing exercises was, 'If you attack an enemy shore it may be muddy!' It might not, I thought.

At lunchtime, eating my bag meal, I thought long and hard about my career choice. Do I want to spend the rest of my Navy time, and maybe the best part of my life, doing this? Being abused, being boiled, then cold and wet (if I ever get diving), and getting shouted at? Why not become a radar operator or maybe a store man, always in the warm, or get into mine warfare?

I couldn't do it. That would be giving up, that would mean they'd beaten me. No way is that going to happen. They had passed, so would I.

The afternoon got considerably better. We started in the classroom, a heated one at that, learning a little about what being a clearance diver entailed. Some seemed shocked to learn that the 'clearance' part of the title meant clearing bombs and mines. One lad just stood up and said 'Fuck that!' and walked out. The instructor didn't try to stop him. He didn't bat an eyelid; he just carried on with his lecture. That must happen a lot, I thought. It was the 'racing snake' who had left the building, the only one to complete the mud run. So, fit as you like, muscles in his piss, yet he was still not quite all they were looking for. They were after people with that, but they had to have a bit extra as well, a bit of mental strength. It was a mental and physical breaking-down process. It was a means of getting the men that 'might' have the right stuff, onto the course.

I don't remember how I dealt with this shocking piece of information. I think I let it just wash over me. It wouldn't be me dealing with bombs and mines anyway, would it? If I did eventually pass, I would only be eighteen; they wouldn't let me do anything like that. That would be a chief diver's job, and they all looked about 50 to me. We weren't at war with anyone and didn't look like we were going to be. And anyway, didn't we have minehunters, minesweepers? If we did find anything, wouldn't we just blow it up? It wouldn't be like the old black-and-white war movies, sitting alongside a bomb trying to defuse it, would it now? I had no idea then how wrong I was.

I took a bit of time to look around at my assembled trainee accomplices. Some were a lot bigger than me, tougher looking, and a good deal older. How was I going to bear up against this lot? They all had thick, black mud in their hair, in their ears, everywhere. I didn't realise I was as bad myself until I got back to my class and spent an hour in the shower.

Just as I started to settle in the classroom, the chief diver shouted, 'AWKWARD!' and we ran outside into the rain and started getting into our dry suits again. There was no way any pair could dress each other in less than two minutes. I and my partner did manage to get it down to just over three, though I couldn't see how it could possibly be done any quicker. The chief didn't seem to think that was very good and made his feelings known by giving us 'a little run in the mud', as he put it.

By 5 p.m. I was shattered, completely drained, but my spirits rose when the four of us left were told to come back the next aptitude day, a week later. Crikey, I'm virtually there. They gave me all they had and I took it, I was meant to be a diver. The four of us were invited back for 'diver training 2'. We were given a sheet of paper with 'DIVER SIGNALS' written on it and were told to learn them by next week. Hey, maybe we'll be going diving then?

A signal is a tug on the rope attached to you telling you what to do, or telling the surface what you are doing. Four pulls (tugs on your line): *come up* – or, if you give it, *I am coming up*. Two bells: *swim away from me* (or *I'm swimming away*). Bells are given faster than pulls, and given in groups of two: ding ding ... ding ding ... ding, equals five bells, i.e. *come back in*.

First dive

If at first you don't succeed, redefine success.

The following Thursday I was adrift by about three hours, be-cause the Torpoint ferry over to the diver training area wasn't running due to bad weather. By the time I got there I'd missed the morning's lectures and some beastings. The chief diver mentioned that everyone else had managed to get there, and I should have tried harder. I didn't see the value in pointing out to him that they were already living over this side of the water, so had no ferry to miss. Two other potential divers had obviously passed their first aptitude test somewhere else and had joined us for DT2. We were a nice round six again.

The weather was obviously my fault so I was severely punished and given circuits. So I missed even more lectures. A circuit involved climbing to the top of an Olympic-height diving board, jumping off with your fins under one arm, then putting them on in the water and swimming, on your back, across the water, climbing out and running around the edge, back to the board, and off you go again. I was joined on this exercise by the two lads I had never seen before. I don't know what their crime was; breathing loudly was enough to get you ten circuits.

The art of jumping from such a great height without hurting yourself was explained to us on the top board by one of the Second Dickies (a qualified diver, who helps the chief). You don't jump out, you just step into nothingness. They don't build you up with the first board, then the second, then the top. Straight off the top you go. If you can't do it, go away. You must hold your neck rings down with one hand and your suit inflation bottle round your waist with the other and tuck your fins under your arm. Heaven help you if you lose a fin.

The other bit of important information, which the guy behind me must've missed, was, look at the horizon, straight ahead. If you look down, you will fall forwards; if you look up, you will fall backwards. Oh, and keep your legs together, for obvious reasons.

'Got it? Right, off you go.'

It's a long fall and it buckles your knees when you hit the water. It seems a long time before you pop up and you shout 'WELL!' I survived my first jump and was wallowing about trying to put my fins on in the water, but at the same time watching the new guy at the top of the board. He was thinking about it for too long. He kept waving his foot over the edge of the board, then bringing it back. It looked like he was practising some kind of bizarre goose step. The SD was shouting encouragement in his ear, such as: 'If you don't want to do it, don't do it, you big tart. Right, this is it, last chance, step out, or go back down the stairs, **NOW!**'

He waved his foot over the edge again, looked down and jumped. Because he was looking down and jumped, not stepped, he started to fall forwards. To try and stop this he was running in mid air. This didn't seem to be working too well for him, so he put both hands out in front of him, in a sort of sleep-walking pose, dropping his fins. I almost didn't want to watch. Not only was he going down leaning forwards, he had let go of his neck rings. He hit the water, slightly feet first, with his legs open. His neck rings smashed him in the jaw, jolting his head back, but from where I was swimming, that was the least of his worries. It looked to me like he would probably never have children. When he eventually surfaced, there was claret everywhere from a nasty-looking gash under his chin. I started to head back to help him, but was told in no uncertain terms that it was nothing to do with me and I'd best get myself across the other side. As I headed off on my first ever circuit, I could hear him whimpering, maybe even crying. When they dragged him out of the water he had both hands over his crotch and there was a big bit of floppy flesh under his chin. So we were back down to five again.

It turned out that the whole morning I had missed was about how to operate the diving equipment we'd be using that afternoon. 'Well, all you've got to do is breathe, isn't it?' I could do that already.

I was hurriedly dressed-in that afternoon and given a run down about what to do if this or that happened, but to be quite honest I was a bit like a rabbit caught in the headlights. I was going to do my first ever dive! I was finally going in the water, to go under it. I jumped in and immediately realised, this ain't going to be as easy as I thought. Two huge great big bottles on your back pulling you backwards, lead weights pulling you another way, fins that seemed to stop you from moving your feet as you would like. A nose clip over your nose to stop you from breathing

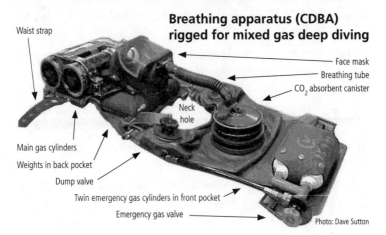

Breathing apparatus (CDBA) rigged for mixed gas deep diving

Waist strap

Face mask

Breathing tube

CO_2 absorbent canister

Neck hole

Main gas cylinders

Weights in back pocket

Dump valve

Twin emergency gas cylinders in front pocket

Emergency gas valve

Photo: Dave Sutton

through it, something you had done all your life. And a face mask covering your face and a hood covering your ears. Essentially all your senses are taken away in one fell swoop. All you have left is your vision – until you leave the surface, that is. Had I ever been diving in the Red Sea, or even in a swimming pool, I'm sure the degree of difficulty would have been considerably reduced.

I had been promoted to a size 4 suit, which, being only twice as big as I required, was much better. On its down side was the fact that the suit was used every week for aptitudes and mud runs so it had no owner or carer; it just got used and abused – and wrecked. In fact, you could say it was a suit of holes, with some rubber in between. But that was part of the game of getting people to give up, wasn't it? Get them cold, get the numbers down. But that won't work with me, will it? Because I'm going to pass, you see.

Splash – and I'm in. I'm in Plymouth docks. It's not quite (in a French accent) 'As Philippe and I make our assent to zer Calypso, zer visibility is only one 'undred feet, so, we both had torches!' Jack Custard for you there! You can't actually see anything at all. It's black-black, and by that I mean black as in pushing your palms into your eyelids, under the bedclothes, at the bottom of a mine shaft, at night. No light gets there. That kind of **BLACK**. You can't see your nose clip at the end of your nose. Not even the slight tint of pink you can see with your eyes closed tucked up in bed. Nothing.

Now this can be a little disconcerting at first. You may get a signal of four bells to go left. Which way is left? Left – to you – may be right to the surface crew, because you don't know which way you're facing to start with. You guess and invariably set off the wrong way, so you get the signal again, only with a touch more violence. It says on your signals sheet that you should turn and face your life line, then go left or right. My problem seemed to be that I kept losing the life line whenever I got a signal. If you didn't answer your signal pretty smart you got it again and again, often taking it out of your hands, which by the way were so cold you could barely feel the rope.

You have nothing to go by – well, look back at the bank. But which way is that? What I'm trying to say is that you have no bearings at all. You have a bit of knowing which is up and which is down because of gravity, but even that is reduced under water. Without light, sound, vision or touch, we're buggered.

Anyway, after a while, maybe half an hour, I was soaked and freezing because of my holey suit but the panic and disorientation had diminished a bit and I hoped I was stumbling the right way when ordered. Two bells: *face your life line and go out.* Off you go. One pull: *stop.*

Now as I said I missed the important stuff about how the air set worked and what to do in the event of running out of air. Whilst getting a quick brief before entering the water I caught something about 'equalising'. I thought he meant my ears.

As you go down in the water you have to equalise the pressure between the inner and outer ear, via the Eustachian tube, the only thing separating the two being a piece of thin and delicate skin, the eardrum. In the Navy you wear a nose clip for this because the face mask covers your whole face down to your chin. Everyone has felt this pressure on the eardrum just going down a few feet in the swimming pool. A descent of only six feet will compress your middle-ear space by 20 per cent, and that equals pain. Keep going down without blowing on your nose and you will burst your eardrum.

Alas, he wasn't concerned with my ears at all. In the Navy if you are wearing an air set you don't have a gauge on it. You start your dive with only one bottle open and breathe normally until it goes tight and starts to run out. If you then open your other full bottle, the air between the two 'equalises' – you can hear it very well under water as a tinny hissing sound. The sound will diminish, and then you close the valve. Now you have two half-full bottles. You breathe down the one bottle again and do the same when it gets tight. Now you have 'equalised twice'; you have about a quarter of your original air left and you come up. Simple!

Simple if you know this, anyway. I missed all that because I was unable or unwilling to control the weather, and was late. The opening of the valve action was never really relayed to me. I know that, because I wasn't there to hear it. Nobody thought about that bit. I learned later that everyone else had the opportunity to wear the diving set, breathe from it and equalise it in the classroom, more than once. Good for them.

I guess I was about 100 foot out on the end of my life line when my air started to go tight. No, it can't be, the chief diver said it should last about an hour. An hour hasn't gone by already, has it, and anyway they would call me up (four pulls), wouldn't they? At this point my short life flashed before me.

I am allergic to not breathing, so I did what all rational, normal-thinking people would do in this situation. I panicked.

I grappled around for my life line and finned and pulled myself to the surface as quickly as I could. You are of course meant to breathe out on a controlled slow ascent or you may give yourself a bend or burst a lung. But I had nothing to breathe out, my lungs were already empty. Air hunger, or the urge to breathe, is undoubtedly one of the strongest human reactions we have and you *will* take extraordinary actions to encourage breathing again. Helped by a large portion of adrenalin, induced by the probability of dying, I hit the surface going full tilt and removed my mask in one swift movement. In fact, the mask may even have been off before I broke surface. Anyway it was in a thoroughly unprofessional manner.

I was travelling so fast I reckon I came out of the water up to my waist. That first intake of breath, that sweet taste of air and water was the deepest I have taken so far in my 48 years. Gasp doesn't do it justice and I don't think you can write down the noise I made. It was probably along the lines of the mating call of a randy caribou. The thing is, I hadn't counted on gravity taking a hold of me now I was briefly out of the water again, but it did, and as I came down from my breach, I went under again. This was becoming intolerable.

The divers on the quay saw this thing shooting out of the water then disappear again, and without pause for thought, three of them began pulling me in, hand-over-hand as fast as they could.

The line I was attached to was tied in a bowline on my shoulder, and with my weight-belt and bottles on I took off at breakneck speed towards the jetty. My speed was so great in fact that a bow wave formed around my head and I found myself under water and unable to breathe again. Only this time I was at a loss as to what to do to remedy the situation. As I began to pass out I just hoped I would soon be at the jetty. In fact I later found out that it was my swift and un-cushioned arrival back at the concrete jetty that might well have knocked me out.

I came to lying in the recovery position and vomiting over some big boots. The chief diver was obviously worried about me and showed his concern by yelling into my face, 'You've not equalised once yet! Why didn't you f***ing equalise?'

'I did clear my ears, chief.'

'Not your f***ing ears, you muppet, your bottles, same as we did in the classroom this morning.'

'I wasn't ... HEEEAVE ... here this morning.' As the second helping of dockyard water and leaves and oil came up and out of me all over the chief's boots, I could see the dawning of realisation move over his face. 'Shit! This was my fault.'

To give him credit, though, his attitude immediately changed from one of anger to apologetic concern. I was wrapped in a blanket and given hot tea and whisked off to sick bay, where I spent a day on bend watch, to see if anything developed, and three days in hospital, throwing up dockyard flotsam and jetsam, and very nearly got back-classed from my basic training unit to boot. If that happened, I would have to drop back two weeks and start again with a completely new intake.

I went back the next week though and tried again, and every week for the next ten weeks. Why? Because I was going to pass, is the only answer I can give.

Bluff Cove, 1982

As soon as we hit the deck, our protectors fanned out to make a secure perimeter around the chopper. We jumped out and made our way to the farmhouse at Bluff Cove. Contact was made with the Officer in Charge of the Second Parachute Regiment, who were still staying hidden as they passed through the area. At the farmhouse we were introduced to the farmer. He was questioned at length about enemy activity in the area, and whether he'd been down the path to the beach. He said he'd been 'banned' from going down there since the occupation, so could not be sure if the path and beach area had been mined. He was pretty intent on telling us his story and he was not happy that the Argentinians had killed around 150 of his sheep and torn down mile after mile of his fencing to use as firewood – probably to cook his sheep.

He was keen to help us in any way he could, and offered us a lift down to the beach area in his Land Rover. We jumped at the chance, saving ourselves the hike down the track, in the pitch black, with all our gear. I remember we got dressed in our dry

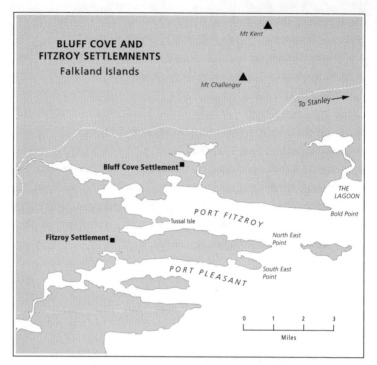

BLUFF COVE AND FITZROY SETTLEMNENTS
Falkland Islands

Mt Kent

Mt Challenger

To Stanley →

Bluff Cove Settlement

THE LAGOON

Bold Point

PORT FITZROY

Tussal Isle

North East Point

Fitzroy Settlement

PORT PLEASANT

South East Point

0 1 2 3
Miles

suits outside the farmhouse, dumped our clothes in the hampers and did another quick check of our equipment. We also talked through every possible scenario for something going wrong. We had done this at the planning stage, but did it again here. One thing we foresaw was if one of us had a problem with our diving gear whilst we were over by the enemy bank. It was decided, if we had to surface and were not able, or well enough, to swim back across on the surface for whatever reason, we should make our way to the enemy beach, and hide up as best we could, until the SBS and Royal Marines effected our rescue. On hearing this, one of the sergeants didn't say anything, he just started to camouflage our faces. He used just the black, to take the sheen off. There would be no need for the green where we were going! There is nothing like a bit of war-paint to give you a false sense of bravado. Every sinew of my body was alive and tingling. It was exciting. I had my camera with me and thought of having a photo taken, but then I thought. 'What if the flash goes off?' How embarrassing would that be? Not to mention possibly life-threatening.

The Royal Engineers went ahead, sweeping the path with 4C mine locators, with some of the bootnecks (Royal Marines), and the SBS lads.

The farmer then hooked up a trailer. We chucked our hampers on the back in amongst the straw and farm paraphernalia, and jumped on ourselves. It was a bit like a motley crew from a set in *'Allo 'Allo*: 'Now listen very carefully, I shall say zis only once!'

The farmer got his instructions to move off slowly and only drive where the Royal Engineers said had been cleared. Then, with no headlights on, he started up the Land Rover and we moved off towards the coast. This was quite a change from the helicopter ride, driving at a snail's pace with the two REs just in view. I can remember sitting on the back wearing my dry bag, holding on to the hamper, which had enough plastic explosive in it to blow us all to kingdom come, thinking 'if we do drive over a mine, we won't know anything about it anyway.'

It was a stop-start, slow journey down to the beach. When he stopped, we unhooked the trailer and the very nervous-looking farmer turned his Rover around and went back to the house.

Now, it was just us. My eyes were immediately drawn to the jet-black east bank opposite our position. Was there anyone watching us? 'Still in enemy hands' kept echoing in my ears. It was spooky, to say the least. Every now and then, the moon would light everything up, including us. In between the bright moonshine, there were bouts of heavy rain.

The Royal Engineers cleared an area for us to work in, then moved along the high-water mark and told us if we stayed in those areas we would be fine. The SBS and marines took up defensive positions around us and the boathouse.

I went behind the boathouse for a PDP (pre-dive piss – 'piss' can be exchanged for 'poop' as and when), always a good idea before going diving. As I did so, something really made me jump.

I almost stood on an SBS trooper; he was right under my feet and yet I couldn't see him. Even after he spoke to me from his prone position, I still couldn't quite make out his outline. I'm sure he would have let me know, though, had I got him wet.

Billy and I got our final brief from Mick, familiarised ourselves with the area we were to be searching and went to get dressed-in. I checked my gear in the pitch black, on the back of the trailer, for the umpteenth time, threw it over my head, and walked to the water's edge. Billy and I checked each other out and walked backwards out into the estuary. You walk backwards so as to make no splashes with your fins. Because of the type of mission this was, it had been decided from the beginning that we would have no standby diver. This is usually unheard off. We would just have to look after each other.

The reason you do so much training, so many times, in the dark, in the rain, in the middle of the night, when you're dog-tired, etc, is so that when you have to do it for real, it just happens. No one really needed to speak to each other, we just got on with the job at hand.

It was approximately 23:00 on the night of 4/5 June 1982. If only my loved ones could see me now, I thought.

School? Not for me thanks

School was never really my cup of tea. I know a lot of people say that, but with me it was true. Some of my school reports are hilarious. One of my favourites was my 1973 Physical education report from Monks Park School comprehensive in Bristol, where my mum and dad's hardware shop was. This one was written by our PE teacher, Mr Gillespie.

SCHOOL REPORT FOR TONY GROOM age 14

Tennis: This game should be played with hand and body, not mouth, which is what Tony most frequently uses.

Soccer: Could do very well in this game, but seems quite happy with his present standard, works better when cornered like a rat.

I was unfortunate enough to be at secondary school in the early seventies, when I can only think the government was 'experimenting' with lessons. Some other examples include:

Home Economics [cooking?]: Tony's work lacks concentration. He could do better. He has been unable to take part in four practical lessons, due to failure to bring in any ingredients.

Typewriting [yes, typewriting]: Tony isn't fair to himself. He has ability but sees no sense in learning typewriting. I understand his father agrees with him on this issue. He can produce good work, when the mood takes him. Room for much improvement in behaviour.

Indefatigable

This wasn't for me. I needed to be outdoors doing things, although you may not think that looking at my sports report! One day a lad in my class, called Ian Dawes, brought in a flyer for a nautical boarding school. I had already been in the sea scouts, but now I was in the sea cadets. I don't understand why, as it's not in my family at all, but I was fascinated with water and the sea. I was always happiest near water. I could stare at it for hours, wondering what was underneath it. Obviously, the glossy pamphlet looked fantastic; these boys didn't seem to be doing maths or typewriting or learning how to cook. They all seemed to be playing sport, sailing, rowing and canoeing, all the things I wanted to do throughout my school days. I wanted to be outdoors, on the water.

I took it home to my parents and said I wanted to go to the TS *Indefatigable*, in Anglesey, north Wales. I prepared myself for a fight, as they obviously wouldn't want to lose me at this young and tender age.

They couldn't believe their luck. I was a pain at home and at school. They immediately gave up golf (mum), and smoking (dad) and spent the money they saved on my boarding fees. Within a few months, we were in the car and driving for what seemed like ever, to north Wales. We drove down a long, sweeping driveway, to this magnificent-looking huge castle-type house. I got out and stared at this splendid place. My parents got out my bags and simply said, 'Right, we don't want to embarrass you in front of all the boys, so we'll be off. Bye then!' and they were gone. That was it, I was here for three months before leave. I waved as they tore up the driveway and I had my first pangs of, 'I hope I've done the right thing here.' I wandered in through the huge oak doors on my own with a due amount of trepidation.

To my astonishment, we did have to do maths, English, technical drawing, science, history and even RE. We were also lucky enough to have one lesson every morning at 06:00, given by the physical education officer, an ex-Marine who did a nice line in torture. At this god-awful time, every single morning, winter, rain, snow, spring and summer, he would have us up doing what he called LAD, which stood for lateral, abdominal and dorsal, the muscle groups. He would basically beast us, so that we would be quiet during breakfast. Being a nautical school, we used nautical phrases and terminology wherever possible. After all, we already saw ourselves as old sea dogs. Beasting is one such term, used across the forces, and it means to inflict pain through physical exertion.

He had many other ingenious way to inflict pain, too many for me to mention here. One was boxing. He would organise it differently, though. Two onto one was one of his favourites. Another was the biggest boy against the smallest, the fittest against the fattest, or 'c'mon lads, it's Fit v Fat today,' as if we were meant to get excited by it! I was queuing up to get beaten by him once, having committed the heinous crime of smuggling a miniature transistor radio to bed, in order to listen to Radio Luxembourg. I remember watching the look on his face as he lashed the poor lad in front of me. This was the first time in my life I'd realised people could get fun out of hurting someone else. His eyes were wide, his face was flushed and he was positively revelling in it. He was undoubtedly a sadist, although I was, as yet, unable to give it that name.

I then watched him more closely when his boxing lessons were going on. He had one of his favourites one day, 'Big v Small'. He would watch avidly as one of the smallest boys would get a beating, and he would never step in until there was blood, tears or even a knockout. Being a tad short myself, I was always determined not to give him the satisfaction he craved. I fought my corner to the point that one of the most keenly anticipated fights was usually between me and the only French lad at the school – known as Johnny Onions! He was a six-footer even then at barely fifteen. I, however, was not. I used to have to go for body shots and be very wary of his long reach. I would knock him out, and he me. I once hit him with an uppercut to his stomach and he threw up over me. The thing is, we didn't even dislike each other, but once we were in the gym it was no holds barred. If I lost, I would have to get badly hurt before it was stopped. Even if I did lose, I would make a point of not letting the pain show; our PE officer loved that. Some lads would cry – wimp out, if you like – and he gave them a right old rough time. If Johnny lost to a much smaller kid (me for instance) he would just put him in with someone else until he learnt his lesson. What lesson? Well, I guess it was not to lose. Some say it's character-building. Maybe, but I wouldn't want my son to go through it.

I now know that these bouts, and my experiences at boarding school, had a more profound effect on me than I ever realised. It may have given me my attitude that I will not be beaten, physically or mentally, and never give up. This belligerence would serve me well later in my life, especially in the Navy divers courses.

Babies course

There are old divers and bold divers, but no old, bold divers.

Having passed out of my basic training at *Raleigh*, still class leader, and being told I'd done enough to grab a place on the next babies course, I was thrilled to bits. I knew there was more torture to come, but I was ready for it now.

I found myself getting a train home to Bristol, carrying my worldly possessions, and a ticket to HMS *Vernon* in Portsmouth, the home of Navy diving since its inception.

I was now a seaman, according to the Navy, despite only ever having been to sea (well, Plymouth Sound) in a bosun's dinghy. Much more important to me, I was on the next Basic Divers Course, Elementary Diver 9 (ED 9). Two of us, out of those hundreds that tried in my ten weeks at *Raleigh*, got on course.

I arrived at *Vernon* in January 1976, and met the nine others who had made it to the beginning. I thought I'd done the hard part – I'd passed aptitude. I was in for a shock. The next three months are a bit of a blur.

When you are not either diving or sleeping, you are running, eating or, it seemed to me, being punished for something you 'might' do in the future and they may not have the time to punish you for it then. A sort of pre-punishment. You would often wake up, or come round, in the water, thinking 'What happened here?'

There is a lovely week they call 'live-in week' that you have on course at Horsea Island in Portsmouth. Horsea is a nine-metre-deep, mile-long lake, built by convicts and prisoners of war in the late 1800s. It was originally built to fire and test torpedoes in strict secrecy. So where better than an island, concealing a hidden lake? The week is about time in the water. That week alone I did in excess of 1,500 minutes. By the end of course, and over the years, I got to know the bottom of that lake far too intimately.

Basically you dive and sleep (a bit), dive and sleep. Throw in a few circuits and mud runs and various other means of torture and, in essence, you are either under water or it seems you are just being punished for choosing this career path.

One instructor of mine, a PO Brian Hutchinson, would wait at the bottom of the board, and as you came panting round on another circuit he would ask, 'Tired?' To which you have only two answers. You could say, 'Yes sir,' to which he would reply, 'You're not fit enough then, are you? Round again.' On your next circuit, in answer to the same question, you might try, 'No sir,' to which he would say, 'Not done enough then, have you? Round again.' Until he got bored or someone passed out.

We had a telegraph pole called George that took at least six men to carry, and it had to go everywhere, and I mean everywhere, with us, including loo, shower, and sometimes the top of the board to throw off and do a circuit with us. At least two course members had to be with it – sorry, him – at all times.

The night we finished live-in week, we even had to take it to the Harbour Lights pub near Horsea Island. The landlord, I remember, never batted an eyelid. 'Oh, it's the divers with George,' as we wandered in with a telegraph pole and ordered eight beers (the thinning-out process was still ongoing). We then had the dubious pleasure of being 'allowed' to buy our punishers a pint. Each one of us was allowed to buy them one, in fact.

On course, the 'circuit' was the second task of the day. Obviously you have to take part in a 'wake up!' run, with George on your shoulders, first. However, I have a slight admission to make here. I didn't really find running with George any harder than without him. It could be because I am only 'four foot and a fag paper', as I seem to remember one chief diver referring to me. Which essentially meant that the taller lads on course took most of the weight. But I never once complained.

When you were meant to be asleep one of the staff would throw a thunder-flash into the sleeping area, sometimes more than once a night. A thunder-flash is essentially a huge firework, a banger, about the size of the biggest Cuban cigar. This was in the days before 'Health and Safety'. In the confines of the small sleeping area, it provided the same decibel level as a stun grenade that the SAS use to momentarily incapacitate terrorists – usually prior to filling them full of holes. For us, it was designed to stun us into an automated response, to move ourselves at the highest rate of knots in the general direction of our diving gear. If they were feeling good or had a hangover, they might just shout 'AWKWARD!'

From the bang, you had fifteen minutes to be blowing bubbles, i.e. swimming up the lake. It's not long.

This gear isn't just air/scuba equipment that you chuck on your back. These are oxygen rebreathers called CDBA (Clearance Diver's Breathing Apparatus); it's not particularly complicated equipment but if you prep it wrong, you will die.

It is a set that gives out no bubbles. Handy if you're trying to blow up someone's ship or simply don't want to be seen. How can you not show any bubbles? You have to breathe out, right? I'll try and explain.

Very simply, when you breathe using CDBA, for example on an attack swim, you would charge your cylinders with pure oxygen. Breathing in and out through a large false lung on your chest (just like a large flexible bag), your body uses some of the O_2 (oxygen) and as you move and work, your body changes some oxygen to CO_2 (carbon dioxide).

A rebreather takes the CO_2 out of the O_2 you exhale, by way of you breathing through a canister full of sodium hydroxide. If you then suck this O_2 in again the CO_2 is 'scrubbed' through the canister and you can essentially breathe the same O_2 again and again. Obviously the oxygen diminishes over many breaths, so you squirt in a little more oxygen as the bag deflates. That way, you can recycle most of the gas. Nothing is wasted or has to leave you, hence no bubbles. Got it? Also, because you can rebreathe it, you need less of it.

Two large 'air' cylinders will give you about an hour on a shallow dive if you're breathing normally. Two of our O_2 cylinders are not much larger than say the old glass Coke bottles, but because you rebreathe most of it, it'll last you an hour and a half.

You have the added advantage of having no need for a demand valve, as on a scuba set, so it's also silent. Handy if you're diving

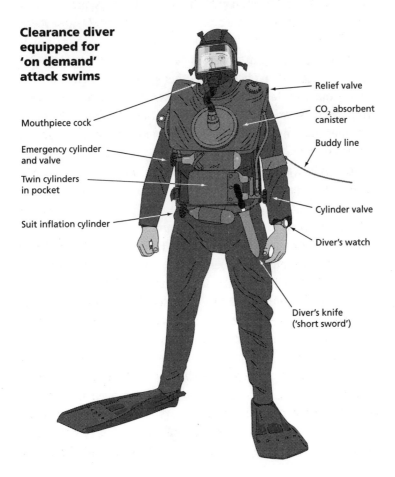

Clearance diver equipped for 'on demand' attack swims

- Relief valve
- CO_2 absorbent canister
- Mouthpiece cock
- Buddy line
- Emergency cylinder and valve
- Twin cylinders in pocket
- Cylinder valve
- Suit inflation cylinder
- Diver's watch
- Diver's knife ('short sword')

on an acoustic mine (one that reacts to the sound of a ship). Also every metal part is made of brass or copper. Handy if you're diving on a magnetic mine (one made to react to the magnetic field a ship makes). If you're diving on a contact mine, you just need to be careful not to touch it in the wrong place.

So we're smaller, hence lighter and faster, sleeker, quieter, we have a better endurance, and we are invisible from the surface. Perfect. I was always 100% confident that nobody would catch me if I didn't want to be seen.

Bang! (goes the thunder-flash to wake you up). Instantly you're off, running to the water's edge at Horsea Island, and you start to prep your gear for a dive. You pour your CO_2 absorbent into its canister, check your gear, get into your dry bag, which has to be within two minutes per pair of divers (we could do this easily by now), then check each other's gear, etc. Then you have to sort out your target in the darkness, take your bearings with your compass and enter the water and be gone within fifteen minutes, and not seen again until your objective is reached.

After three months' hard graft, and I don't know how many hours underwater, I was qualified as a clearance diver. I was a CD! I went straight to the diving stores to draw my wetsuit, and because it was only available once you had passed CD, it was like a badge of honour. All new divers would wear their wetsuit all the time, no matter how cold it was. The novelty does wear off, though, eventually. I was very proud of qualifying, and rightly so. There have been literally thousands of men and boys failed along the way, trying to get one of these standard helmet bubble-head badges. From now on, wherever you went, where there were general service sailors, they would all refer to you as 'Deeps'.

Bluff Cove, 1982

As soon as I left the surface, all the nerves left me. Yes, it was night and a dodgy situation, but this was where I was at home, comfortable, underwater, I was on autopilot. Even if we came under attack now, we were safe. Unless, of course, we were to find mines.

We swam up and down designated courses, using a combination of underwater compasses, depth gauges and swim lines. The visibility was quite good, maybe three metres, although the amount of long kelp usually stopped us from seeing that far. I had been in the water possibly an hour and covered a huge distance back and forth, back and forth, to the enemy bank and back.

While I guess I was about 50 metres south of the boathouse, I swam into something which made me jump. At this point,

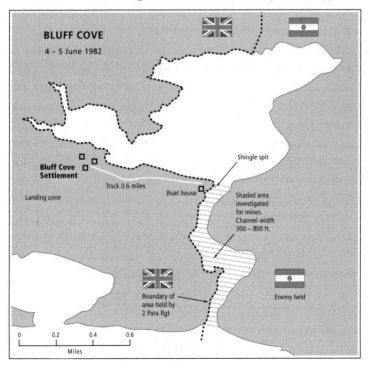

there was no moon at all and I was reluctant to use my torch for obvious reasons. It was about a metre and a half long, cylindrical and metal.

You are trained at the Defence Explosives Ordnance Disposal School (DEODS) to build up a mental picture of whatever it is you are inspecting, especially for situations like this. You might have to surface and tell your supervisor what it is you've found, even if you can't see it. If you're in some far-flung swamp water, with no visibility at all, it's no good coming up and saying 'I dunno, but it's got spikes sticking out of it, it's round-ish and it's ticking. Might be a novelty clock, chief!'

It was too large a diameter to be a ground mine. Unless it was 'improvised'? It had two ridges running round the casing. I moved to one end and gently examined that. We are taught and trained to memorise the lengths of various parts of our bodies (stop it!). From my fingertips to my opposite shoulder was 1 m 10 cm, which was how long it was, and from fingertips to armpit was 60 cm, which was the circumference of the object. The picture I was building in my mind was of a huge bean-can shape. I was just considering whether to signal Billy to come over and have a look, when I found two caps at one end: one large and one small. Mines have caps like this for the fuses. This was not a mine, though, I was pretty sure of that. I went round to the other end and found a long pole sticking out of it. It was an oil drum with the bottom cut out that had been filled with cement. I relaxed and tried to swallow – I say tried, because I realised I had no moisture left in my mouth.

I was just about to swim away from it, with a sense of relief, when Billy swam into a view. He had probably come over to see why I hadn't moved at the other end of the swim line for so long. He was facing the other way when I grabbed his arm to show him what I'd found, Billy spun around like he was being attacked by a shark. He jumped so much it made me jump. I wasn't the only one that was nervous, then? We both just stuck our thumbs up at each other and carried on our search.

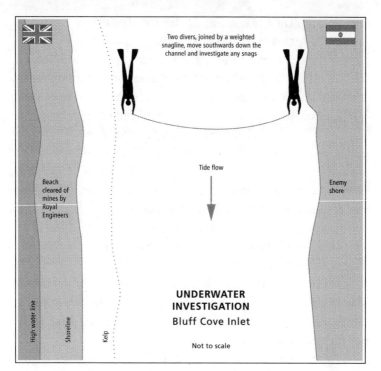

Two divers, joined by a weighted snagline, move southwards down the channel and investigate any snags

Tide flow

Beach cleared of mines by Royal Engineers

Enemy shore

UNDERWATER INVESTIGATION
Bluff Cove Inlet

Not to scale

High water line

Shoreline

Kelp

At the halfway point, we overlapped search areas with each other. I did a bit of his, he did a bit of mine, making doubly sure nothing had been missed. Before coming up, Billy and I used the CD's method for having a sneaky look around, with only a few inches of your head showing above the water. After all, we had no idea what had taken place while we'd been in the water, if anything.

Billy and I both clipped into a buddy line, making us joined together by our right arms. It is a three-metre-long thin piece of cord designed so you always know where you partner is. I was diver one and had the swim board (known as the driver) so I was the one to go up and see if the coast was clear. I released a tiny amount gas from my diving counter-lung by crossing my arms over my chest and slowly squeezing it, and very slowly made my way up to the surface. You do this so as to come to the surface in a very slow and controlled manner. Billy holds the buddy line, which is attached to me. He watches and feels me go up to the surface, very slowly.

For the diver underneath, it is a bit like flying a kite. You are his kite and he is watching the line and feeling your every move. He then releases a small amount of gas, so as to make himself slightly heavy. As just the top of my head and my eyes break the surface, I can slowly spin around, searching the water horizon. I look round at our beach and can see nobody – but then they would be taking cover. When I'm satisfied the coast is clear, I simply lift my right arm under the water; Billy feels this on the buddy line and slowly pulls me back down to his depth. Thus, when somebody breaks surface, or leaves surface, there is no splashing, as white-water and noise would stand out a mile on a moonlit night such as this.

Totally satisfied the area was clear of obstructions and mines, apart from the oil drum and a sandbank running out from the boathouse, which we made note of, we made our way back to the west bank of the cove.

When we came out of the water, it was about half past midnight. The rain had stopped and it was a clear moonlit night. We packed up our gear and made a silent exit back up the path towards the Bluff Cove settlement. The farmer and his wife then made us tea and steak sandwiches. To this day, it was the best sandwich I have ever tasted. She was turning out tea by the bucketful for us and the members of 2 Para.

They then showed us to our quarters, which turned out to be a sheep-shearing shed where the farmer usually kept his flock. When we got inside, it was clear that 2 Para were already there and had bagged the best spots. I wasn't going to moan – these boys had been ashore a lot longer than us – but it made our camp beds on the vehicle deck of HMS *Intrepid* look positively luxurious.

I spoke to a paratrooper called Baz who had just come off sentry duty, I think, and was bedding down next to me. These guys had, of course, already lost friends and their commander,

Colonel H Jones, and they'd been in a good few fire fights and seen plenty of action. I asked him about the Argies. Had he spoken to any? Were they as young as reported?

He said, 'Yeah, some are young, but we've got two seventeen-year-olds in our platoon. So what am I supposed to do, feel sorry for 'em? They're seventeen when you catch 'em, but they still shoot at you. The ones we caught round here were a right bunch of fat bastards. They've killed and eaten enough sheep to keep Tesco's going, that lot. We don't trust any of 'em. I've seen 'em raise a white flag, then you move forward and they just open up at you again. We don't give 'em the chance now, if there's some in a position, we take it out, waste it, grenades, the lot. Sneaky fat bastards.' Then he turned over and went to sleep.

I don't remember much about the night, only that I slept like a log. Why shouldn't we? We had paratroopers and SBS as lookouts. You cannot really get any safer.

I think all the nervous energy had done me in. Also, what with air raids, diving at night, Exocet warnings, working with live new bombs, not to mention our general workload back on the ships, we hadn't had a full night's sleep in weeks.

The Second Dickie
– a star in his own eyes

The PO or Chief Diver was not alone in his duties to make our life a misery. Each course had two or three Second Dickies to help him out. These were usually recently passed divers, or divers 'on route' to a ship, or waiting for a course of their own. They had passed their course, and like us all, theirs was harder than yours. Amazing as it may be, nobody knows anybody that has ever had a harder course than them. Every course has to endure stories such as, 'Now in our day, we had to do circuits until one of us died, and then he was thrown off course for being lazy!' Or, 'We had to do circuits in full Standard Brass Hat and Lead Boots, with the face plate blanked out, at night, if we'd been good!'

The SD's duties included doing standby diver and, more importantly, informing the Chief if any mistakes had been made by the course, resulting in a painful punishment recommended by the SD.

In the Second Dickie's eyes, he was looked up to by everyone on course, and he only punished you when you deserved it, in the full knowledge it would make you a better diver. He wasn't just a Second Dickie anyway, he was Assistant Instructor. He was a Greek god, irresistible to all women and, he suspected, even the Chief's wife. He was fair and just, and would never ask you to do anything he wouldn't or couldn't, willingly, do himself. He would prove this to you by coming on mud runs with you. Admittedly, he would wear a light, tight-fitting wetsuit on a boiling August day, not a baggy dry suit like everyone on course, so he would not be hot and restricted like you. This bit of vital information, I remember, passed me by whilst on course – until I became a model of what a Second Dickie should be after passing my own course. I was never cruel, but then I had been on the hardest course ever.

The SD is also aware that his high moral standards are secretly admired by his Chief. He knows that the chief wishes his own daughter could meet someone like him. Someone who has all the attributes and special qualities to go on and achieve the dizzy heights of 'Superintendent of Diving' one day.

However, in the Chief's eyes the SD is a posing, overweight, long-haired, lazy twat, who should never have passed for diver as long as his arse points downwards, and how he passed course is anyone's guess. If only they made the courses as hard as in his day! He is, of course, unaware that the SD is in fact 'doing' his daughter up on Portsdown Hill twice a week, when he thinks she's at piano lessons. He has to watch this moron as much as the class to make sure he doesn't kill himself, or anyone else.

As for the class, well, they just want to kill the jumped-up little know-all and then bury his dismembered body in the middle of the mud run somewhere near Portchester Castle. Then he could stay where he thought he was so at home, in the black stuff.

The daughter is in the process of selling her story to the Sunday papers.

Capnot

The diver's brain is a wonderful organ. It starts working as soon as you get up, and stops as soon as you leave surface.

As yet, I didn't have my new draft, so I worked at Horsea Island as, yep, a Second Dickie. I joined a legend of a PO diver by the name of Norman Slingsby. He was a huge great bear of a man, and could put the fear of God into his trainees just with his sheer size. He was about six foot four and fifteen stone, and somehow managed to get away with wearing a big gold earring. He seemed to have his own uniform code. Wherever he went, he had a huge diving knife on his belt, a combat jacket, and his white PO's cap at a jaunty angle on the back of his head.

He was a nice bloke, big Norm, and he and I would have a good laugh. It was mostly at our course's expense, though. When I joined him at Horsea Island, he had just started a foreign navy's course. He had been sent fifteen Ugandans, and told not to select them or see who might be a suitable candidate, but to pass them as ship's divers.

The ship's diver course is only four weeks long, and almost any other branch in the Navy could do it. For example, if you were a chef on a destroyer, your ship would need six or eight ship's divers. The idea being, if you're in a foreign, perhaps unfriendly port, or in times of war, and you suspect limpet mines have been placed, you can put in your ship's divers and at least find out.

They could also carry out simple repairs, or seabed surveys. It is by no means an easy course, and the pass rate was probably only 10%. The reward was extra monthly diving pay.

These lads sent over from Uganda hadn't done an aptitude test, they hadn't volunteered, and two of them couldn't even swim. Nevertheless, the Ugandans had paid the British government a lot of money to send back fifteen qualified divers, and that's what they were going to get, no matter how bad they were.

One of these Ugandan divers' names is indelibly burned into my consciousness. He went by the name of Capnot. Whenever you dress a diver in, you know if he is happy and confident. I'm sure it's the same in sports or scuba diving. You also know if he is scared out of his mind. You can see it in their eyes, and in their movements, and by the things they say. When you dressed-in Capnot, you knew he was scared. God never meant this man to go diving, and, to give him his due, he knew that. He had been 'volunteered'.

'An accident waiting to happen' could have been coined just for Capnot.

The first thing you do on your early dives is all your emergency procedures. Before we put any of these lads in the water, they had lecture after lecture explaining everything at least twice. We then did everything practically, as in hands-on, make them do it.

English is Uganda's official language, but there are also about 40 other languages spoken. When they spoke to you, or each other, it was a strange mix of English and Swahili. So how much they understood at any one time was difficult to judge.

When Capnot first jumped into Horsea Lake, it reminded me of a cat in water. He tried to jump in without his head actually going under, and d'you know, I think he nearly managed it. As we pulled him back to the ladder, he hooked his arm into the rungs and held on for dear life whilst I gave him his instructions.

One of the first drills involves flooding your face mask, then clearing all the water from it. These face masks are not like the ones you go snorkelling with that just cover your nose and eyes.

They cover your whole face, sealing around your forehead down on your cheeks and around your chin. The mouthpiece still fits in your mouth like normal, but you have to wear a nose clip in order to clear your ears.

The diver has to put his fingers into the face seal and let it flood up with sea water. Now you cannot drown like this, you just breathe normally. The water cannot go in your mouth, or up your nose because of the clip, but the number of people who freak out at this is amazing. It may be the claustrophobic feeling of the cold water on your face, or not being able to see with salt water in your eyes.

You must then show the instructor your face mask is full, go to the bottom, tilt your head right back and blow hard through your nose clip. If you do this, the air will force all the water out of the mask, you come up and show the instructor you've done it. Then, whenever you get water in, you know what to do.

Capnot's eyes are as big as ever while he is garrotting the ladder receiving his instructions.

'Got it, you fill your mask, go to the bottom, clear it, and come up with it empty, OK?' I say.

He nods. He then puts his head just under the surface and lets about an inch in, and looks back up. Norman and I shake our heads. 'All the way. Fill it all the way up!'

Eventually it is full, and he has kept his now magnified huge eyes open throughout (most people close them because of the salt). 'Right down to the bottom, and I don't want to see you again until it's empty. Leave surface!'

He puts his thumb up and pulls himself down the ladder, which goes to the bottom, only about five metres deep alongside the jetty, his life line being tended by one of his fellow reluctant divers.

At this point I go off to 'wet the tea' for all the 'staff', as I can now call myself. I come back with four NATO standard teas, and notice Capnot's bubbles still at the bottom of the ladder. 'Has he done it yet?' I ask Norman.

'Na, he hasn't come up yet.' All the rest of his class have done it and are doing some other drill. We go over and tell his tender to give 'The Cap' four pulls. He answers and comes slowly up the ladder, till his head is just above the surface. There is about an inch of air in the top of his mask, the rest is still salt water.

Norm starts to get cross. 'What are you doing down there? Get back down, clear your mask and come up and show me!'

Thumbs up, off he goes. We drink our tea and there is still no sign of him. Four pulls, up he comes, and it's about half full. You can now see the big white eyes in normal vision again, instead of magnified. He doesn't look happy. Nor is Norman now.

'Jesus Christ, man. What are you doing? It should take you thirty seconds; you've been in there fifteen minutes. You've got one minute, and I want that mask empty, got it? Get out of my sight!'

He nods somewhat reluctantly and disappears again. We are chatting away and forget him for a while. Then his tender shouts, 'Diver gives four pulls, sir.'

Ha, at last he's done it. He comes up holding onto the ladder. When he breaks surface we can see he still has a third of the water in his mask. This time he is shaking his head, the water sloshing about inside, making it clear he can't do it, and can't go on. He wants to get out.

'Get that useless twat out of there. In all my years, nobody's taken this long to clear his face mask!'

Capnot climbs out, takes off his mask and really doesn't look well to me.

'What's your problem, Cap? What is it? It's easy.'

Capnot lets out a massive burp into our faces, swallows hard and says: 'Please PO ... sir ... buurrrppp ... But I just can't drink any more!'

He hadn't been blowing it away through his nose clip at all. He had spent the best part of a quarter of an hour sucking in salt water round his mouthpiece and swallowing to get rid of it. I was dumfounded. I stood open-mouthed staring at this man. Where did he get the idea he had to swallow it from? How did he do it? I then started crying with laughter, as did the rest of his countrymen who weren't in the water. All discipline left us. I could barely operate as a human, the tears were streaming down my face. He looked ill, but was smiling, in a 'what? what did I do?' sort of fashion, which made it worse.

About an hour later he was sick in the galley queue, which started us all off again. He was still smiling as he was throwing up, which I'd never seen before, or since.

He did actually finish the Horsea Island part of the course without dying, but he had a few close calls even there. This was as safe as it got; next was open-water diving, sometimes at night, under ships, always in the tide, and pretty naff visibility. Norman would go grey before this man ever went home with a diving badge, of sorts. 'The Cap' hadn't finished testing us.

The Cap and deep dips

'You'll never make it out alive.'

'Bollocks! You're just saying that because no one else has.'

As part of their course, they also had to do a number of deep dives. Well, it was deep for them: they had to do some seabed searches at 30 metres.

We got them familiar with the Surface Demand Diving Equipment (SDDE). The big difference with this gear is that you have an umbilical up to the surface which supplies you with your air, instead of carrying it all on your back.

We went over to the Isle of Wight on one of the Navy's 70-ton launches, to a spot just west of No Man's Land Fort where it is possible to get 36 metres, and started diving over the stern platform.

Two of Capnot's class had gone down the heavy shot rope and done their circular search at 33 metres. Having done that, they then had to do a few wet decompression stops, more to get used to the idea of doing stops than because it was really required.

We had been fairly relaxed on a beautiful, sunny, and still day, until ... it was the Cap's turn. I, being standby diver, got myself completely ready in the sense that all I had to do was put my mask on and jump over the side. I hope I wasn't temping fate, but this guy had a way with him of making things go wrong. I asked one of his classmates if they were in any way bothered by Capnot's 'indiscretions' in the water.

'No,' he said, 'we like to have him on our course.'

'Why?' I asked.

'Because if someone is to have big problems, it will always be him!'

I think it made them feel safer having a swimming 'Calamity Capnot' around all the time.

He jumped over the side, with his partner, checked for leaks, and they left surface together. They weren't 'buddied up' together because of the fear of them getting foul around the down line. Their tenders then called out the depth marks that are on the hoses as they went down: 9 metres, 15, 18, etc. As they approached the 30-metre mark, one hose slowed down to stop at 33, but the other kept moving: 36 metres, 39, 42. We couldn't figure it out. Capnot was going deeper than the seabed. Could he have lost the down line and gone off down tide?

'Fifty-one metres, sir.'

'Right, hold him tight, don't give him any more slack, what's the daft sod doing now, digging bloody holes?' said Norman. 'Away standby diver. Tony, go and see where he is, will you?'

I jumped in and swam to the down line, ready to leave surface, when something caught my attention at the edge of my vision. I looked round under the launch's hull and there he was, hanging on to the diving tender's rudder!

Underneath him was 50 metres of his umbilical just hanging there, floating off down tide. He evidently didn't like the idea of going deep and dark. He rather more liked it up here by the surface, where it was lighter and warmer. So why not just pull the umbilical down from under the boat? Who is ever going to find out?

Eventually, later on in the day, I dived with him, to make sure we got his 30-metre dive ticked off in his 'to do' list. From the surface to the bottom, he never took his big doe eyes off me. Even though it was mid-summer and the vis was quite good on the bottom (about two metres), Norman gave me one of the Navy's big torches so that I could see Capnot, and he could see something. We thought it might put his mind at rest. On the bottom, I gave him the torch as I undid the swim line so that we could go out and do our pretend circular search. I had the swim line in my hand and looked back at him, I was motioning him to follow me to the end of the line, but he had the down-line rope in the crook of his arm and I could see that at this moment in time it was the most important thing in his life. I took the torch off him and shone it into his face with the idea of motioning to him we were supposed to do a circular search. I looked into his face mask, and he was bricking it, I mean absolutely terrified. There were beads of sweat pouring down his forehead and into his eyes. All he could do was blink, and nod at my every instruction. He was, I'm quite sure, completely unable to let go of the bit of rope, which in his mind was all that was keeping him from certain death. After a while I just gave up, and we spent our fifteen minutes or so just standing on the bottom. Whatever I did, his eyes followed my every move. When we got our four pulls to come up, I had to start moving his hands, one above the other, to give him the idea that it was time to go, it was all over.

They were supposed to do three 30-metre dives each, but I said to Norman, 'I don't think he's got another one in him.' So we cooked the books to give him his three dives. At the end of the week when he saw on the blackboard that he'd done three, his face lit up, and all his buddies patted his back. Next week was SBS: ship's bottom searches.

The SBS week was arguably Capnot's finest hour. It can be

inherently dangerous, simply because you cannot come straight up, having a ship above your head, and possibly a diver each side of you, attached to a line. The most responsible and arguably difficult job, doing ships' bottom searches, is the keel man. The ships the courses practise on are usually old destroyers and frigates waiting for the scrap yard. They may be up the harbour for years before they finally get made into razorblades. That means they are covered in weed and sometimes long kelp.

If you have, say, six divers on your search necklace, the first one to leave the surface stays on the keel. The rest of the divers then follow his lead. If he loses the keel you are all possibly searching the wrong part of the ship. We made Capnot keel man, and he pulled it off. My God, maybe he is finally getting it.

On their last night dive, up harbour, Capnot was given the easiest job – best not tempt fate, we thought. The other six divers on his course left surface, all clipped to the search necklace, and started searching the destroyer's hull. The Cap was surface swimmer. His job was to wear a snorkel and to swim along the surface, holding the search necklace, right next to the ship's hull, watching and feeling the divers beneath him. He was a sort of indicator as to where the search team had got to. What could possibly go wrong? He didn't even have a diving set on! What we didn't know was, he had watched all the other divers clip on to the necklace, and so he did as well. He would have got away with it, had the keel man not lost the keel and started going up the other side of the ship looking for it.

We were sat in the boat, chatting, watching Capnot making his way down the ship's side, when all of a sudden he left surface. One minute he was there, then he was gone, no bubbles (as he wasn't even wearing a diving set), nothing. 'AWAY STANDBY DIVER!' Luckily, I was at immediate notice anyway, as I always was when he was in the water. I put my mask on and was over the side in one movement, headed straight for his last known position. I ducked my head down and swam like mad down the contour of the ship's hull. About five metres down, I could see him facing me, swimming for all he was worth back towards the surface, but he was still going down. The other six divers were, of course, following the lost keel man, and Capnot had no chance of pulling them all the way he wanted – no, needed – to go. I swam straight past him and cut the swim necklace, grabbed him by his suit neck rings, and dragged him back to the surface. Again, he seemed fine, and the fact that he had so very nearly drowned himself didn't seem to have dawned on him. He wanted to stay in the water, and look for his divers. We dragged him out and into the boat apparently none the worse for wear. We then shot round the other side of the destroyer and found the keel man floundering about on the surface with the other five coming up behind him, all looking lost, which of course they were.

We started the search again with a new surface swimmer, and Capnot just sat in the rubber boat recovering. One of the other second dickies was trying to explain to him what he had done wrong. 'You shouldn't have been clipped to the swim line, you're meant to hold it in your hand, you dickhead! And anyway, why didn't you cut your line once you'd been dragged under? That's what you've got this huge great big f**kin' diver's knife for!' – taking it out of its sheath and waving it under his nose.

Norman Slingsby was sat next to him. He couldn't even look at him, he was so angry. I was sat at the back of the Gemini, still dripping wet and at immediate notice again. I could just see Capnot looking sheepishly down at his side, just the other side of big Norman. It all went very quiet in the boat for a while. What I couldn't see was Capnot in deep thought, bouncing the sharp end of his knife on the rubber tubing of the boat.

All of a sudden, there was a loud 'pop-rip-splash!' He had lifted his knife just too high, and instead of bouncing on the rubber tubing it went straight through. The tubing split, and Norman and Capnot went straight over the side, re-enacting the perfect sports diver's water entry method, feet swinging up into the air over your head. This was not a great problem for the Cap in his dry suit. Norman, on the other hand, was in his daily working gear, combat jacket, boots and cap. For the briefest of seconds, all that was on the surface was Norman's white PO's hat, floating all alone – until he broke surface and was reunited with it. The silence of the night was shattered with the foulest language you have ever heard, and a sort of flailing of arms and gnashing of teeth. Norman wasn't actually trying to swim after the Cap so much as just thrashing the water. Capnot was somewhat lucky in that we were close to the boarding stage of the destroyer. He swam to the boarding stage and ran up the stairs to the deserted destroyer, and hid. The rest of us left in the boat dragged Norman's huge frame (complete with a somewhat moist cigarette still clamped between his lips) back aboard the sorry-looking deflated Gemini. We still had two tubes blown up, so finished the dive, picked up the six other men, and went up the stairs of the destroyer shouting Cap's name.

It took about an hour for Norman to calm down, and for Capnot to come out of hiding. It was about one o'clock in the morning before we got back to *Vernon*, and there was not a dry person on board, including Norman. It was about a week before any of us dared bring up Norman's 'duck diving' incident.

This guy Capnot had so many dices with death. I have forgotten more than I can remember. If he is diving, anywhere in the world, and still alive, I would be amazed. Capnot! Where are you?

Faslane

When I left Big Norm and the school in September 1976, I had a short stint up at Faslane Naval Base on the west coast of Scotland. This is where the big nuclear submarines as well as the smaller diesel boats and hunter-killers would berth. I got a lot of diving in up there and learnt a lot. We would dive almost every day. I did my first screw change there, that is, changing the propeller in the water whilst alongside, without the need for dry-docking. Any damage to a submarine's propeller may cause cavitations, which will make it noisier and change its signature tune, so making it easier to detect. It is rare that you will ever see one of these propellers: the navies of the world jealously guard the secrets of them, as they are what drives a submarine quickly and quietly through the water, and they are absolutely critical to a submarine's stealth.

I could have enjoyed my time on the team, but there was a diver called Skip who took an instant dislike to me. In fact, he seemed to have a problem with just about everyone who was below him – in rank, I mean. Apparently, he told someone that he didn't like the way I walked. I thought putting one foot in front of the other was fairly rudimentary, but obviously not.

We had finished course, so had no need for circuits and beastings and being treated like children. Indeed our chiefs and POs on the team didn't do it. Skip, on the other hand, would take it upon himself to chuck thunder-flashes in our sleeping quarters and shout 'AWKWARD!' He would give us circuits and generally be a right pain in the arse. I think, basically, he was just a bully.

Once I saw him giving one young lad a torrid time for weeks until the lad gave him some cheek back. Skip then said to him, 'Give me your hands.' Then, with his hands outstretched and his fingers splayed, he got the lad to interlock his fingers with Skip's, and proceeded to bend them backwards until he was on his knees and begging Skip to stop and let go.

The fact that we were younger than him and baby divers was a good enough reason in his eyes to treat us any way he wished. Luckily, I was on my way out of there fairly quickly to join HMS *Kirkliston*, but that wasn't the last time I worked with Skip. When I finally caught up with him again, I was a little older, a little wiser and definitely a little stir-crazy, and what I remembered of his finger-bending trick would stand me in good stead.

Mutiny on the *Kirkliston*

It is better to remain silent and appear dumb ... than to speak, and remove all doubt.

The war with the Irish Republicans was raging at the time (1977). On board HMS *Kirkliston*, we had been at sea for a long old stretch around Northern Ireland. We would dive to search the undersides of fishing boats, big cargo ships, harbours and anchorages. We would also dive to investigate suspected 'drop points'. This could be anywhere, but often it was where ships would slow down or stop, for no apparent reason. I'm not really at liberty to tell all the things we did find.

Most of this was to try and stop the IRA from smuggling in weapons, ammunition and explosives. The minehunters were ideally suited to this sort of work, being small (440 tonnes), and shallow draughted: ideal for sneaking up shallow rivers or close to the shore. Whilst on these patrols, they would also carry a contingent of marines, a sniffer dog and his handler and an intelligence officer. They also carried a full team of divers, as part of the crew.

There was an officer on board, and he and I never saw eye to eye. Let's just say he was a 'Darling'. We clashed instantly. I was obviously going to lose, being just a baby diver at the time and he being an officer. But that didn't stop me trying to get even. I could wind him up easily, and did so at every possible opportunity. Well, he deserved it: he had no sense of humour or any common sense. The chief stoker on board put it perfectly one day – 'He could tell you the square route of an orange, but he couldn't peel the bastard!'

On board we had someone dubbed the 'Phantom Piper'. A pipe is any message relaying information around the ship's speaker system. The Phantom would make pipes at all times of the day and night, some of them not exactly being as legal or as informative as they should be.

He would make pipes such as: 'Able Seaman Rocket, missile deck ... at the WHOOSH!' [rush]

Or, 'R.E.M. Brant, paint store!' [Rembrandt]

One pipe that really seemed to get under Officer Darling's skin was 'DARLING ... you make my ring sting!' It was said in a sort of James Brown voice with an American accent. It would happen in the middle of the working day, alongside, and at sea. Sometimes it could even happen in the middle of the night. As soon as it happened during the day, he would be out on deck, looking around suspiciously at everyone – although a lot of his accusations seemed to be aimed at me, for whatever reason, I can only guess.

The pipe would be made, then he would be out. I would be maybe in the diving store on deck, and he would come rushing in.

'Did you hear that, Groom?'

'Hear what, sir?'

'That pipe, that's what.'

Innocently, I would reply, 'Pipe, what pipe, sir? What was it about, sir?'

He would just give me a knowing evil look and be off out and stopping the next person he met and asking them the same thing. I wasn't the only one in on the jolly jape. Almost everyone would say, 'No sir, I didn't hear a pipe, sir.' A wind-up such as this could involve the whole ship's company, and the only person not to understand it would be the intended victim.

Sailors in general have a wicked, somewhat sick sense of humour and evil tongues. Not only is it a colourful language, but it is virtually their own. I have used a few words and phrases in these pages, but there are many more. The language is known as ...

Jack speak

They know that 'Jack speak' is not the norm in the outside world. So to have their own tongue makes them laugh. They do not speak it when they go home, or to newly acquired gronks, but the fact that other people don't 'get it' makes it even funnier to them. With that in mind, I have endeavoured to write an 'extreme Jack speak' conversation between two shipmates who meet in the galley. In reality it was never this intense, but it could, in theory, go something like this:

SMUDGE: Alright Dusty, me ole bucket of s**t? [A real term of endearment]

DUSTY: Ahoy, shipmate. How's me old oppo, Smudge, then?

SMUDGE: Bessie mate, Bessie. [Good, thanks]

DUSTY: What you on tonight? [What watch have you got?]

SMUDGE: I got the Middle, and you? [Midnight to 4 a.m.]

DUSTY: Last dog all night in, me. [6 to 8 p.m., which means in bed all night, afterwards]

SMUDGE: You jammie bastard.

DUSTY: Who organised these watches?

SMUDGE: The 'One'. [The Jimmy, the 'number one', is first officer below the captain]

DUSTY: No wonder! That snotty couldn't organise the duty watch on a two-man submarine, with half the ship's company on leave. He needs Rembrandting, that one. [Snotty is any young officer. Rembrandting – putting in the picture]

SMUDGE: What's for scran? [Any meal]

DUSTY: Ruby, or spithead pheasant. [Ruby Murray – Curry. Spithead is where all the old ships of the line would anchor, off Portsmouth. So the pheasant of the sea was a kipper, sometimes also called a 'one-eyed steak'.]

SMUDGE: The devil-dodger told me to have that, yesterday. I had a ring like a dragon's nostril all through first dog. I wish I was blue card like that sin bosun. [Devil-dodger or sin bosun – the padre; blue card – no duties; first dog is the 4–6 p.m. watch]

DUSTY: Put some wind the slide, ya muppet, and pass us me fighting irons, will ya? [Pass the butter, and a knife and fork]

SMUDGE: I bring me own gobbling rods now; don't want to end up seeing the scab-lifter again. Pass the sea-dust, will ya? [Medic; pass the salt]

DUSTY: You're a right sick bay-ranger you, aren't ya? Were you making pavement pizza, then? [Always ill; were you sick?]

SMUDGE: Was I? I was giving it loads of technicolor yawn all through make-and-mend, I had to go and get some Egyptian PT in me scratcher. [I was sick all through the afternoon off; had to go and lie down on my bed]

DUSTY: You get more time off than Rick Van Winkle's bunk light, you.

SMUDGE: Ease to five, Jack, you're sailing close to the wind, you are. [Watch it, you're pushing your luck. Any sailor can be called Jack.]

DUSTY: You think you're some kinda BAM you, don't ya?
           [BAM – bad ass marine]

SMUDGE: You can talk. You couldn't fight your way out of a
           wet paper bag, you.

DUSTY: You up for a wet before you go ashore? [Drink
           before you go out?]

SMUDGE: Got any Nelson's blood, then? [Rum]

DUSTY: I might let you have sippers. [Small sip]

SMUDGE: Sippers? Gulpers, at least. You owe me! [Big
           swallow]

DUSTY: It's always sandy bottoms with you, anyway. [You
           take a big gulp, anyway]

SMUDGE: You can talk. Every tot is hands to bathe. [The
           pipe 'Hands to Bathe' is made when you stop the
           ship somewhere hot and the ship's company go
           swimming]

DUSTY: Has the paraffin-pigeon come back yet?
           [Helicopter]

SMUDGE: It's up to Professor Fog, innit? He reckons its
           pea-soupers out there. [Navigation officer says it's
           foggy]

DUSTY: D'you reckon he's an ass bandit? I went past his
           kaboosh during the first, and he was wearing
           a brown hatter's scrambling net! [Is he gay? I
           passed his office during the first watch, 8 p.m. till
           midnight, and he was wearing a string vest]

SMUDGE: No way. In this weather, it's Harry Redders out
           there. [Surely not; it's so hot]

DUSTY: Gen up, true dit, no shit, safeguard he was! [Honest]

SMUDGE: He's TUBBIN, that one. [Thumb Up Bum, Brain In Neutral]

DUSTY: Right, it's time for a shit, shower, shave, shampoo, shore, shite-ers, shag for me. [I'm off to wash and go out, and maybe have sex]

SMUDGE: You're not still seeing that gronk, are ya? [Woman/girl – not wife]

DUSTY: Too right! Once the sprogs are in bed, we'll have a bottle of Château crappers – then it's all night in for me. [Once her children are in bed, we'll have a cheap bottle of wine and I may stay the night]

SMUDGE: She's got rug-rats? [Children]

DUSTY: Yeah, the ole man's a sun-dodger. [Submariner, usually away a lot]

SMUDGE: I might just batten down and close the dead lights early. [Dead lights are the brass storm-proof shutters on port holes, i.e. eyes]

DUSTY: Poof. [Gay]

Life on board one of these 'Ton class' (all ending in ton) boats was basic, at best. It could not be compared with swanning around the world as part of the Fleet Team, or even driving around the country living on subsistence on a Bomb Team. No, a sea draft for a diver was not the best thing that could happen to you. My dad used to find it incredible that I would moan so much about getting 'a hunter', and going to sea, when I was, after all, in the Navy! He had a point.

There are usually 40-odd souls on board, as part of the crew, but if you add in a few Royal Marines and dogs, as was *de rigueur* in Ireland, you have a pretty cramped ship's company. The total complement would often be around the 50 mark, and guess how many rain lockers (showers) there were for that many men? Yep, one. Whenever you went alongside in one of these boats, you would have every man due leave trying to get washed at once. The routine went something like this: in the shower, get wet, out of the shower. Whilst wet, you soap and shampoo at the same time; if you are brave that is. If not, you had to go round twice, wasting valuable drinking time. The only place you could lather and wash was stood in front of one of the four toilets, which of course will be in use. You then joined a constantly moving, circular queue. With the soap in your eyes, you shuffle around until it you are back at the front and you get back into the shower to wash it all off. On a very busy night, in a good run-ashore town or country, you would have a maximum of, say, one minute under running water, but it seemed to work.

The mess where the sailors lived was below sea level and only reachable by a very steep, near-vertical ladder. The galley was on the deck above, and there was no dining area, so all the meals had to go on this perilous journey down to your sleeping mess. In rough weather, this could get pretty nasty. Picture yourself halfway down the ladder when the ship takes a violent roll. You have some decisions to make. You can:

(a) Drop your meal and save yourself. Quite a popular choice, until you go back up and see the chef and ask him for another dinner. After you've cleaned up the first dinner of course.

or:

(b) Try and save your dinner, whilst landing in a big snotty heap at the bottom of the ladder, risking serious injury and the derision of everyone eating their meal below you. Also a very popular choice, as you would rarely (or never) get a second dinner from the chef.

On arriving back down in the mess, you could finally eat your exquisite meal. For breakfast this might be cheesy-hammy-eggy-topside – a savoury dish consisting of a piece of toast spread with melted cheese covered with a slice of grilled ham and surmounted by a poached egg. Other culinary delights would include shit on a raft, or 'excreta à la Kon Tiki' as you might call it in the wardroom, which was devilled kidneys in gravy on toast or fried bread. Train smash was always a popular breakfast, which is hot tinned tomatoes, bacon and toast (it looks like a train smash).

If you were lucky and had a chef who cared enough to do a duff, you could always have the 'duff' conversation. Duff in the mob means three things: it means the sweet course, it means sponge-type puddings, and it means that something doesn't work. So, for instance, you could ask, 'What's for duff, chef?' to which he might reply, 'Duff.' Perfectly legitimate if it was just duff, but, 'What sort of duff?' 'Either better-than-sex cake (vanilla, cream cheese and a chocolate glaze) or Chinese wedding cake (rice with currants or sultanas).' Or it might go along the lines of:

'What's that?'

'That's duff.'

'What, broken?'

'No, it's duff.'

'What, sponge duff?'

'No, duff duff.'

'Oh!'

They say the chef's course is the hardest one in the Navy, because no one has ever passed.

You then had to sit on someone else's bunk and eat on your lap or, if there was room, at one of the two tables. The mess cook of the day also had to negotiate the stairs with a bucket of hot soapy water, as there wasn't even a sink to wash up your cutlery. This could make for a most spectacular – and popular – wipe-out.

I remember after one meal in 'Harry Roughers' (rough weather) a young overweight Muppet (Mine Warfare) was taking the bucket with all the plates in it back up to the galley. He missed his footing and his handhold, then tried to save himself, and the bucket, and failed miserably, on both counts. Fatal! As I've said, you have a split second to choose, one or the other. He ended up lying in a big pool of water, surrounded by broken plates and cutlery with a broken nose, and getting roundly cheered to boot, because he tried to do both. It was pretty spectacular, though. He also had to have stitches in his hand, where a knife had managed to land. I almost felt sorry for him, through my laughter.

He was accident-prone anyway, this lad, and was always loosing his beret or his ID card, or hurting himself, or something. He had come back on board one day, having tripped over ashore and split his crown open. One of the chiefs on board was a medic, and he was this lad's DO (divisional officer). He kept going in to see the chief in his mess, trying to get him to look at his cut head. The thing is, the chiefs had been drinking and had two young ladies on board and didn't really want to be playing mother to this young Muppet. On the third request, the chief said he'd have a look. He could see a nasty cut and decided to 'operate'. Now the Muppet was having second thoughts. The chief shaved a huge dinner-plate-size circle around the cut, for 'hygienic reasons'. Being somewhat tubby, the lad looked like a young Friar Tuck.

The chief then proceeded to put some homeward bounders (big untidy stitches) in his head. The thing is, he didn't just stitch him up ... he stitched a big Burberry button to the top of his head. I swear this is true. He then sent the young confused lad away to try and find his beret. 'But, but, chief!' 'Just do it.' When he came back with the beret, his chief cut a small slit in the top, and proceeded to button his beret to his head. 'There,' he said, 'you won't lose that again, will you?'

The poor lad was then forever know as ... you guessed it, 'Buttons'. You know who you are!

On patrol around Ireland we would search trawlers and cargo ships by day, some of whom were very reluctant to stop and be searched. Whether this was because they had any links with the baddies, or just because they all ran a tight schedule, I could not say.

My special sea duty place was either in the Gemini as part

of the boarding party, or loading the 40/60 Bofors. One day we were trying to stop and search a medium-sized cargo ship, about 6,000 tonnes. We steamed alongside him, ordering him to stop, but the skipper and crew just looked steadfastly ahead and kept on going. Our skipper was getting pretty angry. He ordered us to break out a box of HE shells for the Bofors gun. We quickly uncovered the gun, swung it around facing the ship's bridge, and when we were sure we had the skipper's undivided attention, we loaded four rounds into the gun. He still did not stop. We then informed him, over the loudhailer, that it was his last chance before we opened fire. Nothing. So we trained the gun to about 40 feet in front of his bows, and fired one round into the water. A huge plume of water went up into the air and cascaded across the bridge. Funnily enough, that seemed to get the message across really clearly. He slammed his engines astern and came to a halt quite quickly.

Mystery ship

A lot of our work was done at night, sneaking around the inlets of Northern Ireland. One night we were hugging the coast under darken ship. On the radar, a largish ship was seen behaving very suspiciously. We shadowed it for a while, then the skipper decided we would board her to see what she was up to. She was staying close to shore, and as we got closer we noticed on the radar that she had a small boat out as well. We loaded two Geminis with armed matelots (dangerous enough), marines and the sniffer dog and handler.

As we made our approach to the mystery ship, we were told by radio that her small boat had disappeared in towards the shore. We cut our outboard engine and paddled very close to her, but we still couldn't see her lights or outline, she was also at darken ship. Our two small boats approached the ship from different directions and the *Kirkliston* was steaming silently, not far behind us. The plan was, when the *Kirk* was close enough, she would light up the mystery ship with her big lamps, and we would simultaneously board her. The time came, three – two – one – go go go! As soon as our big lights went on, in an instant, so did the other ship's. Then a smaller boat came tearing out of the darkness with an armed crew shouting at us, as we shouted back. It was pandemonium. It turned out that it was HMS *Hubberston*, who was relieving us in two days' time. They were practising their drills and had seen a suspicious ship (us) with boats in the water, hugging the coastline, and so had decided to investigate! Luckily we managed to board them first, which meant we had to drink their beer. Had it been the other way around, it would have cost us dearly.

Darling

Light travels faster than sound. This is why some people appear bright until you hear them speak.

Having been officially relieved, we made our way into Belfast Lough, where we were hoping to get ashore, even into the Army's 'Moscow Barracks'. Anywhere would have been nice, just for a drink and a bit of a wind-down. The officers went ashore, including Officer Darling. The senior rates went ashore, and the marines, but us, oh no, it was too dangerous for us. I was not happy and went to ask Darling, why? Alas, he had already gone. We had a few tins on board but the seed was set, I was not happy. I went up to his cabin and wrote on his door:

I'M ALRIGHT JACK. I'M GOING ASHORE. SOD THE LADS.

I then I forgot about it and went to bed. About 2 a.m. there was a 'Clear lower deck', which means the whole ship's company are woken up. All 50 of us were up and stood in the Burma way (the long corridor that runs fore to aft in every ship) in various stages of undress. Darling wanted to know who'd written on his door. He thought it was me for some reason but I just flatly denied it. I presume because he wanted to go to bed, the buffer (sort of foreman) told him it was me, which in retrospect didn't really help my case. In the end he said he was going to try and do me for 'attempted mutiny', and if that didn't stick he would go for 'inciting mutiny'. What really got to him was when I laughed! Well, I couldn't believe he was serious.

Within a week I was off there. I can't say I was upset, although I could see it maybe wasn't a great career move. I wasn't doing much diving and he was doing my head in. So I wasn't going to shed any tears.

I was sent back to *Vernon* to join the school where Darling thought I needed to go and get re-educated, and learn some respect for officers. I respected officers, ones that showed me they deserved it, that is; all this one deserved was scorn and derision, which I carried with me by the capful, as he would soon find out. He reminded me of many, but by no means all, of the Naval officers I would meet over the years. They are summed up by this scene:

A man is flying in a hot air balloon and realises he is lost. He reduces height and spots a man down below. He lowers the balloon further and shouts:

'Excuse me, can you tell me where I am?'

The man below says, 'Yes, you're in a hot air balloon, hovering 30 feet above this field.'

'You must be a Petty Officer,' says the balloonist.

'I am,' replies the man. 'How did you know?'

'Well,' says the balloonist, 'everything you have told me is technically correct, but it's no use to anyone.'

The man below says, 'You must be a Navy Officer'.

'I am,' replies the balloonist. 'But how did you know?'

'Well,' says the PO, 'you don't know where you are, or where you're going, but you expect me to be able to help. You're in the same position you were before we met, but now somehow it's all my fault!'

I thought I would be Second Dickie to some ship's diver course or some other such boring job, but alas they had nothing for me. So I was told to join a group just being put together for a job. All I knew was that it was called Naval Party 1006. At the time, we just had a classroom and started getting an awful lot of gear together. Then one day we were told what was up and where we were off to.

South Pacific

'We will be going to a group of South Pacific Islands called Tuvalu.' Wow!

'We will be leaving in August 1977 and will be gone for about three months.' Crikey!

'Stopping off at Gander in Canada, Hawaii, San Francisco, and Fiji on the way.' Blimey!

Here I am, one week after being sacked from the *Kirk* for mutiny, if you like, at the age of eighteen, having never flown or been abroad. Then I find myself being told I am off halfway around the world (literally) on some fantastic trip of a lifetime. Some punishment this is, I thought. I toyed with the idea of writing to Darling and telling him, but I thought he might be able to get me pulled. Best keep my head down, until I'm airborne anyway, I thought.

The group of islands, I found out, were an atoll. An atoll, as you may know, is the remnants of an ancient volcano. From the charts you can see that Tuvalu is a ring of coral islands and reefs surrounding a shallow central lagoon, with the coral extending from a very great depth to the surface of the sea. The capital, where we would be staying, was called Funafuti – though Funafuti is not what you would call a typical capital. The width of the island is only about 20 metres at the narrowest parts, and about 300–400 metres at the widest. Yes, 400 metres at its widest point. Another astonishing thing is that the average height of the land, or coral and sand, is only 2 metres, and the highest point is only 4.5 metres above sea level. There are no hills, no rivers, no industry, and Tuvalu creates less pollution than a small village in England. Yet, despite causing no harm to the planet, this group of islands is suffering first. At the time of going to press, the islands are in the process of becoming famous for being the first casualty of global warming. The slowly rising sea levels and increasingly frequent storms are slowly but surely washing the islands away.

Back in 1977 these islands were still a British colony. They were being given back their independence, but you can't really do that if the islands are ringed in mines. The Americans mined them in 1942 to stop the Japanese from using the islands as a base or a landing strip. Therefore, our task was to give them back with a clean bill of health.

Now, arguably the slowest and most uncomfortable aircraft in the world, military or otherwise, has to be the C130 (Hercules), so it would take around a week, including stopovers, at not much over 300 mph to get there. There were a good few reasons why we had to go by 'Herc', though. The main one being, the military had around 90 of them. We also had a huge amount of gear to take, including boats, engines, compressors, diving gear and enough explosives to sink, not a battleship, as the saying goes, but around 100 battleships. Another reason would undoubtedly be because of the Herc's famous short take-off and landing capabilities (STOL). They can take off and land in less than 450 metres of runway. Funafuti's runway was not much longer than this, and it was not tarmac, or concrete, but a runway surfacing material little used around the world called coral. Apparently the biggest thing that had landed there since the Second World War were small twin-engine planes. So the runway was a little short, very narrow, made of coral, and we were going to try and land a fully laden 70-ton flying bomb on it. Should be interesting, but first we had to get there.

We left RAF Lyneham on the 15 August 1977. How do I know this so many years later? Well, when we landed ten hours later, my brain was puddled, and this was just the first of many legs. The noise inside a Hercules is such that if you need to ask the time from your immediate neighbour, you have to cup your hands together and shout, right into his ear, 'What's the time?' That will often not be enough, and you will also have to point at your wrist to get him to understand your meaning.

We landed in Gander, Canada, my first ever time abroad. We checked into our hotel and made our way to the nearest bar. There were about six of us having a drink, when we noticed two girls sat at the bar. They were both crying and, being one of the young-uns, I was 'volunteered' to go and get the beers in and find out what was wrong. Trying to act cool, I sauntered over to them. 'What's up, ladies?'

She said something I thought was a little odd. She looked up at me through tear-filled eyes and said, 'The King is dead, he's gone, the King is dead!'

I took a tray full of beers back to the lads and said, 'Their king has died.' After a few stunned silent seconds someone said, 'Canada hasn't got a king, have they ... has Canada got a king?' None of us had been to university, some hadn't even been to school much. We discussed it for a while and decided that Canada did not have a king. Muggins here got the blame for not listening properly, and was promptly sent back to enquire. 'Are you Canadian? I didn't know you had a king?'

'Not *our* king,' she said, '*the* King ... ELVIS!'

'Oh,' was all I could muster. We were all equally unimpressed with the death of Elvis, but it will forever stick in my mind. So I know where I was on 16 August 1977, the day he died, aged 42.

The day I first flew, went abroad, and found out Canada did not have a king.

Before leaving Canada I wrote a couple of postcards. One was to HMS *Kirkliston*, BFPO Ships, London. To? Yep, the Darling. It read something along the lines of:

> Dear Sir, Landed in Canada today. Off to San Francisco tomorrow. Having a wonderful time, thinking of you, thanks for the holiday. From the now newly promoted, AB Diver Groom. XXX

Military flying is unlike any other: more basic, yes, especially in the case of the C130, but because of the lack of rules and niceties I would say it's more fun. When we took off from Gander the load manager gave us our safety brief, and it went something like this:

'Right gentlemen listen up! This is a four-engine C130, the safest aircraft in the world. Only two have ever crashed before ... aircraft frame numbers 617 and 618. Welcome aboard aircraft number 619! Only kidding, if there is a problem and we are going to crash, you will know immediately, as I will come running out of the cockpit shouting 'WE'RE GONNA CRASH, WE'RE GONNA CRASH!' closely followed by the pilot and navigator, as it is well known that nearly all survivors of air crashes are found in the tail section. Any questions?'

We landed in Sacramento near San Francisco, where we were meant to just refuel and get on our way, but unfortunately we had engine trouble so had to spend the night. We wandered into a predominantly black bar there and as soon as they found out we were 'Limeys' we had a fantastic time. One huge black lad playing pool there was telling me that he had a Rolls Royce. In his American twang, he told me all about it:

'I got me a Rolls Royce. I can't afford to eat, drink or put a roof over my head, but I got a Rolls Royce! Every weekend me an' the boys club together for gas, and go cruising, picking up the babes. They love a Roller man, I'm telling ya. They think I'm loaded, but I ain't got a bean. But I've got me a Rolls Royce.'

Postcard of 'The streets of San Francisco' sent to my Darling.

We then went on to have two days in Hawaii. At the American Air Force base called Hickam they told us the places to go and things to see. They also said don't go to Hotel Street at Waikiki! Well that's just like saying to a small child, don't touch that big red button! We were straight down there, and I had another new experience – no, not that! We were sat in a dodgy-looking bar in Waikiki when all of a sudden the bar lit up, and a scantily clad woman walked out on top of it. She then proceeded to do things with a ping-pong ball and a cigarette I had no idea were possible.

As we left, a cop went tearing by us on a three-wheeled Harley Davidson. He screeched into a dusty bit of wasteland a little way ahead on the other side of the road. So, being nosy, we crossed over to have a look at his bike. He was on the radio and watching us approach him. He pulled a shotgun out of the back of the bike. Wow! They don't do this stuff back home in England. He then told us off for jaywalking. 'For what?' we said.

'Ah, Limey's eh?' Then he was a bit more civil and told us he had reports of gunshots around here. Nothing to do with us, we said, we'll just cross over, at the crossing obviously, and be on our way, officer!

I barely remember having a go at drunken surfing the following day – not a good idea. I nearly died before I'd even got to my destination. Also, I neglected to take my wallet out of my cut-off jeans, which had all my money and my ID card in it. But I did have enough money to send a postcard – one a day in fact. One was from the girlie bar. 'Dear Sir', etc ... Nice touch, I thought. I think you're probably spotting a pattern now.

From there we went on to Fiji, where we had another night stop and I bought myself a Seiko diver's watch for $25, which I still have and it still works. Oh, and some postcards of a beautiful topless native girl, paddling a dugout canoe. The next morning we had a short 1,000-mile flight to a place called Funafuti. I couldn't wait.

Funafuti

As I've said, I loved to get up at the front on the military flights, so I was the first one to bag the jump seat on the Hercules towards Funafuti. Three hours or so later we started dropping down quite low over the bright blue Pacific Ocean until a group of islands came into view. It was an atoll, you could see the classic shape, a group of islands dotted in a rough kidney shape. As we came in closer, I remember thinking how beautiful it all looked, but this couldn't be Tuvalu. None of the islands was big enough to land this beast on. A 400-metre-wide seven-mile-long island in the vastness of the Pacific looks tiny indeed.

I had the headset on, and peering over the pilots' shoulders I listened intently to their conversation. It slowly dawned on me that this was indeed where we were going to land. This was our final destination. We dropped down low, say 300 feet, and the biggest island, Funafuti, started to get a little bit bigger, but still not big enough.

Eventually, we could see a runway, of sorts. In my limited flying experience, all seven days of it, runways should be black, and should have bright white lines down the middle. This just looked like a long straight area, where they had cleared the palm trees; there was a grassy looking stretch down the middle of the island, and palm trees and coral on either side. Surely that wasn't where we were going to land?

The island flashed beneath us in just a few seconds. The RAF crew then banked hard left, and we went over the outer islands and over the beautiful turquoise-blue shallow lagoon, which contrasted starkly with the majestic, dark blue of the deep Pacific on the outside.

We came round again, this time at a little less than 100 feet. They were having a good hard look at this excuse for a runway. Listening to the pilots, I knew they were using full flap and had slowed the C130 right down to its slowest flying speed, which I seem to remember was not much over 110 mph. This time we barely skimmed the tops of the tallest palm trees. I had a good view of the island, and there were hundreds of people gathered to see the arrival of this huge bird. Probably in anticipation of a disaster.

I think it was probably on the fourth pass that I was kicked out of the front of the aircraft, and told to go back and strap myself in with the rest. This was it. Whether it was long enough, wide enough, or indeed hard enough, we were about to find out.

We hit the ground, and after a very bumpy run the brakes were slammed on and engines put in full reverse thrust. That was it. We were down, stopped and safe. The aft loading ramp door was lowered, and out we walked into a different world.

We were told that the whole island was out, including the school. The island's traditional dance troop were there to greet us. It consisted of about ten young females in grass skirts, barefoot and wearing flowers in their hair, in the front, and the young men at the rear. They sang and did a beautiful, swaying, elegant dance, giving us a real customary welcome. We had necklaces of shells placed over our heads, and were given gifts of beautiful hand-woven fans.

During the unloading of our tons and tons of gear, we walked back to see where we had touched down. The furrows the Hercules had carved into the coral runway were over a foot deep and one of the tyres had to be changed, because of the cuts from the sharp coral.

Party time

That first evening we had an official reception laid on for us. We made our way to the island's big hall. It was open on all sides, with pillars holding up the steeply pitched roof. We were then sat at one end so that the assembled islanders could appraise us.

It was a bit like being put on show. It had a perfect setting, right next to the beach – but then if you think about it, everywhere was near the beach, wasn't it? Even in the middle of the island, you can only be 200 metres from the sea.

They started with dancing and singing, which was fantastic. All the songs and dances would start off slow and quite quickly build to a crescendo, then as you were just getting into it, they stopped, then started up slowly all over again.

Then we had a meal, the like of which I have never had since. It started with a bowl of fruit, each. Then a red snapper, each. After the fish course we had a whole chicken and sweet potatoes, each! The thing is we couldn't leave it: they were watching our every move very closely. There was a lot of giggling going on with our young serving girls as well. All along, while we were eating there were small children, who had obviously been banned from the night's proceedings, peering in the sides of the hall and calling to us and laughing.

After the meal, which nearly killed me by its sheer volume, we were sort of challenged to a singing and dancing contest. We were always going to lose this one in light of our beautiful competition. They did a striking song involving all the girls and the men. Taking it in turns, first the men would leap to the front and sing their bit and dance, then the girls would come forward seductively swinging their hips with a slower version.

Then they all stepped back and one of the elders got up and suggested that it was our turn. How do you compete with that? One of the divers, Joe Kennedy, got up and started singing:

I've been a wild rover for many a year,

[So we all got up and joined in]

And I spent all my money on whisky and beer,

And now I'm returning with gold in great store,

And I never will play the wild rover no more.

Then we tried to get them to join in the chorus:

And it's no, nay, never,

No nay never no more,

Will I play the wild rover,

No never no more.

This went down really well. So, buoyed by our lyrical success, Alan Broadhurst, our PO diver, got up and started singing 'I am the music man'. In case you are not aware of this song, it's an audience participation piece. The song initiator will sing, 'I am the music man, I come from down your way, what can I play?' The audience will then call in unison, 'What can you play?' He then sings something like, 'I can play the ... piano!' Then we all sing, 'Pia-pia-pia-no, pia-no, pia-no; pia-pia-pia-no, pia-pia-no' to the tune, whilst carrying out the actions of playing the piano.

Each verse features a different instrument, with accompanying actions. After each verse, singers sing the previous verses in reverse order before singing the main chorus lines again. The music man points at someone and sings, 'What can you play, what can you play?' If he points at you, you have to think of an instrument, such as trombone (oompa-pa-pa, oompa-pa) or bagpipes (sing 'Scotland the Brave'), and mime playing. The longer it goes on, the more difficult it may be to think of your own verse. In addition to the ten divers, there was also the RAF Hercules crew and a few others on the team.

Eventually everyone forgets the order of the verses and, for some inexplicable reason, the song always seems to get faster, the further you go.

'What can you play ... what can you play?'

'I can play ... the Match of the Day' – to the tune of the BBC's famous show, followed by lots of scarf waving and various football moves, fouls, etc. Another favourite is always 'I can play the dam busters, the dam busters, the dam busters.' Then you do the actions, running around making like an aircraft. This is all very well but, after a few beers, you can go on to a less savoury chorus with very suspect actions. Some of which I'm sure the islanders didn't understand, like playing the piccolo or playing the 'shithouse door'.

Whether they knew what it all meant we had no way of knowing, but I could see they were having a wonderful time, and to a man, woman and child, laughing to the point of rolling around the dusty floor.

Paradise

The morning after our party, the Herc was off and we were on our own for at least three months.

It took a few days organising and preparing all our gear before we were ready to go out and see what was out there. During this period, at weekends and during bad weather, we had plenty of time to explore our new homeland.

Life there was very quiet. Back and front doors were always open, and children went and played where they wished with, it seemed, no restrictions at all. If we went snorkelling in our own time in the lagoon, kids that could swim like fish soon joined us. I would swim down ten metres, and look round to find an eight-year-old boy alongside me, pointing, telling me where to look for the best shells or crayfish.

These gentle Polynesian people were always friendly and very generous to us. They lived almost completely on what the islands and the sea would give them; they truly lived off what they could gather. They would decorate their hair with flowers, and wear necklaces of tiny little shells. Shoes had not really been embraced by the locals; flip-flops were worn at dances, but seemed a bit excessive. A group of girls, who sort of adopted us, took three of us to the northern tip of the island one day. We went on their mopeds, and stupidly took no footwear. The girls could easily walk across impossibly sharp coral without a murmur. We, on the other hand, could only manage a few metres without crying out and sitting down. One of the girls, Betty, showed us her feet. She had very thick skin on the bottom and they were virtually impervious to sharp stones or the heat of it. Another of 'our girls', Lasela, would find the sharpest bit of coral and jump up and down, laughing, 'Look, it's not so bad.'

I once had a long conversation with an old man I met fishing. He offered me a drink of toddy. As you wandered these tranquil isles, you would see bottles tied up in palm trees. It was as if they were either growing there or they were some sort of bizarre offering. As I would find out, a four-day-old toddy can give you a hangover to end all hangovers. They seemed to just cut into the palm leaf of the coconut tree and allow the milky juice to slowly run into the hanging bottle. As far as I could gather, the longer you left it the stronger it got.

I asked him what he did for money.

'Money? I want for no money. Every day I catch fresh fish, I have coconuts and fruit here on the land. The coconut gives me drink, food and milk. I don't want any money.'

What an outlook to have on life, I thought. I would catch up with him regularly for our little chats. Before I left, he gave me a perfect replica of his dugout canoe, which I still have. I offered to pay him, but of course he had no use for money, so I gave him my diving knife, which he was thrilled with.

At first we would have a chuckle at the way they walked at such a snail's pace; it was more of a duck-waddle than a walk. The only other place I had seen such a speed was the dockyards of seventies Britain. It was known then as 'the dockyard shuffle', and was designed to take as long as possible to get from A to B, thus wasting valuable working time. As we grew more native, more bush, if you like, we soon adopted the dockyard shuffle in order to stay cool. What was the point in rushing anyway? The island was only seven miles long, and there was always tomorrow.

There were only a couple of cars, one belonging to the British Commissioner. The only other transport was the odd moped, and the old red Land Rover fire truck.

Imagine my surprise and, yes, delight, when one day I found out that the one of the biggest businesses on Funafuti was the philatelic bureau. They make a considerable sum selling beautiful island stamps to collectors all over the world. But who could I possibly write to, every week, for three months?

Mine searching, Pacific-style

One Friday we were ready, and we took off across the beautiful blue shallow lagoon in two Geminis towards the nearest supposed minefield. I say 'supposed' because we had no idea what was there really.

Halfway across we picked up some visitors. A school of bottlenose dolphins zeroed in on us and were playing around the bows. Later in the trip we would stop and jump in and play with these visitors. I can remember grinning from ear to ear. This was great, this was what I joined up for. Moreover, I should still be on the *Kirk*, maybe working day and night around Northern Ireland.

On this first day, we took loads of diving gear with us. In the UK, to find a mine is an absolute nightmare. You need an awful lot of time, thought, energy and gear. You cannot do it visually, simply because, most of the year, there is virtually no underwater visibility. The tides and the weather are always unpredictable. So you need expensive mine-hunting ships, packed with specialist side-scan sonar and electronics, to find and direct divers to suspicious objects. In the 1970s and 80s the Navy had dozens of these minehunters, mapping thousands of square miles of the seabed around strategic areas of Britain, for every rock, wreck, mine or sunken buoy, so that in times of war, anything 'new'

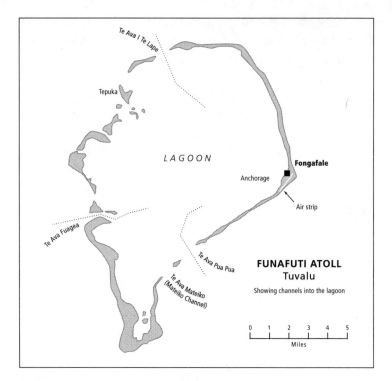

Te Ava I Te Lape

Tepuka

LAGOON

Fongafale

Anchorage

Air strip

Te Ava Fuagea

Te Ava Pua Pua

FUNAFUTI ATOLL
Tuvalu

Showing channels into the lagoon

Te Ava Mateiko
(Mateiko Channel)

0 1 2 3 4 5
Miles

arriving on the seabed could instantly be recognised as a possible threat, mine, or spying device.

Out in the middle of the Pacific, the visibility was such that you could jump in up tide and let the tidal stream take you down tide on the surface, and spot anything man-made on the bottom nearly 100 metres away.

We decided to drop buoys, marking out the limits of the areas to be searched. Then we would go up tide and run the boat along dropping a diver holding a line every 20 metres or so, until we had five of us snorkelling along at a set distance apart, looking down at the seabed.

Where to start the seaward search was easy. You would simply drive the boat out of the lagoon between two of the coral islands. It would instantly go from light blue, inside the lagoon – where you are in reality surmounting the crest of a long dormant volcano, with its head just edging close, and sometimes just above the waves – to the dark blue, seemingly bottomless Pacific Ocean in only a matter of metres of horizontal travel. The drop-off was really quite alarming, and swimming over it was akin to flying very low over the ground, then suddenly passing over the edge of a sheer-drop mountain – only there was no bottom to it, no ground, just dark blue leading to black.

These tiny outer islands were quite incredible. Some looked like they were straight off the typical desert island postcard. The charts we had were 1930s, I seem to remember. No one got out here much to do any hydrography, and one tiny island was written on the chart as having 'one palm tree'. Well, it now had three! However, there were others not marked that had one tree and nothing else on them. There was one enchanting island called Tepuka. It was totally uninhabited, like most of the outer islands. One lunchtime whilst resting up there, Nick Hancock, Paul Middleton and I went exploring.

It had a deep blue, navigable channel into the lagoon to the south (so it was mined, but not for much longer), and a huge untouched coral reef all the way round. We were amazed to find an old American World War II radio shack there. It was mostly a filled-in bunker but bits and pieces of the equipment were still scattered about the island. Walking back to the beach we were startled by a wild pig running across our path. I presume he was put there to graze at leisure, by one of the islanders. Either that or he'd swum, or had been left over since the war. If so, did he even know the war was over?

Sharks and mines

Furious activity is no sure sign of progress.

During our first days and indeed weeks, we were a bit twitchy and you could say nervous. We did have a right to be, though, as there were sharks everywhere. At first, whenever we saw a big one or an overly inquisitive one, we would call the boat over and be out of the water. As the weeks wore on, we got a lot more confident around them. Our eyes were constantly in 'two watches', one eye out for sharks, one for mines.

The first diver on the swim line to see one would give a tug on the line to his nearest swimmer, point out the offender, and make the triangular shark sign, and everyone would pass it on. You then had five or six pairs of eyes on it. If one started circling us to have a nose at what we were, to see if we were edible perhaps, we would call one of the Geminis over and get it to go up and down as fast as possible over where the shark was. This noise would often be enough to get it to move on. Some of the big ones were belligerent and somewhat annoyed at this; then we would be the ones to have to move on to a new area, and come back when it had gone.

On one occasion, we had to move on, and not come back for days, because the biggest shark I had, or have, ever seen, took umbrage at us for exploding mines in his area. He was so upset he tried to eat the best meal we had, our tallest diver, Darby Allen, and was very nearly successful. More on that later.

We started finding mines straight away. They were mostly Mark 13 American ground mines. These were air-dropped magnetic mines, and could be used as bombs if need be. They weighed just over 1,000 lb and used either a TNT charge or the highly effective torpex explosive of some 700 lb. On our searches we also found the sinkers to buoyant mines. Where the buoyant and exploding part of these ended up is anyone's guess, but they're out there in the Pacific region somewhere.

Whilst snorkelling along on our swim line of divers, we could spot anything man-made a long way off. Straight lines, circles, or the rust colour, stand out a mile in nature. Therefore, you may be swimming along on your lines of search for days and find nothing. In the water you go, down with the current. If you find nothing, you get into the boat and shift one lane along, and back up tide, jump in, search again, and so on.

Then one day, maybe after you have been in the water for hours, something at the edge of your vision grabs your interest. It may be an unusual colour change in the coral, or some irregularity in the seabed. It may be the unusual way the coral has grown in an area. Whatever it is, it doesn't look natural – as in not made by nature. It may or may not be a mine; we had already found much wartime paraphernalia, including aircraft engines, shipwrecks, even an old army jeep in the middle of one channel.

Now, having spotted something worthy of further investigation, you increase your hyperventilation (large gulps of air, quite quickly), thus flushing out carbon dioxide from your system. Then you calm yourself, and take in large breaths and hold it, for say 30 seconds at a time. Then as the current takes you closer to your target, you take the biggest breath you can manage. Your head goes down, your fins go up and you make your hopefully long, unhurried descent to the bottom, or as near as you can get to it, to make your positive identification. You soon learn that it is no good thrashing your way to the bottom with rapid fin movements. You may get there quickly, but your body will use all the oxygen you have stored in your blood and

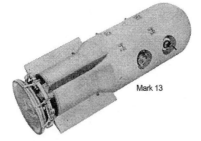

Mark 13

lungs, and you will have to turn straight round and rush back to the surface.

As you become more experienced at duck diving (diving with just the air in your lungs), you start to realise the little ways of extending your underwater time, which increases your bottom time and your depth, thus giving you more time to investigate.

Next time you are swimming, try first just taking a deep breath, and swimming as far as you can underwater, as fast as you can, which is how most people would do it. Then try again, but first hyperventilate for say, 30 seconds, then take long, slow, deep breaths for a few minutes. Try again, but this time, do it slowly. I guarantee you will virtually double your distance and the time you can hold your breath under the water.

All the time whilst snorkelling along you would be conscious of not 'shallow breathing', so you were always ready. Of course, mines weren't the only things worthy of investigation. We would pick up beautiful conch shells and huge clams, some of which decorate my house today, not to mention some enormous crayfish. By the end of two months of this, we could all manage 20 metres depth and maybe two minutes of breath-holding time.

You spot your mine, make a positive ID and turn around to slowly swim up. The other divers will be watching your back and looking to see what you have found. Swimming back to the surface, you give them the thumbs up, they then signal the boat, which rushes over, and drops a lead weight and buoy above the indicated mine. At the end of the day, one of us would dive on the mine and attach a permanent marker to it. Then Saturday would come around and we would attach the required amount of plastic explosive packs. Easy, and not a minehunter or sonar in sight.

Sometimes we would find one on its own. In other areas we would find groups of five or more. On one occasion, we blew five on one ring main (all together), which was very impressive.

Mines can have the housing full of holes and look pretty sad, but if you initiate the remaining explosives, they will go off. These certainly went off with a resounding and very impressive bang, considering they had been in the water for 35 years.

The explosion would kill a lot of fish and other marine life. On one occasion we had to delay the detonation for hours because we couldn't get rid of a school of dolphins. We ended up driving two of the Geminis out to sea for miles to try and compel them to go away. When we did finally blow them, a huge wing of a manta ray came to the surface, which was very sad. He must've been swimming over the mine as it detonated. We would often swim with these gentle giants, and one day we had a beast that was about 20 feet across his back follow us around all day. I am not exaggerating the size of this beauty, and I remember him so distinctly because he had a perfect half-moon piece missing from his right wing. It had grown skin over and repaired itself, but it looked like an ancient shark bite. I was always amazed at how different the patterns on these creatures were. You could snorkel underneath them and tell if it was one you had seen before. On their bellies they had tremendous differences in spots, blotches and a lifetime of scars and pattern of markings as unique as a human fingerprint.

Free-for-all

We told the islanders when the first mines would be detonated. This was usually on a Saturday morning, for their benefit. We then turned up on the first bang day, to be greeted with a veritable flotilla of dugout canoes, excuses for boats and everything and anything that would float, some barely. I thought they were just keen to see these mines go off, but they had ulterior motives.

Trying to get them to stay back before we lit the fuses was an absolute nightmare. In the end, we told them it would be

called off and done without any of them present if they didn't
stay back.

Eventually we gained some sort of authority and kept them
at bay during the countdown. The first bang was huge. It was a
shock to the locals. They now understood why they had to stay
back. The sea lifts in a dome shape, then, out of the middle comes
a huge plume of water over 30 metres high into the air.

As soon as the water came down, the race would begin. The
ones with outboard motors obviously had the edge; some even
had them on dugout canoes. The front of the canoe would come
out of the water and point alarmingly at the sky, until sufficient
speed was reached for it to splash down. Then it would tear off
across the waves. In some of these boats were whole generations,
and they were all here for one thing. Not to watch the explosions,
but to pick up the hundreds of dead fish that would float up
afterwards.

It was a manic free-for-all. First come, first served. No rules,
and no holds barred. By the time they had finished, some of the

canoes would be alarmingly low in the water, but they would smile, wave and thank us as they paddled off with their free booty, sometimes with a ten-mile trip back to Funafuti.

After we had cleared up and checked that all the mines had detonated, we would often head off back, maybe an hour after the locals had gone. We would then sometimes pass some of the boats with engines towing five or six canoes, in line astern steadily plodding their way back home. They would be chatting, laughing, singing and joking with each other; not in the least bit bothered how long it took them to get back home with their free shopping.

Jaws

The film *Jaws* had only been out for two years when we arrived on the islands. It was undoubtedly the film of the decade. I don't know if it was a coincidence or a case of someone just having a sense of humour, but not long after we arrived, *Jaws* was showing at the island's makeshift, roofless cinema. I don't believe any of us went.

One area that had been heavily mined was a narrow deep stretch south of Funafuti called the Mateika channel, between two islands. The tide would rip through there virtually all the time. Whilst searching the area, we found five ground mines close together, and one set apart on its own. However, that was not all that was lying on the bottom.

As we floated over this area at a rapid rate of knots in the rushing tide, there were sharks' tails sticking out of coral caves all over the place. I for one never saw a shark swimming about here. Whether sharks sleep or not, I don't think has ever been fully established. Sharks rely on ram-ventilation, that is, their forward swimming pushes oxygen-bearing water through their mouths and over their gills, which would suggest they have to be moving to breathe. What if they find a place where the current is constantly moving? Surely they could then lie still and breathe? If they were not sleeping, they were certainly resting.

A sleeping shark is fine by me. But they were about to get a very rude awakening.

The plan was to blow five in one go on the Saturday, and then come back on the Sunday morning and do the last one, which was set apart from the others. Now, this was a break in routine for us. Until now, we had always left at least two days, sometimes three, before going back. The Saturday operation went smoothly, and the massive explosion brought the islanders out to collect the dead fish as usual. We also saw a few sharks roving around looking for the fish that were on the bottom.

As far as I remember we had a bit of trouble locating the last mine on the Sunday morning. The float we had left there overnight had disappeared. Darby, being the one who had first spotted this particular mine, said he knew roughly where it was. So we took him up tide (which was out of the lagoon) in the Gemini, and drifted along about 20 metres away from him as he snorkelled along his search route.

All of a sudden, he put his hands above his head, making the triangle shape denoting he'd seen a shark. Then he put two fingers up meaning two sharks. There was nothing too alarming about this. It was the yelp through his snorkel and the subsequent speed with which he moved across the water which made us all look.

He covered the distance across the water in a matter of seconds, and came up and over the side of the boat in one swift movement. Just as his fins came inboard a huge, dark shadow appeared directly behind him, closely followed by another on the surface. This second giant, we think a female mako shark, then bumped the boat. She was around the twelve-foot mark. How do I know this? Well, she was a little over the length of the Gemini.

Now, Darby hadn't had time to open his mouth yet, but

when he did, he said he'd seen these two, tearing around the bottom, behaving very aggressively. They had obviously swum at full speed to the surface and were undoubtedly after a piece of Darbs.

A twelve-foot shark is big enough: they were by far the biggest we'd seen. The thing that struck me was not just the length of these underwater beasts, but the girth of them. The one that bumped the boat must have been more than four feet across her back. All of her dimensions were huge: the dorsal fin was massive, and she looked fat, but lithe. With one flick of the powerful tail, which again clipped the air tank of the Gemini and soaked us all in the process, and a flash of a pure white underbelly, she was gone.

I got the shufty box (an aluminium box with a glass bottom for seeing under water) over the side and got another flash of these two fast and seemingly angry fish.

Maybe they were unhappy at having their sleep disturbed, or maybe it was all the dead fish around that had set them off. It could have been the lone silhouette of Darbs on the surface: at 6 foot 4 inches, might they have mistaken him for another shark, or seen him as competition for their food? We will never know, but they made it perfectly clear that we should not be in the water at this moment. This was their space, and we were just clumsy visitors compared to them.

Someone who hadn't had a good view of the sharks suggested we leave it an hour and then go back in for another try. This was never going to happen. Rank counted for nothing in this situation. If you had seen them and, more importantly, their attitude, you would not dive. A terse exchange took place. Then we were off back to Funafuti for a few well-deserved cold beers and a new shark story to add to our journal of tales.

We left it until the following Wednesday before going back for another nervous look around for the elusive mine. We found it and blew it up that day. The locals, having got wind of the 'monster shark' story, were nowhere to be seen.

This dangerous area was the last in our long list to render the islands 'off of the list of unsafe areas'. In just a couple of months, we had cleared six minefields, totalling 24 mines, without anyone getting maimed – or eaten.

The Hercules arrived to take us home on 22 October 1977 and we had another humdinger of a leaving bash. So with heavy heart and muzzy head, we departed the island on the 23rd. The crew did an awesome fly-past for the islanders, barely clearing the palm trees, then off into the seemingly endless Pacific. It was only a three-and-a-half-hour flight to Fiji, where we quickly refuelled and were on our way.

Or so we thought. Alas! Only an hour out, we had port outer engine problems and had to return to Fiji. We were then met with the 'devastating' news that we required a new engine, and it would take a week to come out from the UK! When, oh when, was this nightmare job going to end? More postcards were soon winging there way to the *Kirk*. I wasn't quite over what I saw as my grossly unfair treatment by my arch-nemesis.

The Fleet Clearance Diving Team, 1978–79

When I arrived back at Portsmouth, fresh from gallivanting half-way around the world for three months, I had absolutely no idea what I would be doing next. I was a little worried that 'you know who' might be waiting for me to complain about all his postcards, even though I'd taken great care to be nothing but polite. For all I knew, in his twisted mind, he might have construed these to be mutinous as well. Perhaps there would be MPs waiting for me and I'd be straight over the wall for a 90-day stretch in chokey? Perhaps he would have an open boat for me at the steps of the Sally Port in Old Portsmouth? Then I would be able to utter those immortal words, 'Cast me adrift would you, Mr Darling? Cast me adrift in nothing but an open-neck shirt? You'll hang for this, Mr Darling! I'll see you hang from the highest yard in the British Royal Navy!' I do realise it was the higher-ranking Captain Bligh that was cast adrift, not the mere Able Seaman Diver Groom, but you know what they say: 'Never let the truth get in the way of a good story.'

Nothing, not a word about my previous indiscretions. I was to join the globe-trotting Fleet Clearance Diving Team. Things were going from good to better. This was the Fleet Team's departmental brief:

> The team's primary role is to provide an immediate-response, world-wide clearance diving facility for the Commander-in-Chief Fleet. To this end, their responsibilities and capabilities are:
>
> (1)   75-metre oxy-helium diving from inflatable dinghies for nuclear weapons recovery, and ship, aircraft or other emergency tasks.
>
> (2)   Afloat dome and propeller changes, worldwide.
>
> (3)   Underwater demolition, IED and EOD tasks, worldwide.
>
> (4)   Provide attacking underwater saboteur forces for ships exercising or work up.
>
> (5)   Provide backup to command CD teams as necessary.
>
> (6)   Being the UK CD commitment to NATO, to participate in NATO and National Mine Warfare exercises, particularly in the team's war role, unknown mine investigation and recovery.
>
> The team's resources include:
>
> (1)   Own transport, including a special-purpose air-transportable seven-ton lorry.
>
> (2)   Air-transportable emergency trailer, carrying a two-compartment compression chamber and salvage equipment.
>
> (3)   A full IED disposal outfit.

The complement of the team should be:

One Lieutenant

One Warrant Officer

Two CPO (Divers)

One MEA (Engineer)

Eight Leading Seaman divers

Three Able Seaman divers

This looked promising. More flying around the world for me, please. I quickly learnt that it was imperative to have a packed bag and my passport with me at all times. One of the chiefs would sometimes come down the stairs and say something along the lines of, 'Right, who's got their passports?' You had to be in the right place, and quick. You could dip in, with a short hop to Bermuda for a screw change, or dip out with a dive up harbour in Portsmouth. We managed to cover just about everything on our list of tasks – except, I'm glad to say, recovery of nuclear weapons. We also covered quite few that weren't on the list. Like 'body jobs'.

Body jobs

On the last day of August 1978 we were mooching around our base preparing gear for a big NATO exercise. A Wessex helicopter landed on *Vernon*'s heliport and one of the crew came over and asked for some divers, ASAP.

I was in the right place, so got dressed in, made up a CDBA set and, along with three others, ran out to the chopper. We soon landed at Netley Abbey on the banks of the Hamble River in Southampton. As we touched down there were police everywhere. The chopper disappeared and began searching the other side of the river. A policeman soon told us the story so far. Apparently there had been an armed robbery nearby, and a major car chase had ensued. The robbers had panicked and taken a wrong turn and driven straight into the river, then bailed out, taking their booty of cash with them. They were unsure if the villains had made the mile-and-a-bit swim across Southampton Water. It was unlikely. They may have drowned not far from the car.

We entered the water by the abandoned car, and had a quick look inside to see there was no SWAG bag and no dead crooks. We then went out and slightly downsteam, which was the way any swimmer would find himself going. Initially we saw nothing untoward, then my buddy Ian Milne gave a tug on our buddy line and got me to look up, not down. Floating around in the water above us was money. Single notes, £5, £10, and twenties. We just started picking them out of the water as they floated gently by in the tide. At first we were chasing after them, then we soon realised if you stood still on the bottom, they came to you. After a while we started leaving the ones and fives and collecting just the tens and twenties. It was like all your dreams coming true – money, as much as you wanted, just help yourself. This put a new meaning on the term 'money laundering'. After a few minutes of this, I had two handfuls of moolah and looked down to undo my wetsuit to stuff it in my jacket, only for safe keeping of course. There, moving slowly along the bottom, were bundles of notes done up in elastic bands. Neat rolls of money, making their escape out to sea. Unless we could rescue them, they would never be seen again. We left the single notes to do as they pleased and now just concentrated on the nice fat rolls. I seemed to be in an area of tenners, Ian on the other hand was predominantly picking up rolls of twenties, so obviously I left mine and went over to where he was. 'Greed is good, greed is right.'

Unfortunately, when we came up sporting new 'lumpy' wet suits, there was a cordon of police and we must have looked sufficiently sheepish to warrant a full body search, not involving rubber gloves, but nonetheless it was pretty thorough.

The next day we were back in Southampton Water searching the car and surrounding area and found the birth certificate and passport of one of the suspects. Not a good idea to leave that sort of thing in the getaway car, really. This time we found no trace of any drowned crooks, and near the end of the second day the search was called off.

We were packing up when another chopper dropped down unannounced onto the beach and asked us if we could dive again, not far away. Off we go again, and this time we fly into Southampton and up the river and land on a bit of wasteland by a bridge. There is a crowd of people behind a police cordon and we are told there is someone missing. A six-year-old boy had been playing with some friends and had gone into the fast-flowing water and disappeared. Body jobs are not nice at the best of times, but a young lad like this makes it a little harder. We searched for an hour or so, moving quite a long way downstream, and found nothing. The area was strewn with scrap and rubbish and the vis was pretty awful, making it a highly dangerous occupation in the increasing flow of the ebbing tide. We moved back to where he was said to have gone in and started again. I was with a lad that was on my babies course, Steve Briggs, and we looked almost directly where he fell in. Right under this spot was an old metal single bed, and we found him under there. He must've gone straight down. Between us we moved the bed and Steve picked him up.

As we walked out of the water, a woman broke through the cordon and ran towards us. Steve turned his back on her to screen the boy's face from the crowd. We, of course, didn't know who she was, but we soon realised she was the boy's mother. She started scratching Steve's face from behind and demanding to be given her baby. Steve gave in and handed him over.

Ouch!

As it says in our brief, we must go anywhere in the world that requires us. It's good to feel wanted! In September 1978 we packed our mobile mine-hunting gear up and drove up to RAF Lynam ready for another Herky Bird or Hercu-Slease flight to Turkey. We were to take part in a NATO exercise called Damsel Fair. Unfortunately, well, for me, we turned up at the RAF base on a Thursday night, disco night. I was doing fine with a petite WRAF girl who had just finished with a Royal Marine who, she neglected to tell me, was on base security there. Can you see where this is heading? After the disco, she and I went to the NAAFI – how romantic – for a brew. There was her ex RM with his mates. Ooops! She decided to bug out and go home, which in hindsight is what I should have done, but no, I needed a cup of tea for some godforsaken reason. So in I went, the picture of innocence. I was just walking out with my beverage when the RM hit me from behind. He didn't even have the decency to let me fall over before hitting me again, and again. Then he allowed me to lie prone upon the ground, and so as not to tire himself, he proceeded to use his feet (large boots, to be precise) to kick me senseless.

I eventually staggered my way back to our transit barracks looking like I'd had the living daylights kicked out of me, which was ironic. The rest of the team were so worried about me they immediately got a camera – because I looked so good, I presume. I had a broken nose, fat lip, a swollen black eye, and they thought it was hilarious.

The next morning about six of us went over to breakfast, and I was with the biggest hardest man on the team, Nev Sharp. He was most put out about his little mate having his head used as a football and was very pleased to see the guilty-as-charged Royal sitting, eating with a couple of his cronies. Nev was built like a brick shithouse, a blond northern lad who loved his Rugby League. He walked straight over to him and was about to ask him about his possible involvement in the beating the night before, when the marine jumped up and said, 'Yeah it was me, what you gonna do about it, I'll take all of you on, come on!' – or words to that effect.

Nev hadn't muttered a word. He just followed the very vocal RM out of the dining room, passing me his combat jacket.

The RM never got off a punch. Nev beat him to a pulp, I mean really beat him. As he was hitting him he was explaining how it was not gentlemanly to hit someone who isn't looking, or someone smaller than oneself, or to kick him whilst he is sparko on the ground. No sooner had he said this, than he immediately broke his own rule, and kicked him again. I won't say where, but if he had two lumps in the back of his throat, he had best swallow, not spit. I was a bit worried as there were two other RMs watching the entertainment, as well as the rest of the dining hall. But the watching marines were quite nonplussed about it all. 'Naa, you carry on mate, he needs a good kicking. We don't like him either, he's a right bully, that one.' Nev was encouraging me to get involved. 'Go on Tone, kick him if you want, like this, look.' Whack. 'No, you're alright Nev, you're doing a fine job.'

Military bases have a knack of attracting the most unattractive women to them, like flies round whatever a dung beetle is eating. I did a Heavy Goods Vehicle (HGV) driving course around this time at RAF St Athan in Wales. For their discos they would send out coaches around the Rhondda Valley, to pick up a troupe of thick-set, ruddy-complexioned, earthy, outdoorsy females with big gorilla hands. They were nicknamed 'the Rhonda Commandos'.

RAF St Athan was some sort of training base. Men could be seen running and marching everywhere. The RAF didn't know what to make of Navy divers, so our arrival brief went along the lines of this:

'Right. Everyone will march everywhere at all times, preferably in groups. If you are alone, you double, except the divers.'

'You will stay on the camp during working hours. Leave

finishes at 23:00, except the divers.'

'You will stay away from the WRAFs' quarters at all times. ESPECIALLY THE DIVERS.'

A hand went up in our number.

'Yes, you?'

'Where are we meant to f∗∗∗ 'em then, sir?'

CD2s course and the bomb team

We the willing, led by the unknowing, are doing the impossible for the ungrateful. We have done so much, for so long, with so little, we are now qualified to do anything with nothing.

Bomb and mine disposal is something you learn as a 'baby diver', but of course you start off as more recognition experts than hands-on disposal. 'Yep, that's a bomb. No, that's not.' As a leading diver you get into the fun side of actually blowing things up and defusing them. Any boy/man would love to do it. I joined the branch really to be a diver. The bomb disposal bit didn't dawn on me until it was too late to change my mind.

You see, it's easier to train someone who has what it takes to be a competent diver how to recognise and defuse munitions, than it is to train someone already proficient in Explosive Ordnance Disposal (EOD) how to dive. Much easier. So much so that they don't even try it the other way round.

I have seen people you would rate 'hard as nails' freak out as soon as you put them in the water, even in good visibility. In nil visibility, well, you lose a lot more.

'Oh no, I can't do it, chief, can't clear my ears you see ... claustrophobic ... rubber aversion ... rubber addiction ... too cold ... too hot [two men died on mud runs from over-heating] ... weak bladder ...' – and numerous other excuses.

Throw them in at night, or in deep water, or in the tide, or with sharks, or when its snowing, or in rough seas, and the numbers drop alarmingly. You have to be pretty thick-skinned and a bit, well, different to be able to cope with all of these. Then throw in a mention of bomb and mine disposal and your volunteers seem to evaporate without you trying. If you get the numbers down from a hundred to just six in a day (quite realistic), and say you only want three for a new course, just see how fit they are with some circuits and mud runs and you'll have your three left who may cope with an intensive course. What's more likely, though, is that you'll end up with one who passes.

Two's course isn't so much about beating you up and getting the numbers down. You've already proved you've got what it takes to be a CD. Saying that, we did do an inordinate amount of time underwater and lots and lots of miles. As a CD2 or Leading Diver in the RN, your boundaries are pushed further and deeper and for longer. If you pass, and plenty did need more than one attempt, you can dive to 75 metres, and much deeper than that if you do a saturation course (more on that discipline later). You can swim unmarked, you get paid more, and more importantly they teach you how to blow things up.

In order to teach EOD and Improvised Explosive Devices (IED, parcel/letter bombs) it is necessary to know how bombs, booby traps, letter and parcel bombs etc are made. The problem is if someone teaches you how to make them, you have to try it – and who better to try out your new-found skills on, than your mates? After two's course I went to join the Portsmouth and Medway Bomb and Mine Disposal team. Bit of a mouthful, isn't it? The Bomb Team and the Fleet Team shared the same building, which was the Triton building in the corner of HMS *Vernon* (now a shopping centre). Both teams had been trained in the art of blowing things up; well essentially we were trained in stopping someone else blowing the goodies up, and just modified it somewhat. To dispose of IEDs and such like, you need the same equipment as to build them. In that building there was everything we needed to detonate someone on a daily basis, as a means of practising of course.

It would start with a simple regular drawer bomb: you open the drawer, and bang! You are covered in French chalk (powdered chalk). Then, whoever got you would have to pay. One lad, Shiner Wright, would always put just that little bit too much bang in his booby traps. If you were 'done' by him, it would leave your ears ringing for hours. One of the favourites was your locker. They were metal and all in the only communal rest room in the block. You never, repeat NEVER, left it unlocked, not for a minute. If you did, well, you would be blown, and it was your own fault. That was allowed, because you left it open. Lockers are simple, you see. All you do is take the gunpowder out of a thunder-flash (it's still explosives, but use a little), and compact about a third of one into an empty thunder-flash cardboard tube. You take a piece of line, fishing line is fine, and attach it to the door. Inside the locker you will have something like a peg with two pieces of wire going to the jaws and maybe drawing pins in the end. When you open the door the line pulls out a piece of card from the jaws of the peg, thus completing a circuit. The batteries set off a puffer detonator and blow the gunpowder and the chalk into the mug's face. Simple, and of course very funny for all sat around in the rest room. Later on they would get more and more intricate and complicated. You might arrange, say, for a few flash bulbs to go off as well – always a good idea to blind your victim first!

Shiner never left his locker open. He had a lot of victims longing for revenge. One day it was 'arranged' for him to go on a little errand up to the vehicle centre to pick up a Land Rover from servicing. Whilst he was gone, his locker was taken away and severely tampered with. He was going to meet with a little accident. We cut a hole in the back of his locker and rigged it up with what he would use. First 'dead crab water', then flash bulbs, then the bang and chalk. So you get soaked (and you stink), blinded, then the chalk sticks to you.

He came back from the vehicle servicing centre full of confidence and, seeing his padlock was still in place, opened his locker. I can remember trying to remain nonchalant and read my paper as he fiddled with his key. You know it's going to go bang, and you're excited about it, and want to see it, but if you give him the slightest inkling that something is amiss, he won't open it. Then you'll be in trouble for giving the game away. Some lads just couldn't do it, I mean stay in the same room as one of their victims. They would be too fidgety, too obviously excited as you went near the 'hot' item.

There was a loud bang, and 'crabby' water was sprayed across the rest room, the flash blurred his vision, then the French chalk stuck all over him. Perfect. Don't listen to do-gooders: revenge is sweet.

On one occasion, there was a big battle going on between the teams. It wasn't safe to move around the building; anything and everything was rigged. As with all these things it eventually came to a head when it all got just a little bit out of hand.

The toilet was always a good and easy place to rig. You didn't know who you were going to get, but equally your victim would not know who'd laid it. It could have been there for hours. The quickest and most frequent was a thunder-flash in a metal bin full of water attached to the door. The added benefit to the bomber was that your victim was in a small room and could not escape.

One day a very complicated idea was tried out, and the toilet seat was booby-trapped with a home-made pressure switch. If you design your booby trap well and with a lot of forethought, you can make the whole circuit, but instead of attaching your explosives to your circuit, you simply attach a small light bulb. You can then test it until your heart is content, watching the light bulb come on to simulate the explosion. When you are satisfied everything is working perfectly, you remove the light bulb and attach the wires to your explosives, and retire to watch the entertainment.

Whoever had set up the toilet was a little over-zealous in how much bang they used. The toilet was rigged with a whole thunder-flash around the U bend, and one in the overhead chain flush. There was also a delayed box of French chalk explosion to come from the ceiling. The idea being, you sit down and bang, the water goes up your chuff then over your head from the one above, then a whole box of French chalk would explode and stick to your now completely wet body.

In theory, a good booby trap. What actually happened was not quite as envisaged by its inventor. It all went off as planned, but the first explosion, being confined in water, and in a small porcelain tube, blew apart the toilet cistern. The sitter (no, I have not missed a letter out of there) crumpled to the floor as the toilet disintegrated beneath him. The top explosion blew apart the overhead water holder, and ruptured the mains pipe, and the complete box full of French chalk went off perfectly. The only one out of the three not to destroy something. Not bad then?

Unfortunately, the bang was so large it brought the grown-ups running down the stairs to see what had happened. When everyone arrived at the rest-room door, the victim was sat on the floor amongst flowing water and broken china, with lacerations around his nether regions and completely covered in French chalk. The excuse that it was only a bit of fun didn't wash, and some lads were severely hauled over the coals. This stopped our IED pranks for a number of weeks, but not for good.

We had to think of other ways to 'do' each other, and preferably out of sight of the grown-ups. Horsea Island was far enough away from *Vernon* to be considered 'fair game'. One somewhat nervous individual went by the name of Beth. At the time he had a Mk III Ford Cortina and was always crowing about its virtues. He was constantly doing something to it, polishing it, servicing it, changing the oil, etc. On one occasion in *Vernon*, he had convinced himself his carburettor was blocked. So without too much thought, he blew it through with high-pressure oxygen. It had the desired effect in that it blew a lot of gunk out of the tiny jets and pipe-work. When he first turned the key, however, the oxygen ignited and blue flames shot out of the back of his Cortina, not unlike the high-octane fuel used in dragsters.

We were all sick to death of his Cortina stories. So we rigged an orange distress smoke flare inside the car. It was very simple: you tie one end to the ring-pull of the flare, the other end to an immovable object, then sit back and watch the show. He had been telling us how he could do nought to sixty in ten seconds, so we convinced him it was necessary to prove it to us. Leading through the passenger door was around 100 feet of fishing line tied to a fence post.

Watchers at the ready, we counted down: three, two, one, go! He shot off up the private road running beside a lake. There was a twang as the line parted, and we thought it had failed to go off as he disappeared from view behind some trees. When he re-emerged he had slowed to a crawl, and had the driver's door open and was leaping out completely orange and gagging from the acrid smoke. The car quickly disappeared in the smoke cloud. It was a most hilarious, if somewhat cruel joke to play on someone. We ran after him to help extinguish the smoke and the small fire which had now started in the back. The smoke had ruined the interior of the Cortina, the orange had got in the stitching, behind the speedo, everywhere. Including Beth. He went home that weekend, with orange hair, orange in his ears, up his nose, the lot.

One weekend we strapped a rotten mackerel to his radiator so he slowly poached the fish all the way home. The smell emanating from his heater made him heave.

Shorty

There was a lad I was on the Fleet Team with called Shorty. This lad was a Geordie (from Newcastle), he was about five foot five, and as hard as nails. He was also one of the funniest men I have ever met.

On a number of occasions we had to drive all the way from Portsmouth to Fort William in Scotland in a Land Rover, a distance of well over 500 miles. This Land Rover would have the rubber boat on the top, six men inside, and a trailer full of diving gear and explosives. Top speed was around 55 mph and it would take us two days to get there with one overnight stop.

On such journeys Shorty would arm himself with a crate of beer and a packet of fags. I don't think I ever saw him eat. These Land Rovers had three seats in the front. Shorty would always sit in the middle seat because under your feet was a small movable panel to give access to the gearbox. He would leave just one screw in this panel, so that when he needed to relieve himself he would kick the panel to one side with his foot, and simply urinate onto the moving road underneath. This was the perfect scenario for him: he could pour beer in one end, let nature take its course, and pass water onto the road, never having to worry about toilet breaks.

We would drive these hundreds of miles, and he would have all of us laughing for the whole journey. Most of his stories were of his sexual conquests. He would maybe take an hour to tell one story, but a bit like Ronnie Corbett, he would diversify all over the place, always coming back to the same theme, sex.

He had got off with this one f-ugly gronk, as he called the ugly ones, which most of them seemed to be in his stories. She had taken him back to her flat in Troon on the west coast of Scotland. He said, because she was so ugly, he had to 'do her from behind.' He said this one was a right double-bagger, meaning one bag over her head would not be enough, to be safe you should use two in case the first one split. 'She had a smile like a row of bombed houses and an arse like a badly packed parachute,' he said. When he got back to her place, she told him to be quiet and not say a word. She opened the front door, ushered him in, and stood him up against the wall and told him not to move. She then opened the door to one side and had a conversation with her mum and dad, who were watching telly. She then proceeded to ask about her two children, had they gone to bed OK, etc. Having said goodnight to mum and dad, she shut the door and they had to creep up the stairs to her bedroom.

She said, 'I dunnegh normally have sex on the first night, but I've got some condoms. So if you wanne, we can.'

He was gutted that he had to wear a knob sock, but he'd do it. She then brought out a selection of ribbed and coloured ones. His Geordie accent made these stories even funnier.

'Anyways up, I wos giving her one doggy-style, reet? An she was gannin, "Oh, Shorty, oh Shorty!"

'An I was thinking, how, Shorty man, you big bastard, go on hort her.

'"Oh, Shorty, oh Shorty!"

'Man, she was jumpin aboot all owar the place, it was like riding a bucking bronco, I was hanging on for grim death like!

'Then she says, "Oh Shorty, SHORTY! ...your cigarette's burning my back!"'

His fag ash was dropping all over her back, that's what all the 'oh Shorty' was about.

You would just about recover from that, when he would just carry on.

'So I wakes up in the middle of the neet, borstin for a piss. I creeps along the hall to try and not wake the bairns and mam and dad, ye kna! An I've finally found the pisser, and I'm having the longest slash in the world, man. Then, I thinks, hang on, something don't feel reet here like. Ah looks down at me ole fella, and me bell end's about the size of a blood orange and bright f**kin red. Ah just started screaming, man, how, the dirty bitch, what has she given me? What's happened to me cock like? Ah must have rampant knob rot or summat!'

Well, he says, only after waking the whole house, who didn't even know they had a guest, did he realise what had happened.

'Ah only hadn't taken me f**kin jonnie off had I? It was full of piss, man. So ah turns round, all still bollocky buff like, and there's the rest of the family like, just staring at us!' Then he announces to the kids and mum and dad, who had gathered on the landing to view this naked stranger in their midst, 'Oh don't worry yerselves man, it was just the red jonnie ya mammy gave us!'

Whilst up in Scotland, he would do his utmost to drink twice his body weight in liquid every night, and then and only then would he go looking for some unfortunate woman. He was hooked up with a long-term girlfriend, but this didn't seem to bother Shorty one iota.

On the way back from Scotland once, we all stayed at his house in a decidedly dodgy area of Newcastle. We had just said hello to his woman, who seemed nice enough, then, as he'd only seen her that weekend, we were off down the 'Club' for some scoops. She had the audacity to ask if she might come with us? Shorty just said, 'How man woman man, it's Frideh, not Saturdeh,' and off we went. As we turned up at his working men's club (with no women in it, as it was obviously Friday) a huge bear of a man was coming out. He had a black eye, fat lip and cotton wool stuffed up his nose. He looked as though he'd been in a car crash.

'Alreet Shorty man. Listen mate, nay hard feelings aboot the weekend, I horpe. It'll never happen again mate. You have my word on it, never!' said the big man.

Shorty said, 'Neh bother George, divvent yer worry yersel aboot it.'

'Champion, Shorty, champion. See ya,' said big George, and off he went.

We made our way into Shorty's club, and he bought the first round of drinks. I asked him what all that was about.

'Arh that? That was nowt, that. He was shaggin wor lass, that's all!'

'Oh ... What happened to his face?'

'Oh, I did that!' he said. 'Who else wants a scoop?'

I asked the barman if he had seen what had happened. He said he had. Shorty just marched in to the bar and told big George he needed to see him outside now! So big George goes outside with Shorty, half his size, not expecting too much trouble. Shorty apparently jumped onto the bonnet of the nearest car and flew at big George with a flying head-butt, and proceeded to beat him unconscious.

Whilst we were having our drinks, I asked him if he had confronted his girlfriend yet. He said no, because it was his birthday next week, and if he said too much he wouldn't get his present, and he knew what it was, and she had been saving for months for it.

Deep work-up

The Fleet Team and the Bomb Team both had to maintain a 75-metre diving capability, which meant regular work-ups. By work-up I mean you don't just go straight to 75 metres, you work down to it. Maybe it should be called a work-down? You dive to 40, 55, 65, and then 75 metres. This really all stemmed from when we used to do 75 metres on air. Not recommended. I for one never enjoyed deep diving on air, mainly because of nitrogen narcosis. It affects everyone differently; I have seen it come on in new divers at only 30 metres, and it is recognisable by people's strange behaviour. Jacques Cousteau famously called it 'rapture of the deep'. The air you breathe is 21% oxygen, 79% nitrogen. That is obviously the same on the surface and underwater, as the air used underwater is merely compressed surface air. Nitrogen narcosis, or 'narcs' as divers call it, is still not really understood, but it appears to be the effect of high nitrogen pressure on the nervous system. It is said to produce a state not unlike alcohol intoxication, basically feeling a bit drunk. As I said, it affects everyone differently and it never really felt like being drunk to me. Whenever I was over 60 metres deep on air, my head would be fairly clear but I would get exaggerated pins and needles in my hands and fingers. Not too scary, you might think, until you are trying to do a job down deep. I once dived to 75 metres on air at the end of a long work-up, and all I had to do was to tighten up a shackle. It took me my whole twelve minutes' bottom time, because my fingers were throbbing with pins and needles. Other blokes I dived with could barely function at all, and others thought everything was funny, just like being drunk. If you do a long slow work-up on air, a lot of these symptoms will slowly disappear.

One of the best ways to see how it manifests in each person is to do a deep air dive, say 80 metres, in a decompression chamber. On my CD2s course, we did one such deep pot dive. The chief diver, Bill Bauckham, chucked in a few things that would be squashed in the descent. A balloon, a child's football, stuff like that. One of the items he threw in was a normal Navy Diver's wetsuit. By the time we got to the bottom, some of our course, namely Mick O'Leary, Jock Lindsay and Bob Sullivan, were in tears of laughter, just looking at a wetsuit, which of course had shrivelled up to a third of its original size and was paper thin. I on the other hand just had my pins and needles and couldn't see what was so funny.

This may all seem just a bit strange to most people – but of course nitrogen narcosis can be severely unpredictable, and even fatal, either from the toxic effects or as a result of illogical behaviour in an already very difficult environment. Eventually, in the late 1970s, the Navy recognised these limitations and swapped the nitrogen part of the mixture for helium. The helium immediately took away the narcosis problem, its only drawback being the famous, ridiculous, Mickey Mouse voice.

Pet

We move swiftly on, from fact to farce. With the Bomb Team we went to Rothesay on the Isle of Bute in 1980, to do one such deep work-up. The diving was fine but the runs ashore were wild in the extreme. I don't know what it is with the little lochside villages around Scotland, but they are crazy places. We were in the only club there and I was just having a few drinks with the team, minding my own business. This woman who, to be frank, was a bit of a butter-head (everything was good about her but 'er head) sidled up to me and said, 'Dance!' I politely said, 'No, it's all right thanks. I'm just here having a beer with my mates.'

She just stayed there looking at me and said, a little bit louder, 'DANCE!' When I looked more closely I realised she had forearms like an all-in wrestler's and fingers like a gorilla's. Best not upset her, I thought, best to dance with her. Every time I went to walk away, at the end of a record, she would just spin me back around, nodding as if to say, another one, another one. Luckily it was the end of the night and I was saved by the lights coming on. I said my thank yous, and as I went to leave she grabbed my wrist and squeezed until the blood supply was severely restricted. I looked down at her forearm, and she had the word PET tattooed there. This was before woman had tattoos.

Then she said, 'Are ye's wanten te tek me awey heem hen?'

I spluttered, 'What?'

'Are ye's wanten te walk me heem?'

My God, I was being accosted. She wanted me to walk her home. If she got me into her house and did the things I suspected she had in mind for me, I might never see the light of day again.

'No, really, I couldn't, I mean, I've got to ...' was as far as I got.

She just said, 'Come on.' And I was walking her 'away heem' as she put it. We went straight into her house at about one o'clock in the morning and she introduced me to her mother (who looked like she'd just come in herself). She said 'Alright Pet?' Ah, that's where she got the name, I thought.

After saying hello, Pet said good night and we went upstairs. I had been in the house 30 seconds and was off up to bed with her daughter and nobody batted an eyelid. She wasn't gentle with me, she was firm, and demanding, but I survived. Anyway, in the morning, after she'd changed my oil again, I made a quick and silent exit, after promising to see her again at the club the next night, or else I don't think she would have let me go.

The next day, after diving, I bottled it and refused point blank to go out. I stayed in the flat we had rented and ironed my smalls, washed my hair, anything. OK, I was scared. I went to bed early and was asleep about midnight, when I was awoken by a lot of giggling and whispering. My bedroom door opened and a voice said, 'Tony, Tony ... why didn't ye go tae the dance, Tony, Tony?' She then got in bed with me again, and I was back to square one. The boys had thought it hilarious that Pet was asking after me all night, so brought her home with them. Not content with that, during the ensuing entertainment, I happened to hear a noise in the bed next to me, and there was Mick O'Leary's eye peering at me from under the bedclothes. He had crept in with Pet and was keeping an eye on the proceedings.

HMS *Bronington*

I joined HMS *Bronington* in May 1980. This time I hoped to make it the whole twelve months without getting run off. I was the Leading Diver this time. I had five divers under me, so to speak. I ran the diving side of things but was also in charge of the Fo'c'sle and had to be second officer of the watch.

The skipper on board was a Lieutenant Roy Clare. He had been Prince Charles's Jimmy (First Officer) when Charles had been on board as Captain. I don't suppose the Navy would pick just anyone as the future King of England's number one. They would have thought long and hard about it, and picked the best young officer they had. I think they got it right with Roy Clare. He seemed to know something, about everything. He also had a good number one himself. His name was Colin Welbourn. It was his job to take the heat off the skipper, just as Roy Clare had done for HRH. I remember having the world on my shoulders one day and slapping in an official request to leave the boat: anywhere would do, I'd had enough.

It came back to me with 'BULLSHIT' stamped right across it. He can't do that to an official document, I thought, so I wrote another one and that received the same treatment, only this time it had 'this man is suspected of being an anal intruder and should never be left alone with forest mammals, especially pretty ones!' written in the comments box. By the time I got to see him, I was over it. On one occasion we swapped uniforms in Burntisland in Scotland and I went ashore as a two-ringed Officer. He went as a Leading Diver. He was a nightmare. Around midnight, I had to drag him off the statue in the square and frog-march him home. I got all the bad press in the morning.

I went AWOL whilst on board as well. Absent without leave is a pretty serious offence in the mob as it can result in you missing your ship – as I did. I had a good excuse, though. I was seriously interfered with the night before, forced to stay the night, and had to perform again in the morning before she would let me go. I came out of a flat in Troon and looked around me. I had absolutely no idea where I was or how to get back to the ship. If you are a lost sailor on land, a good tip is to always head downhill. It will ultimately lead you to a river and hopefully the sea. I used this plan and eventually got a lift from a milk float. Whenever I thought I was getting close to knowing where I was, Jock the milkman would stop and go and deliver a pint or a dozen eggs to someone. When I finally got to the harbour, the *Bronny* was gone! It was one of those beautiful Scottish mornings. It was absolutely flat calm and sunny as I climbed up onto the harbour wall and could see for miles out to sea. There was a faint telltale smoke trail on the horizon from the ship's diesel engines. She wasn't due in until much later in the evening. I was in big doo-doos. I was AWOL.

I sat around the jetty most of the morning until my young lady turned up to see if I'd caught my ship. Her devious plan had worked and I'd missed it. So what was I supposed to do? She looked surprisingly good in the broad daylight, so I went back to hers for the afternoon and went back to bed. To sleep!

When my time came to leave the *Bronny*, this is the letter Colin Welbourn gave me to give to my parents:

Returning Home Letter

Issued in solemn warning this 1st day of May 1981

To the neighbours, friends and relations of LD Groom (RN)

Very soon the above named Diver will be in your midst once more, dehydrated, confused, and demoralised. Eager to regain his place in society as a human being, entitled to liberty and justice, whilst engaged in the somewhat delayed pursuit of happiness.

In making your joyous preparations to welcome him back to civilisation, you must make some allowances for the crude environment which has been his unfortunate lot for the last year. In brief, he may be suffering from various diseases contracted abroad including, 'sweatitis', 'rashitis' or even the shakes (a common local complaint brought on by the consumption of too much NAAFI canned beer, or C.S.B) and he may have become a trifle 'Scottish' in his outlook.

His diet, to which he has grown accustomed, should, for the first few weeks at least, consist of beer. Fresh or rich foods, especially milk, should be avoided for the first few weeks and then only introduced gradually. His only meat should be corned beef or spam. If he should prefer to eat his food with his fingers instead of the normal eating utensils please smile nonchalantly in an understanding manner.

Show no alarm if he prefers to sit on the floor instead of a chair, always kicks his boots off before entering the house, wears only a towel and flip flops when visiting the neighbours, or has a tendency to avoid anyone important. Side track him from partially filled coaches for he will almost certainly regard them as organised parties to the local brewery.

Do not allow him on the roads unaccompanied for it may prove his undoing. Traffic he has forgotten, and rather than walk he will sit on the pavement for hours muttering things about 'Fast blacks, rattlers or dockyard treaders' waiting for some tourist to take pity on him and offer him a lift.

Do all his shopping for him, gently establishing in his mind that all bartering, haggling, or threatening of shopkeepers is taboo in your land of civilisation. Always check his socks before washing as you'll usually find a few hidden Pound notes, Dollars, Yen etc. he has put there for emergencies.

His language may be rather embarrassing at times, but in a short time he can be taught to speak English again. Never make flattering remarks about the Army, RM or RAF in his presence.

For the first few months (until he has become house-trained), be particularly watchful when he is in the company of women, especially young and beautiful specimens, for he is liable to enter into discussions on prices, services rendered and money matters in general. His intentions are sincere but entirely dishonourable.

Keep in mind that beneath his rugged and tanned exterior there beats a heart of pure gold. Treasure this, as it is the only thing of value he has left.

Treat this man with kindness, consideration and tolerance and on occasions take him out for a good drink and you will be able to rehabilitate that which is but a hollow shell of the once happy person you knew.

Signed

Chief Medical officer. RN

Fleet Team again

The second time I joined the Fleet Team, it was an altogether more exciting affair, not that it was boring the first time around. I had only been on the team for a month when we were off to Crete for three weeks. Our job was to find about ten mines. Well, it all went a bit too well. We found five on the first day and five on the second day, and a Spitfire engine to boot. They had nothing else for us to do so the boss gave us a pocketful of money and said, 'Be back here by Friday.' We hired mopeds and off we went on a tour around the Greek islands. It was fantastic. The following week the same thing happened. There were a number of bike accidents and injuries, though. One lad, Mick Beal, wrote off three mopeds in a week and fractured both his wrists. When he got back to Pompey with them both in plaster he came round to our flat and picked up a weight-lifting curling bar in the flat and both wrists went 'pop'. They were now properly broken, not just slightly fractured.

As soon as we got back from Crete, we had to pack again for a trip to Turkey for two weeks. It was a bit like getting paid for going on diving holidays. I could live with that. It was a nice sabbatical after being cramped up on a minehunter for a year.

We had a new piece of trial equipment with us, an underwater mine-hunting sledge. Some trials can be boring and repetitive, like finding out how deep something will go before it implodes, or what happens if you smash it with a ball-peen hammer because it's a load of old rubbish and you don't want the Navy to buy it. We of course would never think of doing this, but it was an option considered perfectly legitimate by many.

The new sledge was none of these. It was about twelve feet long, bright yellow (we painted it matt black), with four control planes, two forward and two aft. It had a Perspex dome in the front for the pilot to lie in and be protected from the rushing water. Inside the dome were a few controls. You had levers to operate the planes to make it go to port or starboard, or you could push the levers forward to dive or back to make it rise. There were also controls to operate a quick release from the towing boat, and you could also use small air cylinders to blow tiny ballast tanks to make it surface in an emergency. We also rigged up a good system of communications between the diver and the boat driver that was towing you. It was of course only any good in very clear visibility, so was perfect for Turkey and the usually calm, blue, sheltered Aegean Sea.

It had cost someone a huge amount of money to develop and then try and sell to the Royal Navy. In reality we knew the Navy wouldn't buy it as it was too good, and generally the waters we searched mines for were too murky for a piece of kit like this.

That didn't stop us having great fun with it, though.

The first trick you had to try was a 360-degree barrel roll. Once you had mastered that, you would then try the breach. That is, you told the driver to go as fast as he could, while you drove the sledge as close as you dared to the seabed, then pulled up in the steepest possible climb to the surface. If you got it right you could nearly get the sledge completely out of the water. If you got it wrong you crashed it into the coral seabed and parted the towing line, much to the hilarity of the towing team. Another thing discovered by one of the divers, during these strict military trials, was that if you stuck your head outside the dome whilst going flat out, the water would rip your face mask off, hence causing a cessation in breathing, and much panic. By the time we gave it back to its rightful owners, it looked as though it had been dragged through a coral forest then dropped off a cliff. We just gave it back to them with a note tied to it that said something along the lines of 'No thanks'.

Being thrifty in Turkey, we put our extra accommodation money into our pockets and camped it up, if you catch my drift. After two weeks camping near Izmir, I was packing up my tent and found a huge scorpion had made its nest right under where my arse had been parked.

If we were back in our home base, HMS *Vernon*, any longer than a few weeks, the boredom and often heavy drinking would start to take over. We worked hard, although it may not sound like it, and we played hard. It was and is the diver's way, in the military and out of it. The only people I have met who seemed to have the same party ethic as divers are nurses. I don't know why this is, but it seemed to me that wherever we were based, the divers and the medical staff seemed to develop close personal relationships, if you get my meaning.

Jock Stewart, one of the team's CD2s, was on his way back from one such DTS (dinner time session) with a group of nurses we had become friends with. He arrived back at *Vernon* a little the worse for wear. Unfortunately for him he was driving one of the team's bomb wagons. This is a Land Rover with bright red front and back wing panels, a blue flashing police light for emergency bomb disposal jobs, a massive Gemini on the top and 'Navy Bomb and Mine Disposal' written on the back and sides – basically, not a vehicle for covert operations. Jock made it through the main gates OK and probably thought he was home free. Maybe because he relaxed too much, he wasn't as steady in his driving as he should have been.

The Jossman (the head Navy Regulator/MP) unfortunately was also using the same piece of road as Jock, on his push bike. Now normally this shouldn't be a problem, as the road was both long and wide enough for the two of them to share. At the court martial, however, the Joss apparently explained how he was neither quick enough, nor agile enough, to avoid the impending collision.

'On looking behind, I saw the accused driving erratically in the LR. I took evasive action and turned left, whereupon the LR did the same, so I turned sharp right. It seemed he was following me.'

Jock in his defence said, 'He rode backwards and forwards across the road until eventually I got him, sorry, I mean accidentally hit him.' Jock hit the poor Jossman a glancing blow and a sent him spinning into the wardroom hedge. Jock then drove on a few metres before realising that fleeing the scene of the crime in this eminently recognisable bomb wagon was not in his best interests. Like a gent, he stopped and reversed to see if the third party was OK. This is where he made his last mistake. Not by returning, but by reversing over the Joss's new bike in the process.

The Captain weighed up the evidence before him and decided to err on the side of caution. He found Jock guilty. On hearing the judgment, though, Jock didn't see it like that at all. He was flabbergasted that he had been stitched up with this fabricated tissue of lies and innuendo. Instead of apologising to the Navy for drinking in their time and using their vehicle for an illegal purpose, Jock just got angry. He went off on a rant to the Captain and told him he was sick of the Navy's petty ways and was sick of it all and would be 'Slapping in my eighteen months notice to leave forthwith.'

The Captain asked Jock, 'What is it you don't like about the Navy, Stewart?'

Jock thought long and hard about this and said ...

'The bits between leave, sir!'

Digs

Whilst on these shore-based teams, the first thing you would do was find a flat. Otherwise, it meant living in HMS *Vernon* or whatever Naval base the team was attached to, and being submitted to the draconian laws and rules that went with that, like Captain's rounds every week. This would involve some goon following the Captain around your bedroom wearing white gloves, looking for dust, checking inside your wardrobes, or telling you off for having pictures of scantily clad women on your walls. No, that would be no good at all. You had to get out of there and join the local student fraternity, in one of the cheap, but often dank, flats in the area.

At the time, I had a room in a flat at Yarborough Road in Portsmouth. This was the mother of all party houses. It was a huge flat with a small garden, a kitchen, a massive lounge, two reasonable-sized bedrooms and one you couldn't swing a rat in. When you took up your tenancy you would start with the matchbox-sized room and as people moved on you would be promoted to one of the bigger bedrooms. The only problem with the biggest room was it had the flat's only toilet in it. So, whatever proceedings may be going on in that bed, you would be interrupted at regular intervals throughout the night by the other residents, or their guests. The other highly desirable part of the flat was that the electricity meter was broken, so once a week someone would have to put the same 50-pence piece through the slot about 50 times. It got so hot in there that even when it was snowing we used to walk around in shorts.

We had that many parties there that some of the local taxi drivers used to call it 'the 21 Club'. They were quite convinced there was an illegal drinking den in one of the flats.

Tim Horner and I threw a party one night for our other flatmate, Garfield Rowland. It was his 23rd birthday so we pulled out all the stops and everyone on the team clubbed together to buy him something really special. We had just enough money to buy him a full-size black blow-up doll named Susie and a long black strap-on penis. He was thrilled to bits, so took both his new presents out to the pub with him. Gary being Gary saw no embarrassment in these gifts at all. He would find a way to use them to help him in his favourite hobby of 'trapping' women. The first pub we went into there was a reasonably attractive barmaid. Gary walked straight up to her with Susie under his arm, put the strap-on over the beer pump handle and said, 'We'll have eight pints of that one please.'

To give her credit, she did put her hand straight around it and pulled the pints. This was Gary's kind of woman, and he proceeded to give her his Inspector Clouseau rendition, which went something along the lines of 'Come on, my oven-ready chicken, my little vol-au-vent,' in his rubbish French accent. Within a few minutes they were usually laughing and he would have their phone number. His success rate was astounding. He was basically a slut and I was jealous. Sometimes I would be up in the morning and he would walk through to the kitchen with his previous evening's used johnnies and a big stupid grin on his face. The following night it would be someone else.

We met our usual crowd out in the Cambridge pub – usually a lot of divers – and all the girlfriends and women we knew. When there was about fifteen minutes to go until closing time, we would have a whip-round of about a fiver each and carry it all back to the 21 Club for our usual impromptu and un-organised party. Back at the flat, we would quite often, for some reason which evades me now, swap clothes with the girls. I know it sounds a little odd but the girls would go upstairs to Dolores's (live-in landlady) flat and come down wearing basques, or leotards, or little black numbers. Of course, it was nice to see the girls in this get-up, but they did have an ulterior motive, and that was that when we swapped clothes, we would look totally ridiculous. On the night in question, I was wearing a slinky black pinstriped mini-dress of Liz's and Gary was wearing a black and red basque. He had now taken to wearing his strap-on either on his nose or on the top of his head. I seem to remember that the girls were fascinated with the working parts of Susie and we were all in stitches and so possibly making a bit of noise.

In the building where the 21 Club was situated there were about seven other flats, and at the time all seven were taken up by women. The girl directly above our flat I do have some sympathy for (despite the fact that she was a miserable, sour-faced cow). Whenever we had a party, she would come down and moan about the noise. Fair enough. This night, Gary had foreseen this problem and beaten her to it. He had gone up to her flat, wearing a basque, with Susie under one arm and a dildo on his head. He somehow had her laughing and convinced her to come to our party. When she came in we all welcomed her as a new guest. It was better to have the devil within than have her upstairs phoning the police as usual, which is what we told her.

She put her hand to her mouth and said, 'I'm sorry, but I've already phoned them, about fifteen minutes ago!' Sure enough, the doorbell went.

Now, being somewhat short of seats for all the people in the flat, we had been using Susie, the blow-up doll, as a settee. The only problem with that was that it had turned her mouth inside out, so it now looked like she had a very long pink tongue. The same thing had happened to her nether regions. This thing was obviously soundly built in preparation for the pounding it was

▲ Prince Charles commissions his old ship HMS *Bronington*, 1980. New captain Roy Clare nearest camera, Leading Seaman Diver Groom on door opening duty.

◀ Placing a 4lb plastic explosive pack on a Mk13 American WWII ground mine. Funafuti Atoll.

▲ 55-metre diving, Rothesay.
L to R, TG, Alex,
Mick O'Leary, Gary Welch,
'Clint' Lynch.

▼ WW1 mine with PE pack.

▲
Typical bomb team
work. 250lb German
bomb.

▲ Satisfying bang. Gemini with us in foreground.

After losing to Royal Marine's boot at RAF Lynam. ▶

Torpedo dragged up by trawler, Old Portsmouth. L to R: Worried Copper, Nutty Carr, Mo Crang, Mick O'Leary.
(Photo: *The News*)

Recovery of Sikorsky passenger helicopter, Scilly Isles, July 1983.

Fleet Team at work (play?), Turkey, September 1981.

Underwater Christmas card photo, sent to other teams.

meant to take, as it had not popped. Poor Susie now looked like some twisted Frankenstein's monster. Her eyes were bulging, her once deep throat poked out like a tongue, and her vagina now looked like a long pink penis. When the doorbell went, Gary left his new-found girlfriend from upstairs with us and dragged his largely inside-out Susie (they were now inseparable) to the front door. What the two policemen beheld before them no doubt went right around the station.

There stood Gary, in a basque, complete with beard and hairy legs, and on his head was a very long strap-on black cock. He was towing behind him, by the penis, a black blow-up doll with very strange appendages. Instead of arresting him, which you would think would be the obvious course to take, the two policemen succumbed to Gary's usual charm and accepted an invitation to come in, whereupon an even stranger picture was brought before them.

I seem to remember they stayed for about an hour and reported over their radio they were 'Sorting out a domestic, sarge.' We had run out of mixers for the inordinate amount of duty-free booze that we always had and I remember one of the police officers quizzing me about the nature of my somewhat fizzy drink. When I told him I was drinking gin and 'Shake n Vac' he pulled a funny face and just left.

There was a communal hall in the house, and a communal payphone right outside our flat. It was before the days of mobiles so it was a race to the phone whenever it rang – because if it was for any of the other flats you would have to go up and bang on the door, hopefully catching them in all stages of undress. One day it rang and I got there first. On top of the phone was a vibrator, nobody else around, it just sat there all alone, so I rescued it. One of the girls had obviously gone down to the phone, put in on top and gone back to her flat, completely forgetting the most personal of all items. Gary, seeing a perfect opportunity, unselfishly used a great deal of personal time and effort to find its rightful owner. He would not rest until he had thoroughly grilled each member of the house. Alas it was never claimed and spent many a lonely month on top of our telly until, during another party, it disappeared.

Gibraltar 1982

On 22 March 1982 (only eleven days before the Argentinians invaded the Falklands) the Fleet Team had flown by Hercules from RAF Lyneham, with all our kit, to Gibraltar to take part in a big NATO exercise with ships from all over Europe and the Americas. We expected to be staying at the Navy shore base in Gibraltar called HMS *Rooke*. However, we were met with devastating news. There were no rooms at the inn. The Navy couldn't put us up. There were so many extra staff from all the different navies staying for the exercise. This was terrible. It would mean having to draw subsistence money (about £35 extra a day, back then) and go and find our own digs in a hotel or bed and breakfast. It was so busy there was nothing on the Navy side of the island but we were told we might get rooms in the posh part of town – Catalan Bay on the far side of the rock.

I knew Catalan Bay quite well from previous trips to Gibraltar, one of them having been eleven weeks long. I had been participating in some of the first live firings of the then new Mk 24 Tigerfish heavyweight torpedo. One piece of useless information that sticks in my mind is that a double gin and tonic cost 19 pence. An allowance of £35 a day could go a long way. I was out there with my 'Sea Dad', Dave Southwell. The border was permanently closed back then, to all service personnel, anyway, and there is not a great deal to do on the rock. We would try to stay out of the bars but we would fail miserably. When I returned home after my eleven-week sabbatical, my mother barely recognised me.

Anyway, about twenty of us pitched up at the doors of the

Caleta Hotel, the biggest and most spectacular hotel on the rock, trying to look smart in our number eights (the Navy's casual blue working uniform). Sometimes we would wear tracksuits and travel as a 'football team'. One or two, who shall remain nameless (Wilki, it was his birthday), had secretly been drinking on the Herc on the way over and were being hushed up by the rest of us.

Bill Bauckham, one of our chief divers, was at the desk trying to arrange twin rooms for us all. We, on the other hand, were told to remain inconspicuous, as we were not the normal clientele the hotel was used to, or indeed seeking. From the reception area you could see into the piano lounge bar and dining room, which through huge glass windows had a spectacular view overlooking the entrance to the Mediterranean. There was a sweeping, majestic stairway running down the middle of the dinning room and some very wealthy-looking guests, scoffing their scran.

Nobby Newborn, a bit the worse for wear, and a wild card after a few beers, looked through into the dining area and saw the huge grand piano. Instead of staying with the rest of us in reception, he walked straight across the dining room as bold as brass and sat down at the piano. 'Can he play the piano?' No one seemed to know. He then proceeded to make a big fuss of looking through the music sheets, adjusting his seat, flicking back his hair and un-tucking his shirt, so as to have the classic pianist's coat tails. 'He must be able to, I didn't know, did you know he could play?' No one did. All along, he was getting more and more attention from the diners, the waiters and the maitre d. Some had even turned their chairs, expecting a free concert of sorts.

He then made a show of looking around to the now expectant diners, and, nodding at them before turning back to his music, lifted his hands ... as if to say, now ... I shall begin.

What came next was just a noise. It wasn't anywhere near as good as Les Dawson used to manage. He just smashed all the keys with his fingers like a naughty, somewhat stroppy child.

It sounded more like someone dropping a piano down the stairs than trying to play it.

The maitre d, with the help of a couple of other waiters, was over in seconds, and Nobby was unceremoniously escorted onto the pavement, closely followed by us. Poor Bill Bauckham had not even finished signing us in when he was asked to leave, and he didn't even know what had happened. Within ten minutes of our arrival, we were scouting around for cheaper B and Bs, and splitting the team into groups of two and three to try and fit us all in somewhere. The boss was not impressed. We had yet to dive or do any work and we were well and truly in the ka-ka.

The next day and night we made our preparations for the following night's sabotage attack on the warships. The harbour was chock-a-block with grey funnel lines from all over the world. We were going to use three teams of two divers, and each team of two would attack four warships each. It was always a bone of contention with us that we had to give up on the last warship. It was a bit like they had actually caught us in the act of sabotage. We knew full well, had we not wanted to be caught, and had simply swum away, none of us would ever have been spotted.

We practised attack swims around the marina area so the warships couldn't see us, and consequently did not know what to expect the next night. Then we did some in the harbour at night. It is probably a good hour's night swim across Gibraltar harbour, from Rooke to the outer walls. So we hatched a shrewd plan to reduce the swim by half.

We made two large banners, which in red letters on a white background said, 'SAFETY BOAT'.

The day before, and the evening leading up to the attacks, one of our rubber Geminis, with these signs on it, would steam all around the harbour showing itself to the warships. The lookouts and the marines got used to this 'safety boat', and so weren't suspicious of it at all. 'WHO GOES THERE?', the traditional cry in the forces to seek whether you are friend or foe, was simply met with 'Safety Boat', then you just pointed at the big white sign and raised your eyebrows as if to say 'Obviously!'

Underneath an identical Gemini in *Rooke*, we built an underwater platform which sat just aft of the outboard engine and about three metres below the surface.

Our brief was to attack anywhere between 9 p.m. and midnight. Then we had to give ourselves up on the last ship we had mined, pretending we couldn't speak English, until told to by the controlling safety officer.

Come the night of the assault on 25 March, all six of us slipped silently into the water wearing O_2 rebreathers. We then put our cunning plan into operation. We slipped under the Gemini, grabbed hold of the underwater platform, and were towed silently, slowly, and invisible from the surface, out into the middle of the harbour.

When in the correct position the engine went quiet and was lifted clear of the water to simulate a foul propeller scenario. The supervisor cleared the prop, of nothing, and checking we hadn't been rumbled, he then tapped 'two bells' (go out or away, if you remember?) on the metal casing of the engine. We silently swam away from the platform towards our prearranged first target.

The Gemini engine was then started again and, free of its human load, moved away. To us, when the engine noise diminished sufficiently and all was quiet, we used our 'sneaky' technique to slowly come to the surface and take a bearing with our compass on our first ship.

Each diver would carry two limpets, one for each ship. These were obviously dummies that were made to look quite real, complete with a yellow band across the middle. Even when you know they are not real, if you are searching a warship at night in a strange port, in one of these exercises, it is a bit of a buzz to come across one.

I had seen some real ones that were made by the Israelis. These were completely smooth and looked like the classic fire-bell shape. They were held on by magnets like most limpet mines but these had one deadly difference. In the middle of the area that would be stuck to the ship or your target was a piston protruding about an inch. Once you armed the limpet by pulling a pin and pushing it onto the hull, there was no taking it off. If you did, the piston would spring back out and it would explode. Once it was on, it stayed on, until it exploded. The only defence was to flood the compartment adjacent to the limpet inside the ship and burn or cut a piece of the ship's hull away with the limpet. All along, not knowing what time was set on the mine or what would trigger it. Ingenious.

I only surfaced once, not long after the Gemini had moved on, to get a bearing on my first target. As the 'driver' of the pair of swimmers, I had the swim board. On this board you have attached a luminous compass, a depth gauge, and a watch. As you are swimming, you only have eyes for the compass, with occasional glances at the depth. When really worked/trained up on attack swims, I could come up under a plastic bottle and pull it under at a distance of some 100 metres. One somewhat cruel trick I have seen is to come under a duck or seagull and pull it under! Now that is sneaky-beaky diving. The swim itself is always tinged with excitement: it is always dark, you have no float and you two are truly alone and free agents. You have to look after each other totally, the trust must be complete. The glowing phosphorescence would sweep over your swim board, occasionally the moon would come out and you might get the eerie silhouette of your buddy diver just below you and to one side. There is utter silence. I always enjoyed it, even with the anticipation of the impending orchestrated capture and questioning at the back of your mind. When it was for real it was even more exciting, but if I wrote about that ... ! These were always nervy times for the supervisors too because if something were to go wrong, you could not be traced. Staring ahead and judging your swim speed by your watch, you could estimate your ETA (estimated time of arrival) pretty well, especially in a harbour like Gibraltar where there was no tide effect. The dark hull would suddenly leap out at you, and it always made you jump, even when you were expecting it. We attached our mines on the three other ships and then moved along to the fourth, a certain HMS *Coventry*.

We slowly surfaced and made our way to the boarding ladder that went down to the water's edge. We were on the surface and I guess about two metres away before someone spotted us. Then there was utter pandemonium, lots of lights shone on us, shouting and guns pointed at us. I remember one of the ship's Royal Marines, taking it very personally and acting like we were really attacking his ship. He was screaming at us and gesticulating for us to get out of the water, or he was definitely going to shoot us! We climbed leisurely out of the water while he continued to threaten us. We both took our masks off and waited for instructions. We had already decided before entering the water that neither of us could speak English. We decided, for one night only, we would be Russian.

We were persuaded up to the top of the steps at gunpoint, where it was made clear we were to remove our diving gear, which we duly did. But when I reached down to my calf to take off my eight-inch diving knife, again, I had the barrel of a 7.62 mm self-loading rifle (SLR) jammed into my ribs from this over-zealous Marine. He was really getting into this, and beginning to get to me. Eventually the officer of the watch came along and put bags over our heads and had us marched along the Burma way inside the *Coventry*. We were then put into the stress position, i.e. spread-eagled up against a bulkhead.

Then we were questioned. 'How many mines did you place?'

In answer to my interrogator, I gave various replies in my best Russian accent, such as, '*Your suitcases are too heavy for my donkey.*' That gave him something to think about!

The Marine who had stuck to me like my underwear was virtually growling at me by then. 'When are they going to go off?'

I replied, '*The last train for Moscow left three days ago.*'

Then, as we all do if someone doesn't understand us, he just said it a little louder. 'Where did you place them?' he shouted.

'*You are homosexual, ... No?* was my reply.

I was still in the stress position during my interrogation and had been unable to see because of the bag over my head. During these exercises, there is usually a safety officer around in case someone gets a little over-zealous, and he told them to remove my bag. As soon as I could see I looked up to see what my hands had been on, only to notice I had spent all this time with my hands on a fire axe! I thought about unshipping it, and maybe making a threatening gesture, à la Jack Nicholson in *The Shining*, just to see what would happen. Then I looked to my right to see my ever-present, personal, snarling Marine and thought better of it.

Eventually the safety word was called out, usually 'Safeguard', which means everyone back to reality. Then we had to tell them where the mines were, how many and what other ships had them on. They then, of course, put their own ship's divers in the water to search the hulls (Operation Awkward). They couldn't do important work like this now as the powers that be have decided in their wisdom we have no real use for ship's divers any more. In today's world – full of threats from terrorism – try and explain that one to me.

I then had a little word with my own personal Marine and said, 'You do know I'm English, don't you? You do know this is all a big exercise and I'm really on your side, don't you? I'm not really Russian, you do realise that, don't you?' I think he'd got a little caught up in the moment and just stared at me with hate-filled eyes. Weird, I thought.

What is really the point of me telling you all this? Well, I checked my RN Diver's logbook and on 25 March 1982 it says:

GIBRALTAR. NIGHT ATTACKS ON FOUR SHIPS.

VIS GOOD. GAVE UP ON HMS COVENTRY.

DEPTH 9 m. DURATION 65 MINS. CDBA O2 ON DEMAND.

It seems a bit ironic that on 25 March I was placing a limpet on HMS *Coventry*, and exactly two months later to the day, on 25 May, she was fighting for her life and eventually sinking with the loss of nineteen men in the South Atlantic's icy waters. There had been no hint then that she would meet such a violent end. Her crew were a happy bunch and after the 'interrogation' looked after us well and even 'spliced the mainbrace' for us in the mess. I never saw the Marine again, but I suspect to this day he has anger management issues.

Sounds like the buggers mean it

All the arms we need are for hugging.

The second of April came along and everyone found out where the Falklands were. The then Governor of the Falkland Islands, Sir Rex Hunt, on receiving a signal from the British Government, had an emergency meeting with his two senior Royal Marines in Government House. 'Sounds like the buggers mean it!' is what he said to them after reading the warning from England of a possible Argentine invasion, received on 31 March.

In HMS *Vernon* we watched a number of ships leave Portsmouth harbour on their way down south. They had a fantastic leaving party and one of the minehunters about 200 metres from our building had the famous white poster on the sweep deck. It read 'Don't cry for me, Argentina!' It still wasn't really anything to do with us on the team, was it? They would soon leave when they saw what we were sending their way, wouldn't they?

As the days went by, though, it seemed we might well go. It was only hints and rumours at first. Then we started packing stuff. After half a dozen false dawns, we got the call on 12 April and blue-lighted it, complete with police escort, from Portsmouth to RAF Lyneham on the 13th. We flew all the way to Ascension Island and then, for want of a better word, we bummed around the island trying to find a decent place to sleep. We had a couple of nights in what was dubbed Lunar Camp, because it really did look like the surface of the moon. It was just a load of Army tents pitched up near the black golf course. The poor souls that were posted there had tried to make the most of it by building an eighteen-hole course on pure volcanic rock. It is still in the Guinness Book of Records as the world's worst course. Eventually we managed to get a roof over our heads and stayed up the hill in a big communal hall of sorts. On one side of us was a large contingent of SAS and on the other side were the SBS. Now these boys don't much care for each other, and some comedian had put us in the middle. Whether we were supposed to keep the peace I don't know, but we just sort of stirred it up and then stood back and watched the fireworks.

After a few false ships, we wound up on the *Sir Tristram*, with most of our gear, and were ready to go.

It's started

On 2 May 1982 at around 17:00 we (the Fleet Clearance Diving Team) were steaming south towards the Falklands listening to the BBC World Service. Aboard the *Sir Tristram*, we heard the news that the *General Belgrano* had been sunk. It was just a warship to us and many thought that it might be enough to stop any ideas the Argentinians might have of starting a war. We had no idea that 300 or so sailors died that evening. Saying that, it wasn't too much of a shock; we were so confident in our ability and superior seamanship and technology, it was pretty much what we thought might happen some time or other. It meant it was going to kick off now, though. It was looking increasingly unlikely we were going to all make friends and go home any time soon.

Two days later I was virtually alone in the mess, listening to the World Service again, when I heard that HMS *Sheffield* had been sunk by Exocet missile. I ran up to the galley, where most of the ship's company were watching *Flash Gordon*. I was so shocked that when I made the announcement I could hardly speak. My voice was distinctly unclear, 'They've sunk the *Sheffield*.' Stunned silence. 'They've sunk the *Sheffield*,' I managed to blurt out. Some wouldn't believe me. This was not meant to happen. Utter disbelief, shock, now we will have to go in, I thought.

Sunday 20 May 1982 RFA Sir Tristram

Steaming around in a nautical box inside the 200 mile limit. This is the fourth day we've done this now. Boredom has really set in. One day just runs into the next, with no difference.

Practise action stations a few times again. At 1800 got the world news very clearly for a change.

At 1810 all ships received this signal from Admiral Woodward.

THE EYES AND THE EARS OF THE WORLD ARE UPON US.

BE STRONG IN RESOLVE

BE BRAVE IN BATTLE

BE MERCIFUL IN VICTORY.

(We go in tomorrow morning)

This was the first day I had decided I was going to keep a diary, just in case something happened. It was the first day I would realise I was going to war. It's a wake-up call when that dawns on you.

I was on the *Sir Tristram* with 400 or so Booties (Marines) and an assortment of specialist troops like the Mountain and Arctic Warfare Troop. Being essentially matelots (the French word for sailors), we never really had much of an opportunity to mix with these guys in the daily run of the forces. However, four weeks at sea in what was essentially just a cramped troop-carrying mess is enough to get to know your fellow 'sailors'. They may not appreciate being called that, but for those four weeks, they certainly knew they were at sea.

On the steam south from Ascension, you have to go through what mariners call the Roaring Forties. This refers to the latitudes between 40° and 50° south. I had been through rough weather myself in the Navy but I had never seen anything like this. The wind down there has hardly any land mass to slow it down. Great atmospheric depressions sweep unhindered around the cold, endless seas at the bottom of the earth, building the icy green water into an endless succession of mountainous waves. These heavy winds predominantly roar in from the west, so you're either rolling heavily or smashing your way through the huge seas. *Sir Tristram* took most of these 'goffers' on her starboard bow. As they slammed into her they made a noise like a metallic explosion.

Up on the bridge is always the place to witness these spectacular demonstrations of nature's ferocity. The waves march on at you in perfect formation, relentless and menacing. Looking out from your secure location behind inch-thick glass, there is nothing but white madness and howling wind.

Then, every so often, on the horizon, you can see a bigger one. As it gets closer, you track the 'rogue' wave. There is the taller than normal summit, yes, but before you get over that, you have to negotiate the deeper than normal trough that falls away before it. The ship's head drops into this dark basin, where the screech of the gale lessens as you are blanketed from it by the towering slope of dark green coming your way. The ship buries her bows into the valley, and then starts the gut-wrenching climb up the advancing wall of water. Your knees bend as you hang on and you have to lean forwards to counteract the steep angle of the climb. The vibrations of the engines increase as they try to drive the faltering 6,000-ton ship uphill. Then, just as you are about to stall, the bows burst through the top of the crest, sending the white water smashing into the bridge before it is snatched away in the storm, only to repeat the cycle over and over again, day after day, night after night.

The *Tristram*, when going through these walls of water, would bend and vibrate alarmingly. All the craft heading south were loaded down to the gunwales with heavy equipment. We had armoured personnel carriers, light tanks, 105 mm light field guns – the lot. One thing that did concern me a tad was the ageing 'double front doors' of the *Tristram*, getting battered in this relentless hammering.

Some of the Marines spoke longingly of getting ashore. One lad, I remember, could only stop throwing up when on the upper deck, lying down. When walking around the upper deck at night, it looked like there was a body up there under one of these guns.

They were a great bunch and we got on brilliantly with them. The amount of abuse flung about may seem to an outsider to be totally over the top, but that is how the forces are run, and it works. Whoever can give the other the most grief is seen as the winner, for that exchange, or that day. We, numbering eighteen, were outgunned, big style, but I think we more than held our own in difficult circumstances. It helped, of course, that we were the 'senior' service!

What boosted our egos enormously was a little bit of Dutch courage, and we were helped in this respect by an old Naval tradition called 'splicing the mainbrace'. The mainbrace was one of the most important – and heaviest – pieces of running rigging in an old ship of the line, and it was essential for manoeuvring the ship. In the old sea battles, the British would customarily aim at their opponent's hull, hoping to take out guns and personnel. The French on the other hand took the view that it was best to shoot out the enemy's rigging: take away her ability to manoeuvre, and you will have the upper hand. Both sides would use the normal cannonball, but the French also used a lot of chain shot. This was two half-cannonballs joined by a piece of chain. When fired from a gun it would be sent spinning through the air, grabbing rigging, masts and ropes as it went. The mainbrace essentially took the weight of the main yard, which in turn carried the sail. If your mainbrace was shot away, repairing it quickly was very important. In fact it was probably seldom spliced if damaged, but renewed in total instead. Splicing this line would have been among the most difficult chores aboard ship, and one on which the ship's safety depended. The operation was one of such rarity and difficulty as to warrant the issue of an additional amount of rum to the ship's company. For sailors today, the term refers to congratulating the crew. In common usage, it means an invitation to have a drink after a hard day (or not so hard day).

When Mick Fellows (our Fleet Chief Diver) summoned us to his cabin to splice the mainbrace, we had no intention of fixing *Sir Tristram*'s masts. Where Mick got such an extraordinary amount of Pusser's Rum, to enable the team to have a tot every day for the four-week voyage, I have no idea. I have never asked him. It would take place at 13:00 every day and we would leave his cabin with a ruddy glow on our cheeks and ready to do battle with anyone.

The Cadre (Mountain and Arctic Warfare) lads were in our mess, along with all sorts of other units. One night making our own entertainment, I noticed a Cadre lad cleaning a weapon in the mess. He had made some attempt at concealing what he was doing by drawing his bunk curtains. Crikey, I thought. I sauntered over and started asking stupid questions a sailor might ask a squaddie about guns, like 'What is it?' To which he replied, 'Oh this, a Colt 45.'

Christ, says I. Isn't that what Dirty Harry had, 'The most powerful handgun in the world, PUNK, make my day ...'? etc.

'Yeah,' he says with a grin. I had no idea it was so huge, a Colt 45 I mean. You couldn't point it with one hand without it waving around like a flower in the wind. I had trouble picking it up with two hands. I also had no idea you could take your own weapons along with you. Can you take your own hand grenades, ammunition, maybe? He unwittingly answered what was to be my next question.

Next to his cleaning kit was what looked like a fishing tackle box – you know, the ones that have a see-through top so you can see what lead or float you want. You can spin the top round and select what you want from a small opening. Looking at this more carefully, I noticed it was carrying not fishing tackle but a selection of the most evil-looking shells I've ever seen. Noticing the direction of my gaze, he proceeded to give me a run-down on the killing potential of each garish slug.

One delight he had in his Pandora's box was an armour-piercing round. What?

'Yeah,' he said. 'If you know your target's wearing a bullet-proof vest, you use this and prove him wrong!'

Of course! Well you would, wouldn't you? Keep him close I thought; well, don't make an enemy of him, anyway.

Later in the campaign, we learned that these lads were heavily involved in the battle to take Top Malo House. All nineteen of them, in fact.

We had about four weeks at sea and time to kill. There were all sorts of activities going on to keep the boys busy. You could go for a run, well, a 'dodge' – the decks had so much extra gear on board you could hardly go a few paces without having to go round, over or under some piece of military hardware. You could join 42 Commando for PT sessions, where lots of shouting and cajoling and even threatening of violence was commonplace. We did a lot of weight training and there were weekly sit-up and press-up competitions. What a laugh they were.

They also organised lectures. The team had one on Conduct after Capture, the usual stuff: name, rank and serial number. Also, what to do in the event of us getting lost and 'rescued' (captured) by the Argentinians. Although I think the correct term according to the Geneva Convention is Prisoner of War. Maybe they would want to torture us to see if we could actually remember anything.

The team had one about being caught and made a POW. Then there was one about escape and evasion techniques, dealing with torture, living rough in the Falklands, etc. Personally, I thought the torture lecture was very good and could be put to use in everyday life, such as when getting grilled by a loved one as to why you are three hours late and you only went out for one. Others seemed to have an even more light-hearted response to the correct way to behave in a torture situation. One of our Chief Divers, Ben Gunnell, came up with one of the best quotes I heard in my whole time down there. He said, 'If I were caught, they'd have to threaten me with torture ... to shut me up!' The thing was, he meant it.

The lectures were usually by a stern and serious sergeant who obviously knew his craft very well. One lecture I remember was given by one of the marines who had served in the Falklands garrison. In fact, I am not certain, but I think, he may have even been there during the initial invasion.

The sergeant lecturer was telling us about things to eat if you're living rough: where to find water, make a shelter, move at night, etc. All very interesting, but we were after all meant to be sailors, of a sort. We were quite convinced that if anything did ensue – and some on board were sure it never would – we wouldn't be going ashore anyway, would we?

I remember one talk going particularly badly for the lecturer. It was about 13:30 so, unfortunately for him, just after one of our very private splice the mainbrace sessions. He was telling us the best animals to eat and where to find, trap and cook them. Then, after finding out how to kill just about everything that lived there, he seemed to think better of it. He paused, looked at us, and said, 'Actually ... you lot are probably best sticking to penguins. You don't have to catch or trap them; they'll walk up to you, and you just smash 'em round the head with something heavy!'

To which came the reply, 'Do they have red ones down there, sarge?' (Jan Sewell, I believe it was.)

'Red ones?'

'Yeah, they're my favourite. I like to suck all the chocolate off the outside then eat the biscuit underneath.' We thought this was highly amusing; our lecturer just sighed and carried on regardless of the sniggering.

We learnt that there were all sorts of islands and areas named after the most prevalent animal to live on it, like Penguin Point, Fox Island, Rabbit Hill, and Swan Island. 'It must be like a f**king zoo down there,' was one comment. This time Wilki stuck his hand up and asked, 'Where's the Virgin Islands, sarge?' which we thought was hilarious; he evidently did not, and ended the lecture early.

It was a bit like a war on the way down there some days. So much firing would go on, I was a bit worried we might run out of ammo before we got there. It wasn't just small arms that were firing either; the 40/60 Bofors would have a go as well. One day I came up on deck to see two 105 mm light field guns lashed to the deck and aiming over the side, with boxes of ammo alongside. Surely not! You can't just fire them over the ship's side, can you? Yes, is the answer to that. Anyone who was of a slightly nervous disposition would have been shaken to the core that day. Walking along the vehicle deck without prior knowledge of the firings would have been akin to being on the middle deck of the *Victory* when she fired her twelve-pounders on the deck above. Loud, is what I'm trying to say. These things fire a 34.5-pound shell about ten and a half miles. So it has to have a big bang.

Everyone, it seemed, was shooting something. Except us, that is, but there was a good reason for that. It is said in the Army and the Marines that there is nothing on earth as dangerous as a matelot with a gun. We were to prove this proverb correct one day. On the helideck, which was high and aft on the *Sir Tristram*, a lot of shooting went on. They would chuck something over the stern, or sometimes tow it, and the bootnecks could blast away at it to their hearts' content. 'Can we have a go?' must have come up somewhere, and I'm sure much to their disapproval someone said yes. I loved it. I had a go with a GPMG, the American Armalite M16 and various assault rifles. My favourites, though, were the sniper rifles. I seem to remember the guy teaching me to use a wooden-stock 7.62 mm L42A1.

I loved the precision of these weapons. Even I managed to hit a bag of gash, which in my imagination was at least a mile away, that I had consistently missed with the GPMG. But it came to a sudden and, in my mind, untimely end when one of our lads had a premature discharge. Now you normally go and see the scab-lifters (medics) about this sort of complaint in the Navy, as it more often than not comes about by an illicit liaison with a lady of ill repute. But in Her Majesty's Army it is called a 'Negligent Discharge' and is a court martial offence.

I won't say who it was but the round hit the deck and bounced off into the sunset. No harm done? Hardly. 'You would think I'd shot someone!' said the culprit after coming back to us following a rigorous dressing-down by a Sergeant Major (SM). 'Well you nearly did,' we pointed out. My sniping days were over. It was fun while it lasted, though.

Prick on a stick

Now I know one shouldn't generalise about SMs, but these chaps didn't appear to have much in the way of a sense of humour. Once, a couple of years earlier on a Leading Divers course, we were doing an Explosives course at DEODS in Rochester, Kent. It's a Tri Service School, training all three services in the art of explosives disposal, but as it is in an Army camp they naturally assume total superiority.

The Army and Navy have always had a little misunderstanding going on. You tell a Corporal you are a Leading Diver and he doesn't have a clue what that means. Who's senior? Who knows? Who cares? You tell a sailor you are a Colour Sergeant and he might ask, 'What colour?'

Anyway, to cut a long story short ... We were on our way back to classes at DEODS after visiting a local hostelry as part of a fact-finding mission. This usually included facts such as, what particular beer they sold, how many pennies one had to part with to purchase a flagon of their finest ale, was the bar-maiden sufficiently endowed to fulfil her duties? Important questions that could keep one awake at night if unsure of the answers. After pooling our resources, we found we did indeed have sufficient funds to purchase more than just the one beverage. Wherever we went, we would always endeavour to support the local economy by buying as many as we could.

So, with an alcohol-fuelled sense of bravado, we took a short cut across the parade ground, sacred turf in the Army, and used for marching, shouting, and parading only. This was a heinous crime in itself, but we weren't just ambling along. We were doing 'Baggy Trousers', the Madness song that has you all walking along very close behind each other, in step and swinging your arms in unison. When we hear this god-awful shout come from the guardroom area.

'Right! You lot! Stay where you are!'

We all stopped to see what the noise was, only to see a Regimental Sergeant Major (RSM) marching our way. He's immaculate. He's got the hat on with the doctored peak so you can only just see his eyes, the pace stick under one arm with a silver engraved end, boots you could see your face in with ironed laces, gaiters, moustache, the whole shebang.

What does he want, we wonder. Before we can even ask him, he begins shouting.

'The only ones allowed to walk on my parade ground is me, the Colonel, and God ... and the only reason God is allowed is 'cos I can't phuqin see him!'

To which Spider Webb, one of our lads, asked, 'Well, how do

you know that he does it then?'

More expletives followed. 'What do you lot think you are doing on my parade ground?'

Spider just looked him in the eye and said, 'Madness marching, sarge.'

He went ballistic, calling us all sorts of horrid things. He even cast doubt on the authenticity of our parenthood.

Well, calling Spider a bastard is red rag to a bull. In his eyes this was a challenge. He'd have to break him, if not mentally then physically, and I could see it was going to get ugly. The RSM and Spider were still eye to eye, neither of them flinching or giving any ground. The rest of us, on the other hand, were inching backwards. The RSM then tapped Spider on the chest with his pace stick. 'Oh no. Please don't do that,' I was thinking.

'I've got me some kind of little prick at the end of this stick, haven't I'? says the RSM.

'Maybe sarge,' says Spider, 'but it ain't at this end.'

Ouch, it got nasty then and all sorts of higher ranks got involved. I seem to remember, however, that they were unable to show us anything in any DEODS Operational Standing Orders to say you 'Couldn't do Madness Marching' across the parade ground. It probably says it now, though.

Later on, whilst giving his account of the confrontation to our Chief Diver, Spider explained, 'I wasn't really arguing with him, it was more like a theological debate with some pongo [wherever the Army goes, the pongos, allegedly] who kept swearing at me, Chief.'

Spider's ability to stay calm and detached was later recognised by the forces, and he went on to become one of Her Majesty's finest Interrogation Specialists. All chosen for their gentle easygoing attitude and unnerving ability to stay composed and focused in stressful situations. All nice people, though. Spider will tell you he is perfectly normal, but he will admit that his Yin and his Yang have never quite been in equilibrium.

Falklands

Late in the evening of 20 May I went up on the bridge wing, and the whole invasion fleet were crammed up close to each other and steaming in a tight group. All the civvy ships and RFAs (Royal Fleet Auxiliaries) like us were in the middle and all the frigates and destroyers were on the outside. It was a brilliant sight. Usually at sea you spend a great deal of time, thought and energy making sure you never get too close to any other shipping. This time we were all very close. I think the idea was to steam at Port Stanley and give a huge radar image to the Argies. Maybe have them think we were going to gatecrash straight into the capital. Quite close in, we turned to starboard all together, went round the north of the islands, and headed for what was going to be the beachhead landing site, San Carlos Water.

The night before we went in, I don't think anyone really slept. I know I didn't. It was very quiet on board; most people were keeping their thoughts to themselves. Writing letters seemed to be a popular occupation.

Friday 21 May 1982. D Day for us!

DAY ONE UNDER ATTACK.

We entered Port San Carlos 04:15. In line astern were HMS Antrim, Sir Galahad, Sir Tristram, Sir Percival, Sir Geraint, two large ferries Norland and Europic, Canberra, HMS Fearless, HMS Intrepid, HMS Argonaut, HMS Antrim, HMS Ardent, HMS Brilliant, HMS Broadsword, and a few more civvy ships.

Troops had gone ashore all night. As we came into Port San Carlos, at darken ship, shooting could be seen (tracer) but not heard, up in the hills around us. Hearts were racing.

It was very eerie as we came in quietly and

totally unopposed. All through the early morning while at anchor, troops, tanks, jeeps etc. were pouring off all of the ships. I was given a job as Gun crew as it was known I'd done it before.

Around ten o'clock came the pipe.

'Hands to action stations, Gun crews close up, Air raid warning red IMMINENT'

This time was for real. Five Skyhawks and three Mirage fighters attacked the fleet. A missile landed between the Elk and us, it was meant for the Elk. It was terrifying but fantastic. The noise was incredible. 4.5 inch guns going off from the warships, Bofors, Sea Cat missiles, Blowpipes etc were coming off us. They were dropping 1000lb bombs, 250lb bombs, and firing 2 inch rockets etc. The jets were low and going very fast. The Rapier missile systems were on the hills around us but no ammo had got up to them yet. Our missiles could be seen going up but we saw no planes come down. They were so fast.

They attacked 3 more times, in waves of four. The gun I was on got four rounds away at a Pucara jet but missed.

At the end of the day many of their planes were shot down. Nig, Jan and Mick went to the Antrim to deal with a 1000lb UXB. It had gone through the Sea Slug launcher, through the magazine then tuned upwards and hit the deck head (which was the underside of the helideck), dropped down and landed in the senior rates heads. It took all night to lift and get over the side. During this the Ardent could be seen exploding about two miles away. It sunk about 07:00, 22 dead. Some of the survivors came on board the Antrim and other ships.

Got no sleep. Nigel and Jan told me the chopper
on the flight deck was riddled with holes and
a sergeant who was manning the GPMG machine
gun might have been killed. The flight deck
was covered in blood and holes from shrapnel
and rockets. The injured were in the wardroom.
Crying could be heard.

Sneaking into Port San Carlos at four in the morning was exhilarating. Whenever something was going on, I could be found hovering around the bridge. It's amazing the tit-bits you can pick up just listening in the background. The bridge is not only the eyes and the ears of every ship but also the buzz centre. It is said in the Navy, 'This one is hot off the galley stove,' meaning this is a new buzz (story). The truth is the galley is the centre of the ship – everyone goes there, and everyone talks and listens there. Then from the galley it goes to the bridge in the form of tea, sarnies and buzzes. 'Got any buzzes? Heard the latest buzz?'

I could see tracer going from one hill to another across what looked like the entrance to San Carlos. A quick burst of tracer fire, then quiet, then another burst. Then one of the warships (*Antrim*, I think) up ahead of us fired a single 4.5-inch round at where the tracer was heading in the hills. It soon became apparent that the sneaky boys (SBS) were telling the ship where to aim using a thermal imager.

Another burst slightly further along, then another shell. Then I can only presume they said something along the lines of 'Yep! That's the spot – let 'em have it,' because then the frigate up ahead let loose a lot of shells. Well, I thought, if there was anyone there, they aren't there now. Then it all went quiet again.

A later search found eleven Argentinian bodies on the hill, from where they would have had a grandstand view of the landings.

We then slid silently into our anchorage, still at darken ship. Which means no, and I mean NO, light is allowed to escape the ship to give away its position. Ships signal each other and tell them if they have any 'light leakage'.

As part of our CD2s course we once had to attack HMS *Bulwark* around midnight just off Portland. We had to pretend to be hostile divers, saboteurs if you like, and attach inert limpet mines to the ships to test their reaction. We would then give ourselves up and test their interrogation techniques (which varied enormously from good to hilariously bad). We were out at sea in a little rubber Gemini in the middle of the night and I swear, no more than half a mile away on a moonless night, you couldn't see this whacking great aircraft carrier because she was fully darkened. Halfway through my 'attack swim' I popped just my eyes up level with the surface, to get a fix on the carrier with my compass, and could only tell it was there by the outline in the sky and stars. Only when close in could you hear the generators on board through the sea. Even then, it makes you jump when you swim into it.

Mind you, despite its bulk one team (who shall remain nameless) still managed to miss it. 'You missed the *Bulwark*?' It was hardly mentioned in the pub later.

My point is, darken ship works. It's amazing, but dark grey is the perfect colour to camouflage a ship. Look at the horizon at sea on any given day, what colour will you see? Maybe that's why they use it.

We finally anchored about 04:30, the first time I think we'd stopped and gone without engines for thousands of sea miles. Although it came to my attention that the perfect quiet came at a price. It was dark and seriously hushed in San Carlos Water at that time of the morning, until the assembled ships had to anchor. The noise of the fathoms of cable racing through their hawse pipes would have woken the dead, never mind a sleepy Argentinian lookout. If they didn't know we'd snuck in here before, I thought, they do now.

No sooner had we anchored than a monumental effort to get

as many men, machines, artillery, ammo, etc as possible ashore got under way. Landing craft went back and fourth constantly. Before daylight, the sky was alive with choppers. By the end of the campaign we would all become very good at chopper recognition just by the sound. Even now when I'm out and about in Hampshire, I recognise a Chinook or Sea King sound instantly, and it takes me straight back there.

Sea Kings would form an orderly queue over the most urgently required supplies, pick up, move off, next ... Some 3,500 troops were put ashore that day.

Whilst at Ascension Island, the RFAs had hastily fitted 40/60 Bofors guns on the fo'c'sle, in some vain attempt to make troop ships look more menacing, and perhaps give them some fire power. I suspect it was more of a morale booster than anything else. Not only this, anything that a ship had that could fire was on deck. I even saw GPMGs tied to guard rails.

Like a mug, I volunteered to load for the gunner on the *Tristram* as I'd done it as my special sea duties a few years back on HMS *Kirkliston*. Well, I didn't think anything would come of it, and I want to know what's going on. I don't want to be below decks if we do get attacked or sunk or hit. As a diver I'd rather take my chances in the water. So if I can see the sea, I'm happy. I'm still the same now.

I had a quick brief from the gunner, along the lines of, 'Push down another clip when they start dropping into the breach.' **I know!** 'Don't force it down.' **I know!** 'We'll fire three solid shots first to clear the barrel.' OK. 'And come here as soon as you hear ACTION STATIONS.' **I KNOW!**

When you first hear AIR RAID WARNING RED, IMMINENT, you think, Christ, it's gonna happen. That word *imminent* means it's gonna happen *soon*.

There's only one other pipe more scary, which I would hear in my days down south, but I'll come to that later.

I wrote in my diary (above) that it was around 10:00. I don't really remember running to the gun on the *Tristram*. I do remember the noise. The noise of your first engagement is mind-numbing. It makes the hair on your neck and arms stand up. All your senses are alive and buzzing. It gives you butterflies. The adrenalin rush is so intense I don't think I even registered fear. You want to do something: you want to hit back, to fight.

The first attack was about four planes. They came over the hills towards us. Boy, were they low.

There were guns going off, including mine, and the incredible noise of low-flying jets, and small-arms fire and missiles, but I hadn't seen a thing. I was on my 40/60 spinning around on its mounting when I saw my first jet. I could say it was a Mirage or a Skyhawk, but it was just a plane, and to all intents and purposes it was shooting at me! We fired four rounds in the rough direction of this plane. Later I remembered that three of these rounds were just solid shot. The reason I think it took me so long (seconds) to see my first jet was simple: they weren't where you expected them to be; they weren't really up; they were more, level.

Where our only HE round went I have no idea. To say we missed is to be polite. It's not like they were high and flying at us or away. Then you would have a chance to bring your gun to bear. These were very low, very fast, and very close. They also seemed incredibly small. And they were going across our line of sight. Left to right, on the first attack.

It has to be taken into account that the 40/60 Bofors was around in the Second World War, and the jet was travelling at about five or six hundred miles an hour. If the two should ever meet to make the intended explosion, it would be more by luck than judgment.

We saw it, shot at it, and it was gone. A few seconds had passed. Was that it? I looked up, trying to take it all in. Then they came back, from the other direction. We swung our gun one way towards where they were coming from and they went the other way, our barrel crossed their path for the briefest millisecond, by the time we realised we were under attack again they had gone.

How many times this happened, I couldn't say. It was a blur of brutal noise and aggression. It fried your brain until you didn't know what was happening.

Now I must say something about the Argentinian pilots. They had balls. I mean it. No one who was there that day and witnessed the wall of lead that flew up at them could fail to be impressed. It was a lot of fire power, and they didn't just scream over, drop their ordnance anywhere near a target and get the hell out of there, which would have been perfectly understandable, after all – it's not as if they were defending their homeland.

They came in hard, fast and low. The word 'low' doesn't really do them justice. I have a photo which is widely available that shows a Mirage below the height of the *Fearless*'s mast and about level with her bridge. They would survive that, and come round again, and again, and back on different days as well, if they survived.

Most readers of this (me included) cannot imagine the difficulty of flying fast and low, being shot at, and still having the guts, skill and sheer determination to drop a bomb in the perfect trajectory to hit a ship (which may also be moving). Have you ever tried to lob a ball into a bucket at ten paces? Well, try it whilst running along, and from the height of a house while someone's throwing things at you, and you may begin to get an idea of how impossible a task it is – but they hit their target on many occasions.

That was it for my gunnery experience. Ships had been hit with bombs, ones that hadn't gone off. The call for bomb disposal assistance was up before we'd been stood down from action stations. This wasn't what our war was going to be about, was it? I thought we might do some mine-hunting dives, some repairing of warships, maybe making some munitions safe. But UXBs?

HMS *Antrim* had a 1,000-pound UXB (unexploded bomb) on board and the *Argonaut* had two.

In 1940, one of the first bombs to be dropped on Britain fell in the city of Canterbury. At this point in the war it was unclear which service took charge of which bombs. So in August of that year the three services thrashed out some basic rules that still apply today. They are:

- Royal Air Force: responsible for all unexploded ordnance, including Allied ordnance, and all ordnance of whatever nationality found on or near to crashed aircraft.

- Royal Navy: all unexploded ordnance on its property and all underwater weapons (hence the need for clearance divers).

- Army: all unexploded ordnance on Army property, or not on RAF or Navy property or crashed aircraft.

As a clearance diver, I had dealt with quite a few mines, bombs, shells, and even IEDs (improvised explosive devices). But, and for me it's a big BUT, all except for IEDs were left over from some distant conflict, usually WWII.

Therefore, a mine you go to deal with in a fisherman's net isn't and doesn't look new, and if you were to open it up, it is not going to have working batteries or ticking clocks to make it go bang. The salt water soon puts paid to delicate moving parts. As long as the explosive has been held in its rusting casing, even if it's waterlogged and full of holes, it will still go off. You just have to make it go off. You do that by diving with a 4 lb plastic explosive pack, attach that to the mine, and retire to a safe distance to set it off. You can initiate this either by lighting a safety fuse attached to detonating cord, which runs around the PE, or by pushing a detonator into the PE, and setting it off by using an electric charge to set off the detonator, which in turn sets of the PE, exploding the mine. You can even get a little casual, if not blasé, about dealing with old rusting relics from another era.

What we were faced with during the Falklands conflict was a world away from a rusting mine in the sea just off Folkestone, or a WWII bomb in the nets of a fishing boat off Portsmouth. These ones were painted green, with a yellow band round the nose (denoting high explosive), and written on them in red was PLEASE HANDLE WITH CARE – in English! In fact, they were British-made 1,000 lb Mk 17 free-fall bombs, and they were shiny and new. When you sell a bomb (and someone does have that job), I doubt you ever expect it to land back on British sovereign territory.

This isn't a rusty heap that's been in the sea for 40 years. This has just been manufactured. This will go off how it was meant to, and everything in it is new: batteries, timers, wires, fuses, explosives. This bomb has been armed that morning, just before take-off. It should have gone live not long after leaving the aircraft that dropped it. For some reason it hadn't done its job and gone off. Why? Did it have a timer? Unlikely, but something to mull over whilst studying one. So, what are you going to do about it? The bomb on board *Antrim* was the first UXB of the war so there was no precedent to follow.

Whilst considering whether I should write this book, I phoned a few friends who were in the Falklands with me in 1982. I got hold of Jan Sewell's number from Mick Fellows. They both still work in the bomb and mine disposal industry today. I spoke to Jan for the first time in maybe 20 years. We chatted for about an hour; it would seem none of us really talks about our time down there unless we are talking to someone who has similar experience. I don't know why, maybe it's because you think you are boring people, maybe it's because they might think you are bragging, or even bullshitting? It may be a bit of them not really being able to understand what it was like. I can never quite put my finger on it.

The thing is, once you get started, talking about it, you can't stop – it all comes flooding back. I hadn't talked about any of my experiences down south for more than a few minutes in 25 years. When I started to write this down, I thought it might be a struggle, but as soon as I looked at my diaries for the first time ever, in February 2007, I couldn't stop. I would be up until two in the morning, I would go to bed thinking about it, then I would come downstairs in the morning having remembered something and start again.

I have tried to address the reasons why I had never read my diaries before. Maybe I'll find out before the end of this book, but as yet I still don't know.

I was not in the party that went over to the *Antrim* to deal with that first unexploded bomb. But when I told Jan (Gary) Sewell that I was writing a book he wrote at length of his memories of being on board the destroyer on the morning of 21 May 1982:

Once we got tasked to the job on HMS *Antrim* from RFA *Sir Tristram*, we departed by chopper ASAP. To be perfectly honest we had taken so much kit out there, but it never really occurred to me that we would we be dealing with a UXB on board a ship!

Most of our work involves diving, or ordnance on the seabed or beach. Once a bomb has hit a ship, it should no longer be a threat as it, and probably the ship, are no more. Divers do now train at getting bombs out of ships, but I certainly did none of that before April 1982.

So Nigel Pullan and I were given some kit each at very short notice that might be of use, and I think I got the short straw. Shortly after taking off, I found myself dangling like a conker on a string above HMS *Antrim* on the helicopter recovery wire, looking out for the nearest incoming enemy aircraft. We had to be lowered onto the flight deck by a winch wire because there was a dome in the centre of the flight deck where the bomb had smashed into the underside of the deck and nearly managed to make its exit.

I had a det box in one hand containing electrical detonators and in the other hand another box containing plastic explosives, and I remember thinking, What the f***g hell am I supposed to do with this? Also running through my mind was how electrical detonators and static electricity (a huge amount of static is created between a helicopter and a metal warship) is really not a very good combination.

It was like a scene from a war movie. HMS *Ardent* was on fire on the horizon; it and several other ships were still under air attack!

The flight deck had been strafed with cannon and rocket fire, during the bombing run. A pool of blood could be seen next to an abandoned GPMG pointing skyward on the port side of the flight deck and the ship's helicopter was stowed on the port side of the hangar – full of holes.

The ship's company told us that three aircraft had attacked from the stern just above sea level, close together and in a line. The huge outdated Sea Slug missile, which was probably bigger than the attacking aircraft, was situated at the very stern of the ship. Essentially a long range missile, one had just been launched at point blank range!

This massive missile with a ton of explosives and four huge booster rockets resembles a slightly smaller version of the space shuttle. When fired it sits rumbling on its massive launcher for several seconds building up thrust before hurtling towards its target. The missile apparently passed between the first and second aircraft only a short distance from the ship. Had the missile left the launcher a split second sooner or later it would have taken out all three attacking aircraft.

One of the bombs was right on target and entered the Sea Slug magazine just to the port side of the launcher. It was deflected up into the pyrotechnic magazine, then back down into the Sea Slug magazine; it then went back up through the senior rates' heads, with not quite enough energy remaining to penetrate the flight deck. Finally, it dropped back down onto the deck of the senior rates heads close to its entry hole. The Sea Slug magazine runs two-thirds the length of the ship and can hold 36 missiles. There is an armoured door that lowers shut between each missile, to stop them all exploding together, should one detonate – at least in theory.

I had been a gunner before changing branch to clearance diver and had served on one of the *Antrim*'s sister ships, HMS *Norfolk*. I worked on the Sea Slug part of ship, and was well aware that the Sea Slug magazine goes right under the Port and Starboard Sea Cat Missile Magazines. Down there is also the helicopter torpedo magazine, up to four Exocet missiles and the 4.5 inch shells for the gun. Effectively, what we had here was a bomb on a bomb, hence my thinking, What the hell am I supposed to do with this?

Mick went to the bridge to talk to the UK on the sat phone, while Nigel and I watched the war raging around us. HMS *Ardent* was on fire, and we eventually saw her beginning to sink.

Because of the state of the fuse, Mick contacted Northwood/DEODS and, between them, they decided it would be best to leave the fuse as it was. When Mick returned, we were taken below to view the bomb by a Chief Stoker. I feel sure he said he was in the heads when the bomb had entered. The bomb had wrecked half of the toilets while he was in there; he said he looked at the devastation not knowing what had happened. He was standing right next to the bomb for a while before he noticed it.

Next to the bomb you could see a Sea Slug missile just a few metres away on the deck below, through the hole made by the bomb's travels. I remember taking my first look at the bomb and thinking, if it goes off, it's not going to hurt, but it really will upset my mum and girlfriend.

The ship was mostly stationary, but every now and again we felt like we were going full ahead using 35 degrees of port and starboard wheel in order to dodge incoming aircraft. This was a bit worrying as the ship was vibrating like mad and listing heavily during these manoeuvres. As this was the first bomb to have hit a ship and not detonate, or made it over the side, we really didn't know if it was going to have a happy ending. You couldn't help thinking that a freshly dropped unexploded bomb and a good shaking is not the ideal scenario.

During the violent manoeuvring we could hear the 4.5 inch gun firing, followed, a second or two later, by another slightly different bang. I think that sometimes the second bang was the 4.5 projectile hitting the water close to the ship. The aircraft were flying so low, and the deck was sometimes at such an angle, that the gun was firing down at them, not up, as in all of the anti-aircraft gunnery training I had ever done!

During the day we also had a spot of fire fighting as a fire started while a hole was being cut in the flight deck.

We were fighting the fire wearing 5665 smoke masks with an air hose (which is a bit like wearing goggles with a garden hosepipe to breathe through). We only had hand-held water fire extinguishers working at the time to fight the fire, which we kept filling by throwing them in the ogin [sea] on a bit of string, then changing the gas cartridge.

It took several hours to prepare the bomb for lifting. We made the wires safe as it was a concern that the wires might earth when they hit water. It was dark and the air attacks had stopped by the time we got it onto the upper deck. The buffer's party rigged sheer legs above the hole that had been cut in the flight deck and we lashed the bomb with a helicopter securing strop. The three of us plus the buffer and one or two of the ship's company hauled it up through the hole and lowered it onto a torpedo trolley (like the one that takes the Tesco's shopping to the car, except we all had our fingers crossed). We then very gently pushed it from the centre of the flight deck to the starboard side.

The bomb was lashed to a long rope that passed through a block on the ship's davit, which we hauled taught, lifting the bomb off the trolley, swung out the davit, lowered it to just below the surface of the water.

As the bomb was in such a state, nobody could say what would happen when it was first submerged, or if it would explode as it hit the seabed, acting like a mine. So the skipper was ready to go full ahead as soon as the bomb was released. He wound up the engines, the bomb was let go, and so the ship survived.

Once the bomb and the Antrim had parted company, it was a quite a relief, having just spent several hours knowing that every second could be your last.

We were then all invited to the wardroom for a spot of Pusser's Rum.

Jan Sewell

Thankfully, the decisions about that *Antrim* bomb were up to Mick Fellows, our immediate boss, and not any of us. Mick was a Fleet Chief Diver who had seen and done just about everything. I'd worked with Mick many times over the years in all sorts of situations, and he is unflappable.

For some reason my memory lets me down a little here. I don't know if I was in shock, but it seems there are long bits of time I cannot account for; bits of my mind are somewhat vacant. It had been one hell of a first 24 hours, so it's hardly surprising. I know I went over to *Antrim* in the morning with some equipment for the lads who had been on there all night, but something blanked out some of the night. I remember the state of the senior rates' heads where the bomb had been, but to embellish too much would be tantamount to guesswork. So I'm not going to do it. Best to rely on my diary.

Saturday 22 May 1982 (DAY TWO)

Just about daylight on the Antrim. From the bridge came: 'Air Raid Warning Red Imminent'.

Five minutes later we were lying in the main

passageway. We could hear the two inch rockets hitting the ship's superstructure. There were many lying face down, hands over their heads in the main passageway, praying!

Two Army helicopters were shot down today, both crews killed.

Got back to Tristram and we were sent away again to HMS Argonaut. She has two UXBs – both 1000 lbs. One has gone through the port side a foot above the water line. It went right through the boiler room and came to rest under the ladder of the engine room.

The second bomb went in the forward magazine 5 ft below the water line, ripped right through the ship, hit the hull of the starboard side, there is a 4ft long rip in that side, it then went up hit the roof and landed back down on top of two Sea Cat anti-aircraft rockets. One of the rockets partially ignited and welded itself to the bomb. There is broken ammo all over the magazine.

The Magazine flooded when the bomb went in and killed two young sailors. The REs did the one in the boiler room, defused.

Earlier I said that AIR RAID WARNING RED, IMMINENT was not quite the scariest pipe I'd heard 'down south'. That honour goes to what I heard on the *Antrim* during the early-morning air raid, when AIR RAID WARNING RED, IMMINENT was followed by BRACE BRACE BRACE!

Now that takes the biscuit for clenched butt-cheeks. It means you're going to be hit by something so best brace yourself Jack. The rockets were thumping into the ship's superstructure. You just wait for the big one, the bomb; you hope beyond hope that this one will be a UXB. Everything is out of your control. If you are hit, you are hit; if not, great, get up and carry on. This sort of action and no sleep at all may account for my memory lapses.

HMS *Ardent* has had scant mention up to now, but that's because most of us in the fleet barely saw her, then she was gone. She went down fighting, though. She was outside Bomb Alley, partly to provide a sort of buffer to the landing fleet in Bomb Alley, and also because she had another very important role. She had been constantly bombarding Goose Green airstrip with her highly accurate 4.5-inch gun. This had two effects: it kept a large garrison of Argentinian troops pinned down, and it made sure the Pucaras there were either unable or unwilling to take off. This was of course very important during the landing phase, as they were unable to effect any counterattack. She even destroyed three and damaged more Pucaras on the ground.

During the war, hundreds of canisters of napalm were found at Goose Green by the Paras as they took the airstrip back. Whilst at DEODS training, we saw the effects of most weapons and bombs either on film or in use. Napalm fills everyone with foreboding. It's not a complicated bomb, in fact it's barely a bomb in the true sense of the word. It's simply a thin canister that has no fuse; all it has to do is break open on contact with the ground and it will spill its deadly jellied gasoline out and burst into flames as soon as it comes into contact with the air. Because of the speed of ignition, it creates a deadly shock wave before burning everything flammable in its path. If you are caught by the huge 'hot area' of say 100 metres across, you will have the jellied petroleum stick to you, engulf you in flame, and simultaneously starve you of oxygen. Fire fills everyone with dread, so to be bombed with fire is truly horrific. It was there in Goose Green to be used; there is plenty of photographic evidence.

Were the Pucaras there ready to bring napalm into play? Is this why they hammered the *Ardent*, so that they could take off with it and use it on the troops trying to land? Can you imagine the British casualties had they been able to use it? It was on the islands for a reason, complete with canisters. It wasn't there as a fuel to keep the troops warm.

Therefore, when *Ardent* moved to take her position outside Bomb Alley, the AAF wanted revenge or they wanted to stop her gunfire. Either way, they attacked with a vengeance. First, planes that had survived her bombardment on the islands attacked her. She was straddled by two bombs and shot one of the Skyhawks down. Then the next wave came from the mainland, and it would seem they had the same orders: 'Attack *Ardent!*'

Two more Skyhawks attacked and scored a direct hit on the stern, and with this she had lost her anti-aircraft Sea Cat system and was on fire. *Ardent*, pretty much out of it, tried to steam into the comparative safety of Bomb Alley. The crew apparently still brought weapons to bear on the attacking aircraft by way of attaching GPMGs to guard rails. One of the crew was killed whilst doing this. She was then again attacked by Skyhawks and again hit by no less than three more 500-pound bombs. The AAF had not finished yet, though. *Ardent* was next attacked by no fewer than five Mirages skimming low over the water. The Mirages, thinking they had the upper hand, were then jumped by two Sea Harriers. They 'splashed' two, and two more took off, having been hit. One of the Mirages was astonishingly shot down by the ship's NAAFI manager with his GPMG.

In the final attack, *Ardent* was hit by two further 500-pound bombs and sprayed with 68 mm rockets. How many bombs hit her in all is almost impossible to tell, but by late evening, she was a tangled wreck, on fire and listing heavily. Twenty-two of her crew were dead. The order to abandon ship came not long afterwards. The *Yarmouth* backed her stern into the *Ardent* and most of the crew simply stepped onto her deck. She eventually sank in the hours of darkness. One of the nearest headlands is appropriately called Wreck Point.

Overall, it is reckoned, *Ardent* withstood around six hours of air attacks, with about a half-hour break in between each wave.

HMS *Argonaut*

I don't know why the REs (Royal Engineers) did the bomb in the boiler room. I guess you could argue it was above the water line. But the second one, in the magazine, was not. That was ours. The magazine was obviously locked down and watertight during action stations, and because the bomb had gone in below the water line it must have instantly flooded. Before we could do anything, we had to get her watertight. We quite quickly made heavy metal patches to cover the bomb holes, with the help of the *Fearless* engineers.

This second bomb had very nearly gone clean through the ship: through the port hull, through a few bulkheads deep inside the ship and nearly out the starboard side. Think about that, and the amount of energy required to go through a warship. There was a rough split in the starboard hull, where the bomb had so very nearly gone clean through the ship. I had the pleasure of diving, during an air raid, to hammer soft wooden wedges into the split, in an attempt to slow the floodwater down. This was done from the outside, obviously. Whilst diving and hammering away, I was very conscious that on the other side of this split was squashed ammo and all sorts of distorted, mangled, and shall we say unstable ordnance, which I could see through the split from my position on the outside. Oh, and there's a 1,000-pound bomb in there. Hammer gently, I thought. If you can hammer gently, I did.

I really felt for the ship's company of the *Argonaut*. Not only were they living in the now-christened Bomb Alley, but they had just lost two young lads and to top it all had to go about their daily business with a huge UXB on board. To a man they never complained, though. I remember our every word being scrutinised by everyone within earshot as we discussed the job over dinner in their galley. So, hot off the galley stove that day was whatever the 'bubble heads' had said at scran! 'When do you think you'll get it out?' seemed a very popular question.

Around this time we were hearing a 'buzz' that two Royal Marines Gazelle choppers from 3 Commando Brigade Air Squadron had been shot down and, more disturbingly, that the crew of one of them had ditched in the sea and were then machine-gunned. It later tuned out to be true. Attitudes hardened instantly.

Sunday 23 May 1982 (DAY THREE)

Another Clear Day.

Some of the lads went over to Argonaut to measure up the holes to make patches. Hope to do the job at night because of constant action stations during the day.

PANIC.

We have half an hour to get all our gear off of the Tristram as she is going to sea. Loading our gear onto small landing craft to go to HMS Intrepid. Air raid during the loading. Got a letter from Marie, it took half an hour to read because I was under the table in the dining room sheltering from the air raid. A very bad one.

Antelope, Fearless, and Yarmouth hit. Antelope got two UXBs above water. All we could see was two holes like that on Argonaut. REs left us to defuse them. Left Tristram. Stopped at Argonaut to drop off a water pump. Approx 19:00 while alongside Argonaut a huge explosion took place. Everyone hit the floor because it was very close. The UXB on Antelope had blown up while the REs were defusing it. There was a hole in the ship's side about 30ft wide and four decks high. The fire took over immediately.

All landing craft and choppers went to assist. We and others got fire hoses into the hole but it did no good. The ship's company were taken off after about 10 mins, all boats told to get clear as it was very close to the Sea Cat and other magazines. We waited and watched for about 3 hours totally helpless and almost silent.

Returned to Intrepid 04:00 unloaded our gear and slept on floor of the vehicle deck.

Although exhausted not much sleep was got by any. I felt sick, because of what we'd seen. I think that's when it really sunk in.

HMS *Antelope*

HMS *Antelope* had just arrived in San Carlos Water, and was now covering the northern end of the sound. Not on the gun line like the now-sunken *Ardent*, but in a precarious position nonetheless. She was there to fight, as frigates are built to do, and to take the heat off the RFAs and civilian ships deeper in the sound in San Carlos. Frigates have always been expendable, that's their job, to take the flak (literally) and do the dirty work. You are on your own at the end there, little protection from the hills, and of course you are the first big grey target sitting there.

In my view, flying into San Carlos, a pilot would have a few seconds to pick a target, depending on where he might find himself after desperately weaving around to avoid the wall of flak put up at him. If he was not near his first choice target, he could pick another.

Not outside. If you are an attacking pilot, you now had one ship firing at you, not dozens; you can settle and focus on the one job, lengthen your run-in maybe, get it right. In addition, you must imagine, as the pilots surely did, 'the ship is trying to kill me – I must try to kill it.' It was probably a bit more personal. If a pilot survived this ordeal, all he had to do then was make his way out of the sound, avoid getting shot down by the high and waiting CAP (Combat Air Patrol) of Harriers, then negotiate a 400-mile flight back home, on a very limited fuel load.

Early afternoon, the first two Skyhawks attacked her. Straight after this came the main attack of the day. This time waves of them had a go at the fleet: Mirages and Skyhawks, in groups of say four together, then another four of five. Nobody was counting. They were heading over us toward the exit from Bomb Alley, where *Antelope* lay.

We later found out she had been hit, by two bombs, yes, but also by a Skyhawk. One attacking plane had come in so low it had hit *Antelope's* main mast after dropping its bombs, and then disintegrated in mid air.

One was killed on board *Antelope*. A young steward.

Later on, as we watched her come into San Carlos Bay, we could see she was still fighting fires on board and that her mast was leaning over at an angle as a result of being hit by the Skyhawk.

Soon after witnessing this, we got the order to change ships, *Tristram* to *Intrepid*. *Tristram* had been tasked to leave Bomb Alley, and our work required us to stay amongst the ships. This was by no means a simple or quick task: it had taken two C130s (Hercules) full to the brim to get all our gear to Ascension Island. Because we didn't really know what to expect down there, we played safe and brought everything. Often this extra stuff is referred to as Justin's Kit, on account of 'just in case we need it.' As usual in the forces, the move had to be done NOW as well.

No ordinary bang

Because the clearance divers were not available, Staff Sergeant Prescott and Warrant Officer Phillips of the Royal Engineers were tasked to board *Antelope* and render any munitions safe.

My memory of this is very clear. It was just dark and we were in one of *Intrepid's* small landing craft loading all our gear on board, it was 19:00-ish.

What happened next was 'No Ordinary Bang'.

It was a mammoth explosion, and we were too close to it. You felt it and smelt it. It penetrated your body. I can remember the sensation that all the voids in my body moved as I'd never felt before. My eardrums stretched, my lungs deflated, my heart felt like it missed a beat, or if it didn't miss, it stirred. I'm struggling really to explain it. It was like having your innards shaken. My hair moved. It was a total-body experience. This was a full-order detonation of a modern 1,000-pound bomb, encased inside the comparatively thin metal canister of HMS *Antelope*. I would guess it was between 200 and 300 metres away. We all hit the deck on the 'B' of the Bang.

One thing to remember about being close to an explosion, which I know from experience, is – don't be too hasty in getting up to see what's going on. One of our lads, Billy Smart, did, and there was still incoming shrapnel flying past. He was quickly dragged down by Jan Sewell. There were splashes all around and that horrible noise of hot metal shearing through the air. Peering over the gunwales towards the *Antelope*, it was immediately apparent what had happened. One of the bombs had gone off whilst being defused, or moved.

We were meant to be dropping off a water pump at *Argonaut* at the time so the lads could start pumping out her magazine. Immediately we cast off and covered the distance over to *Antelope* in a matter of minutes. We started the water pump on the way over to them and had fire hoses running before we got there. Steering straight at the massive hole in her side, we trained the landing craft's and our fire hoses into the huge hole. Upon arrival, it appeared like a gaping black cavern; strangely, I thought, there seemed hardly any fire. It was black but hot, in places glowing hot, but still no fire. We could easily see right into the guts of the ship.

The crew hadn't been taken off for the disposal part of the operation. They all had fluorescent orange suits on that are designed to be put on over your clothes in a hurry and to give you a semblance of a chance if you have to go over the side because they would keep you dry, for a while at least. They had been mustered as far away from the bomb as possible during the dangerous defusing phase. They were all stood on her stern and bows when it went off. The shock under their feet must have been enormous, and some men were knocked down and clearly injured on the deck.

I don't know how many landing craft came to her aid. It was a few – but I think the heat stored up in that huge explosion was always going to win. I also remember seeing one or two brave souls of her ship's company, still dressed in their 'once only suits', quickly getting hoses into the hole from the deck. Six or eight hoses spraying into a huge hot hole. It quickly became apparent it was a pointless exercise. The hole was getting hotter and fires were breaking out everywhere. All the helicopters that were in the air gathered at *Antelope*, and were hovering around taking off the crew.

I say in my diary that the hole was 30 feet wide and four decks high. That is just what came to me later that day, writing my diary to try to explain it. It could have been a lot bigger; what do you judge it against? Who can say I'm right or wrong? I had my camera with me and I could have taken pictures right inside her, but I'm no hard-nosed journalist and I couldn't do it. People had just died in that very spot, I was pretty convinced of that.

It was crippling terminal damage, as far as I was concerned. It wasn't just wide and tall but deep into the ship's hull. At least half of the ship's beam deep. The innards had been ripped out of her and a large part of her 'bulk', for want of a better word, had gone, just disappeared. I later realised that the glow, and the extent of the destruction, may have been due to the large amount of aluminium making up the *Antelope*. In a steel ship the bulkheads would merely buckle, but the *Antelope* was melting before our very eyes.

The modern idea at the time was to go light and manoeuvrable, in theory more difficult to hit, and faster. But maybe you should go back to World War I and have eighteen-inch-thick armour, which means bigger engines, bigger ship, bigger target, less manoeuvrable, but indestructible. There isn't a right or wrong answer. What you gain with one idea you lose with the other, it seems, which is why it's impossible to build a perfect warship.

We tried for ten maybe fifteen minutes with the hoses, but it was no use. It was building heat and ferocity at such an alarming rate that everyone, in the various landing craft, was having to retreat backwards, and we were soon unable to get close enough to bring our hoses to bear on the fire. On top of this predicament I, and I'm sure others, were acutely aware that in our landing craft, right under our feet, were all our explosives. We shouldn't be getting anywhere near such an unpredictable exploding fireball.

This was obviously a no-win situation and a very dangerous one. We knew there was another bomb on board as well, and this fire was perilously close to the magazine. It could all go off again pretty quickly. The word soon went round for all personnel to stand clear. We backed off and just watched. Helpless. It was horrible, and we all felt pretty useless and low. I don't know how long we watched. We all just sort of drifted backwards, not wanting to give up on her. The choppers got all the men off pretty quickly, then there was nothing for us to do.

Eventually we went back to the *Sir Tristram* and continued to unload our gear, all the time periodically looking back at the *Antelope* as she continued on her path of self-destruction, burning and exploding, showering the bay with white-hot debris. All along fanned by a steady South Atlantic wind.

Eventually we moved a little further northwest to where the *Intrepid* lay at anchor and continued unloading and moving onto her, all along deeply aware of the bonfire-type light being sent out all around Bomb Alley. Never had a place deserved such a nickname now. We sort of carried on working for hours because we had to – but if you ask any of our team about that moment or the time immediately afterwards, I don't think you'll get much out of them. I've tried. I think we were all dumbstruck, our senses were shot though.

As I said in the diary, we must have got to bed about 04:00. But sleep was hard to come by. We had just seen what one of these bombs does to a ship when it goes off, and guess what we would be working on in the morning.

We knew one of the Royal Engineers was killed. We later found out it was Staff Sergeant Prescott, and that Warrant Officer Phillips had lost his arm. If we hadn't been moving ship, would it have been one of us?

A ship has a certain life to it. People always get attached to ships: it's human nature, we can't help it. If you take a long passage on a ship you will generally talk fondly of the voyage and the ship because it will invariably look after you, protect you from the elements. Even if you've had a bad experience or a rough passage, the ship has still been your home and brought you out the other side. I think also it may have something to do with the nature of the sea, the calming effect it has on most people. Also you can always be alone on ship, you can always find a place to lean on a guard rail and stare at the constantly changing scenery. Never are two days the same at sea. We call ships affectionately 'she' and 'her' for these reasons.

If someone says they aren't moved to see one sink, especially such a violent end as this, then they are either lying or have no feelings. It was sad and emotional. I remember getting up at about 07:00, unable to sleep, and going up on deck and watching the *Antelope* still afloat, still burning.

Later on Monday the 24th we were out in the Gemini, going to fit patches on the *Argonaut*, and we went quite close to the *Antelope*. You could now see her ribs and right through her in places. She was a tangled heap of molten metal around the midships area. Only the bow and stern still resembled a grey warship.

The famous picture you see of her exploding was taken on this early morning, I think it was possibly the second bomb eventually going off after 'cooking' in the fire. It was another huge bang. Not long afterwards she broke her back and her midships settled on the bottom. The sea then quenched the worst of the heat and fire, and the plumes of mainly white smoke and steam towered hundreds of feet up into the air. I was diving on the *Argonaut* that morning, and under water I could clearly hear her breaking up. Sound travels extraordinarily well under water. It was a series of long and painful sounds of slowly creaking and tearing metal, not unlike the noise of a whale.

Later in the afternoon the stern went down, leaving just the bow stuck up at about 45 degrees, her 4.5 inch gun just visible above the water, pointing up at the sky as if in some defiant last shot at the plane that put an end to her commission.

You have to wonder if this would have happened to either *Ardent* or *Antelope* had they been inside Bomb Alley; but then, it might well have been a troopship that was hit – or a civilian one such as *Canberra*.

You have to remember that this whole spectacle was taking place slap bang in the middle of Bomb Alley, in full view of the thousands of mariners and soldiers on the hills. It was like some sick reminder or warning to all ships: 'You might be next!'

Monday 24 May 1982 (DAY FOUR)

Five weeks at sea.

08:00 Antelope still burning and exploding about a mile away. The fire helped by the wind had gone from the bridge to the stern, gutting it. We were amazed it was still afloat. One explosion broke her back.

Dave Boss and Stan went to look at bomb on Argonaut, not a popular job after last night's viewing. Ben, myself and others went to patch hole on Argonaut, also not a popular job. Not many popular jobs about.

While working on Argonaut an Air Raid was said
to be imminent!

We left the ship in the landing craft to head
for the nearest beach. Before getting there,
four Mirage fighters came over the southern
mountain, sheltering one Canberra bomber. One
bomb hit the Sir Geraint and one hit the Sir
Percival. The one we were on the previous day
was in between these two before going to sea.
Again neither bomb exploded, both 1000 lbs.

The Canberra came over our heads with one
Mirage. Both were hit. Rapiers, Sea Cats, and
all sorts of missiles were chasing the jets.
It was like star wars, but real. We saw the
smoke appear from two fighters and the Canberra
hit a hillside rather quicker than he ought.
We had just left the Sir Geraint 10 mins ago.
Bullets were coming across the water from all
directions. Another air raid followed 5 mins
later.

We had gone aground by now but we weren't too
bothered about that. The next wave came from
completely the opposite direction. Five Mirages.
Two didn't get halfway along the valley, one
got by Sea Cat and one by 40/60 Bofors and 100s
of marines with machine guns. The other three
came over us and the rest of the ships. We could
see a rapier missile chasing a Mirage. We were
jumping up and down screaming at this missile to
go faster, and it did. The Mirage let out black
smoke and visibly slowed down. Not one of the
five left the valley. The shouting and cheering
could be heard for miles as one by one they hit
the water and the hills around us. All this took
no more than a minute as the jets are going
flat out.

> Thirteen aircraft were shot down by the fleet
> and the Harriers today. One was killed on the
> Sir Percy, three on the Sir Geraint. If the
> bombs had gone off? Hundreds maybe?
>
> Boss Dave and Stan spent the night working on
> the Argonaut. The plan will take four days to
> get it out.

As with all these extracts from my diary, the above is as written on the day, and was what we knew there and then, so the details may be incorrect. I was actually diving on the 24th when I got four pulls on my line (*come up*). I came up and was dragged unceremoniously out of the water and into the landing craft. No sooner was I in than we were off across the water towards the nearest (west) bank of the sound. Nigel Pullan told me it was an air raid.

We were not even halfway there when Mirages sheltering a Canberra bomber come over our heads. The Mirages where fighters, small and agile, with a full camouflage paint job and the classic swept-back D wing configuration. The Canberra on the other hand was not meant for this low-level stuff, you could see that instantly. She looked big and cumbersome up against these lithe menacing fighters. She was painted shiny black and stood out like a sore thumb.

The Canberra was in the middle and the Mirages looked like they were shadowing her every move. I'm pretty sure they were all hit by something. There was an enormous amount of flak going up at them in the way of everyone with a weapon on the ships and everyone on the surrounding hillsides. There were also shoulder-launched Blowpipes being used, and Sea Cats and Bofors all going off from different directions but all converging near-about the jets.

They didn't explode in the Hollywood style, but to me one minute they were beautifully agile, the next sluggish and smoking. What those pilots thought when they first came into range of the fleet I can only imagine.

One of the Marines who was aboard the landing craft with us was firing from the hip (well, not aiming in the traditional sense anyway). When we saw a jet slow and let out a puff of smoke he was yelling, 'I got it, I got it!' Well, yeah, and about 500 others will be claiming it as theirs as well, I thought.

I have a photo of us at this point. It doesn't show any planes, I was too slow with my camera, but it shows us huddled down behind the gunwale of the landing craft looking back at the ships at anchor, as the planes were going over and in between. I distinctly remember seeing splashes where bullets were making their way across the water towards us, and they must obviously have come from the ships' gunners. We were, after all, in their line of fire, well, -ish. As I said earlier, I had no idea where my rounds ended up when I had been firing my 40/60 shells, and I obviously wasn't the only one. Friendly fire is a term which comes to mind. It doesn't seem friendly at the time, I can tell you.

One of the larger landing craft from the *Fearless* had her life raft shot off by a 'friendly' missile. The raft was situated right alongside the wheelhouse and, get this ... it was shot off by a Sea Cat. Those things were fired by our ships, at aircraft, and it hit a boat. Luckily nobody was injured, but it must be some story for the crew to tell.

We went aground. Then they came back, from the north this time. One Mirage had a missile on its tail, whether it was a Rapier or Blowpipe I couldn't say but it was quicker than the jet. I do remember cheering it on. The moment of impact again wasn't what you'd expect. I for one saw no bang, just a sort of kick from the tail and a change in the jet's manner, from agile and sleek to labouring and struggling. It made it over the nearest hill but I doubt if it got much further.

More ships were hit during this raid. More work for us? Only time will tell.

<u>Tuesday 25 May 1982</u> (DAY FIVE)

Fine again.

Up at 05:00. Some ships thought they had heard
something on the ships' bottoms (limpet mines?).
Split team into 3. Searched all, nothing found.
Rest of the day the raids were said to have been
beaten off by Harriers. The first happy day
we'd had for a while. Reports came in every time
the Coventry shot down a plane. Cheers went up
accordingly. 4 planes she'd got. That's why we'd
not seen any today. They'd all been attacking
her a few miles away.

At 18:05 Gloom and despondency set in again as
we were told the Coventry was being abandoned.
Twenty two dead, twenty odd casualties. An hour
later the Atlantic Conveyor was hit by Exocet.
She was carrying RAF Harriers, and choppers.

Broadsword was also hit by one those non-
exploding bombs. It hit the flight deck at an
angle and went out over the side. Morbid and
high tempers set in again. Not had a wash for
three days now, what's new?

Some of this is written a day or more late.

Not getting any sleep is one thing. Not having a proper home or
bed is another. Throw in air raids and more work than we could
handle, and not an undue amount of stress, and you can imagine
how we needed our sleep. All you need to throw into this was an
operation 'Awkward.' That is Navy terminology for 'Oh my god
we're under attack by enemy divers' and the possibility of them
putting limpets onto the ships at anchor.

More than one ship had seen or heard something.

Of course it has to be at 05:00 when you're at your lowest
and weariest.

When doing basic clearance diver training you do this day in day out. Wake up and get into the water pretty damn quick, I mean. Just like the live-in week at Horsea Island.

Awkward

The point of all this horrible treatment is lost on you during the course, but in a war situation, when it's real, it all just happens. You don't have to ask or speak to anyone else, everyone knows what to do. From bang to splash on this occasion was well under fifteen minutes, and we got a hearty well done from all the masters of the vessels involved.

We had also had the pleasure of doing this at Ascension Island before we even got to the Falklands. Someone just entered our land of sleep and shouted, 'AWKWARD'. No other words were necessary. It says in my diving log that this was also at 05:00. There wasn't anything found and we came up thinking what a waste of time, and longing to go back to bed. But hanging over the stern of the ship was virtually all the ship's company shouting, 'Thanks lads!' Obviously their night had been ruined as well – but with fear for their lives and their floating home.

This time in Bomb Alley it was the RFA *Fort Austin* for us, but other ships had heard and seen something as well and other parts of the team went to their aid. I knew we'd trained for this for years, but this was for real. Was there really a mine on one of the ships? *Fort Austin* was a perfect target, after all, full to the brim with everything a fleet of warships needs, ammo and fuel, to name but two. It would make a tidy bang.

We all attach ourselves to the light line, or necklace as it is called, and enter the water searching our adjacent piece of hull. Halfway along we get one tug on the line from one of the lads, Ian Milne. He is in the middle of the sweep. We congregate around him. He has eyes like dinner plates and is hovering away from the hull and pointing. We all move in slowly, looking. There is something round on the bilge keel. It looks new and dark. I don't remember who, but someone is brave enough to get real close, and comes back and smacks Ian round the head. It is an anode. A piece of zinc that helps stop the metal hull from rotting. It's meant to be there. My heart was coming through my chest at the time.

After our rude awkward awakening on the 25th, some of us went over to the *Argonaut* and we worked out a plan to get the bomb out ASAP. We figured it was going to take about four days. The patches were holding and the magazine had been pumped dry to reveal the 1,000-pounder, sat on some mangled Sea Cat missiles and every other sort of ammo a warship carries.

There's a reason why a warship's magazine is where it is. It's because it's the least likely place to be hit. It is low down in the ship, well below the water line, safe – how can it be hit? Except maybe by torpedo, but even then it will flood. Logically the ship would have to burn to below the water line to cause trouble, by which time it's all over anyway. If it does catch fire, it is instantly floodable. Since, if you lose the magazine, you stand a good chance of losing the ship. So, what are the chances of having a huge UXB sitting in there? On board the *Victory*, the powder magazine was below the water line and was protected by double doors and wet blanket-type curtains in case of fire or sparks.

Our team boss was a two-and-a-half-ringer (Lieutenant Commander), Brian Dutton, and this was his job. The logical thinking was, if it's fallen from a jet, hit the water, then the warship's hull, gone through the hull and through at least two other metal bulkheads, hit the other hull, partially set off some Sea Cats and still not gone off – then it ain't gonna go off if you move it gently. Leave the fuses where they are. Let sleeping dogs lie. It worked on the *Antrim*.

We knew of at least one that went off whilst trying to remove the fuse – on the *Antelope*.

So we were first going to move all the dodgy mangled ammo

from around the bomb. There was a lot of unstable ordnance under the bomb as well, but that will have to wait until the bomb has gone. Then cut a hole through the deck head (roof) and through the ship's side and lift it up and out and lower it into the sea. Dump it on the bottom and move the ship. Some of our brave compatriots can then come back at a later date and blow the shit out of it. They'll love that.

Dave Southwell, the Boss and Stan Bowles stayed on the *Argonaut* and the rest of us went back to *Intrepid*. We had air raid warnings but saw nothing. A relatively quiet day really. We were informed the air raids were getting beaten off by the Harriers and the *Coventry* was doing a damned good job of shooting down any that attacked her, about ten miles away. We got a sort of countdown each time she shot one down, and cheers would go up accordingly. The CAP were shooting down their share as well. Things were looking up. Was this the beginning of the end? Were we getting the measure of these Argie pilots? Surely our superior technology will prevail?

The lads came back from the *Argonaut* and we were all together having dinner. 18:05, I wrote in my diary. That was the time we were told on *Intrepid* that the *Coventry* was being abandoned. We heard there were 22 dead and 20 or so injured. How can this be happening? Talk about depressing. An hour or so later the *Atlantic Conveyor* was hit by Exocet. She was brimful of essential stores, if you can call them that, stores like Chinooks and eight Wessex helicopters. There were also twelve fatalities on her, including her master. She had the dubious honour of being the first British merchant vessel lost at sea to enemy fire since World War II.

Then we hear that the *Broadsword* has been hit by one of these non-exploding bombs. You don't troop merrily off and sleep soundly when you hear this sort of report. No matter how tired you are, you will consider if you are going to be sat astride an unexploded bomb during an air raid before the night is out. It turned out she was hit by a bomb which hit the sea first and did a Barnes Wallis and bounced up, hit the helideck, destroying the ship's Lynx chopper in the process, before disappearing off harmlessly over the side. She was also hit with multiple rocket strikes, but we never did attend.

Fuses

Something I have to address is the non-exploding bombs. What was happening? Were the British just selling dodgy bombs? It might be nice to think we were selling dummies to the Argies but I'm afraid that wasn't the case.

We had our suspicions early on as to what was going on. When you put a bomb on a plane it is armed, in a sense, but it isn't armed to the point were it'll go off if the said plane were to crash on take-off for example. It shouldn't anyway. It'll have an inertia fuse in the nose, like an air bag in a modern car, in that it will have to stop quickly to arm the fuse. But to be safe it'll have another fuse in the tail. This is in the form of a tiny propeller in the middle of the tail fin. When the propeller is wound in, it isn't armed. This is the position it'll be in as your attacking pilot taxis towards his take-off. Drop it from the plane and a long fall through the air will unwind the propeller. Fully unwound and a long way from the dropping aircraft, the bomb goes live. All it needs to do now is stop quickly, and bang! Good for the pilot, bad for you.

Now ... What if your pilot is not very high? What if he has to come in low and fast to deliver his payload? Will the bomb have time to arm itself on its considerably shorter journey? Can the propeller unwind fully? Probably not. Drop one into the sea, smash it through metal walls, do what you will with it, but if it isn't yet armed it's safe. As safe as when the ground crew happily slung it under the wing of its host. Make sense? It did to us. Leave the fuses where they are.

Wednesday 26 May 1982 (DAY SIX)

The four o'clock raid came at half five today.
Three waves of four. The first two waves were
said to have been chased off by the Harriers. We
were lying down under cover on Intrepid waiting
for news on the third raid. We couldn't see
what was going on as we were three decks down.
The frigates opened up on the other side of the
valley. Thirty seconds later we were told a jet
had just crashed in the water about a mile and
a half up the sound. The pilot had ejected. The
first one to get out I think. He was the only
one out of the three.

We thought maybe they'd been attacking one of
the ships further out again, but luckily nothing
was heard.

As it got dark six of us went over again to
shift the ammo etc from around the bomb on HMS
Argonaut. It took all night. The patches we
put on are holding well, not much water at all
is getting into the magazine. Found one of the
lads' wallets who was killed.

The SAS went ashore at midnight to cause havoc
around Port Stanley (about 30 SAS and SBS) –
should pick them up in a few days. They're not
trying to take Stanley, just frighten them a
little. Good boys.

Something really tragic happened today. We ran
out of beer!

I couldn't for the life of me figure out what
day it was today, or the date. Nor did anybody
around me know. It makes no difference what day
it is or what time it is, it all just rolls into
each other.

The SAS

The SAS were homeless like us in the sense that they didn't have a base or a ship. We weren't attached to anyone, we were a separate unit. I don't think anyone who came across us knew what to make of us. We would turn up on a ship and you could see them thinking, 'Who and what is this lot?' We didn't have any duties on board, we didn't have a mess, we were just there. I think they were confused because we adopted the 'pirate rig' philosophy and made it our own. Combat rig with maybe a hint of blue, to confuse the enemy (officers). From the outside most people probably couldn't even tell which arm of the forces we belonged to, and that's how we liked it. No one gives you any grief if they don't know who you are. There wasn't ever much Navy uniform on show. 'It's the bubble heads I think.' Oh?

The *Tristram* wasn't our ship, the *Intrepid* wasn't our ship. We were a bit like the gypsies of the task force and went where we were required, hunkered down and made it home for a while. After all it was only a place to sleep; we were working 20-odd hours a day. It seemed one part of the team was always away doing something, and had I not kept a diary I'd have had no idea where I was on what day. For a long while we slept on the vehicle deck of the *Intrepid*, some on camp beds and some even in our Land Rover. I had a feeling the *Intrepid* wouldn't be the only place we'd be getting our swedes down either. The SAS were down there, homeless, or at least bunk-less, as well.

I came back from a job one night still in my dry bag, covered in diesel oil, pretty cold and feeling a bit sorry for myself, and one of them said to me, 'Christ you wouldn't catch me doing your job!' What? I was flabbergasted.

'You wouldn't catch me doing yours,' I said.

One night I watched four of them getting ready to go on a mission, I had no idea what it was, obviously. Boy, did they carry some kit with them. They are always on top of the best gear available anywhere in the world and they had a lot of their 'funny gear' on board *Intrepid*. Shh gear. I swear if I ever got one of those rucksacks on my back, I'd never be able to stand up, never mind walk anywhere. None of what they were packing looked very friendly either. Anyway, we said cheerio to them and off they went by chopper. Give 'em hell!

About three days later I saw a couple of them making their way down from the helideck and they had nothing left in the way of ammo and things that go bang in the night. 'What happened to that lot?' I said.

'Well you don't want to carry it all back,' he said, grinning. 'Anyway, it's heavy.' Christ, I thought, I wonder who was on the end of all that?

I had the pleasure of taking some of the SAS boat troop for a diving course at Horsea Island once. I don't think they do a lot of diving, that's more SBS and us, but these four guys were with us for weeks doing attack compass swims. In preparation for what, I have no idea. One freezing December day they had just finished their swim and hit their target. Now for some macho reason whilst on course you are not allowed to wear diving gloves. Something to do with the 'well we never had them in our day' syndrome. There was ice on the lake and it was not nice.

One of them came up the ladder with his CDBA on looking blue and said something along the lines of, 'Kin hell it's cold, I can't feel my fingers, this is ridiculous.'

To which Eddie Kerr, the Chief Diver, said, 'Oh, roughy toughy SAS, are we? I thought you guys were meant to be hard. You can't go behind enemy lines and say, I can't shoot anyone today, my hands are cold.'

He turned to the chief, very close, looked him straight in the eye and through gritted teeth said ... 'Hey! I tell you this ... if there's a kill in the air I'll be there, don't you worry about that!' Then walked off.

Eddie and I just looked at each other. Oops. 'If there's a kill in the air.' That's not a phrase you hear every day. Best not upset him again, eh Chief? Na, best not. In the afternoon we gave them gloves.

They would dive all day, doing the miles, yes, miles and miles, of swimming underwater; we all have to for it to become second nature, and it's hard graft, I can vouch for that. These guys would then go back to Nelson barracks and go training. Running, weights, the lot.

I've heard it said in football sometimes that such-and-such a player is fit: 'He's got a good engine.' Meaning he can go or run all day. I think that's what the SAS guys all have. Stamina? You can build stamina, a bit anyway, but I think you have to be born with a good engine.

They were obviously not used to Pompey, usually being based in Hereford. So one night they were round my house in Southsea because I was going to show them around town. My lodger at the time, Liz, came in from work and was quite impressed to have a house full of SAS. One of them took quite a shine to her for a while. I say for a while because she wouldn't stop asking him, 'Have you ever killed any one? Have you? No, but have you?' He wouldn't tell her.

I remember one bolshie doorman telling them they weren't coming into the Cambridge Pub because they wouldn't show him their ID. It would have been fun to watch it kick off, but they just walked off. One did say he wanted to slot him, though. Don't know what that means.

Day seven

I spoke to one of the lads who had picked up the Argentinian pilot who had ejected in San Carlos Water. It was one of the *Fearless* boats that picked him up. Apparently he had broken both legs and was in a right state. His knee caps weren't where they were meant to be either, having been smashed into the cockpit as he ejected. He spoke the Queen's English perfectly and was trained by the RAF in Blighty! Lucero they said his name was.

He said he was told that they were attacking unarmed merchantmen. What a shock then to come over the hill into San Carlos Water and see the wall of flak, lead, missiles and sheer aggression that came up at him. And what a shock to come to in the water being dragged into an English Gemini with busted legs. He lived, though, unlike a great many of his flying buddies.

Thursday 27 May 1982 (DAY SEVEN)

Got to bed early last night half twelve. Got next to no sleep. My long awaited wisdom tooth has started poking its head out and I have an ulcer to go with it.

Dave Stan Boss went over to Argonaut this morning. Ship's company have started cutting holes in roofs and ship's side to lift the bomb up and over the side. During the cutting, sparks caught fire to something and the forward part of the ship caught fire. The compartment with the bomb was flooded immediately (by ships damage control part). We stood on the upper deck of Intrepid and watched the smoke billowing out of her. Eventually the fire was brought under control. Thank God! Dave was somewhat worried.

Lots of the ships have gone now (Canberra to South Georgia with Norland to pick up QE2 troops). So, that leaves us a better chance of being hit! Intrepid was missed narrowly two days ago I'm told. It was while I was on the beach on the landing craft.

At one o'clock, went over to look at bomb on Sir Galahad. It was in a fairly easy place to get out. The fuse from the front had disappeared and the one in the back was smashed with all the wires hanging out. It had metal wrapped around it where it was spinning as it came through the metal walls. FCDT3 made a sling and lifted it out into a gemini by crane. They had sent the ship's company to HMS Intrepid during this. They didn't need much pushing. Then they took it away to deeper water to sink it. They sunk the gemini as well. All that could be seen was thousands of cornflakes on the surface, which had been used to stop it rolling about. Different!

All day went by with no attacks. I was on the flight deck with George and Wilki waiting to go to Argonaut. Three Skyhawks came over the nearest shore to us dropping parachute-retarded bombs. We saw it as clear as daylight, four at least went off, the one that hit the ammo dump certainly did. We learned later that three had gone into the field hospital. Their intelligence must be good for them to know there was an ammo dump there, so who in their right mind would bomb a hospital? The casualties came on board the Intrepid most of the night. Four dead (very lucky) 40 injured (some from the hospital).

The day before it was argued whether us or the other diving team should go ashore. They went ashore, which was considered to be the safest place! It seems nowhere is safe now.

Some of the team left under the cover of darkness to do - yes, you guessed it, Argonaut. Tonight it comes out and over the side.

Bloody tooth!

In a war zone a toothache doesn't really cut it when there are people walking around with horrible burns and injuries. The emergency hospitals set up on most of the big ships were all very busy. Can you walk in and say, 'Excuse me sir, I've got a tooth-ache'? I couldn't. I'd have to suffer.

Saying that, when it's you, it drives you insane. The only way I could sleep was to put an aspirin actually on the offending tooth and let it soak into the ulcer, and then as the pain-killing effect wore off, I'd have to do it again. This may be why I appear to have written a lot on some of these days, because (much to everyone else's disappointment) I had virtually stopped talking; maybe I was writing instead?

The dentist

The other thing holding me back was the dentist. He wasn't from the *Intrepid*, I have no idea where they had prised him from, but he was a nervous wreck. He would stalk the galley from dawn to dusk wearing full anti-flash, hood on and gloves on and sporting a gas mask on his hip, life jacket round his waist and once only suit at the ready. He had a permanent sweat on and would chat away to himself, pacing the same route, back and forth, back and forth, looking up at the deck head seemingly listening, waiting, for the next impending disaster. It seemed everyone else on board had come to the same conclusion as me, just to leave him be.

Once during the night I went down to the galley for a tea and there he was, walking his walk. I was in agony and thought about asking him what he might be able to do. I walked up close to his route and waited, hoping for some inkling that he even knew I was there ... Nothing! He was alone in his world. Do I want this tormented soul working on my teeth? I think I'll wait. I just popped another pain-killer onto the tooth and went back to the glorious surroundings of the vehicle deck.

One of our lads, Lester Geoffreys, had a wacky sense of humour and was maybe not far behind the mystery dentist in the madness stakes, and that was before the war. The galley was completely cleared most of the time in Bomb Alley as it doubled up as part of the hospital for emergencies, so you could make 'a clean sweep' as you would say in Nelson's day. One of his jolly japes was to come running into the galley during scran shouting, 'Look out! Here comes a Mirage, eeerrrgghhh!' He would have his arms stretched out (and swept back for authenticity) in a schoolboy aeroplane mode and dive headlong into all the piled-up boxes and plastic chairs, making crashing and exploding noises.

I remember the look on the dentist's face on witnessing this drama being played out before him. Anyone on our team who over-reacted from now on to a bomb blast, rockets or any general bang, was then compared to 'the dentist'.

The thing is, how are you going to react when the shit hits the fan? Do you know yet? Ask yourself now, really, how would you conduct yourself under fire or in a close air raid? If you haven't done it, you simply don't know. You can't say, 'Oh I'd be all right,' because you don't know. Some people can function and just about do their job, others go through the motions but don't really achieve a lot, and some excel – they actually improve with the adrenalin rush. Experience helps, but only if you don't lose it the first time, because from what I saw those sort rarely got any better. That first air raid loading a gun and actually getting shots off at the enemy helped me no end. I'd done my bit to fight back and I got better as time went on – not more relaxed, but I could certainly function better.

Dave Wilkinson, a lad on our team, told me whilst I was preparing to write this about one lad he had seen who was meant to be loading a 40/60 Bofors gun during an air raid, but as the planes appeared and the noise started he locked himself into the little temporary magazine under the gun and put all six clips on the door. Probably not the safest place to be, amongst ammo, but that was his place. Maybe it was 'out of sight out of mind' for him. He didn't know he would react that way. Another time I remember seeing someone I knew well, laughing at an enormous explosion we'd witnessed and nearly getting himself chinned for his reaction. Until we realised it was a nervous reaction. It was his way of dealing with it.

Fire

Dave Southwell, Stan Bowles and the Boss were on the *Argonaut* again, cutting holes in the deck head and bulkheads ready to ease the passage of the bomb to its new home in Davy Jones' locker.

Fire is a word you don't want to hear at sea. You don't want to hear it at sea in a war zone, and you don't want to hear it at sea in a war zone with holes in your ship and a bomb in your magazine, of all places. Somehow in the process of burning the bulkhead, a rogue spark caught something alight. If you cut metal at sea using cutting torches, someone is always on the other side of the bulkhead with fire hoses and extinguishers at the ready. So how it happened, I really don't know. The magazine was immediately flooded, as per the ship damage control procedures in the event of a fire.

However as I came on deck of the *Intrepid*, the *Argonaut* was undeniably on fire. We, the rest of the team, watched with trepidation as the smoke billowed out of her and I knew one of my closest buddies was on there. Dave, or Saggy Southwell, as he was affectionately known, was an ex-flatmate, drinking buddy and golf partner. He was my Sea Dad, i.e. the bloke who takes you under his wing and shows you the ropes.

When we spoke later he admitted he was at times 'concerned' (though what he actually said was more descriptive and involved a spontaneous movement of the bowel area). The fire was eventually brought under control, then put out. The magazine now had to be pumped out again, fire damage checked and made good, our patches checked (dived on again) and a multitude of other things. The bomb's impending departure would be delayed again. Not good for the hosts of this unwelcome visitor, the crew of the *Argonaut*. Their stress levels were being incessantly tested.

Where are you safe?

Around this time it was decided it was not a good idea for both diving/bomb disposal teams to be staying on ships that were constantly getting bombed. Both teams volunteered to go ashore. Someone higher up had realised we were doing a decent and very important job. Well, it had to be safer ashore than out here. FCDT3 won, or lost, depending on your point of view. They went ashore to Red Beach (Ajax Bay in San Carlos). They had been living on the *Sir Bedivere.*

The number of ships in San Carlos was now diminishing, as ships were getting tasked to go all over the place. Good for them, but, I would argue, bad for us. My logic was simple: more ships equals more targets, less chance of getting hit. Fewer ships gives the attacking planes less choice of targets and the *Intrepid* was now one of, if not *the*, biggest target in the sound.

If I hadn't kept a diary of events, I'd have no idea that all this happened on the same day. I wrote on 27 May that after witnessing the fire some of us went over to the *Sir Galahad*, where Fleet Team 3 had their own problems. They had two 1,000-pound bombs of their own to deal with, one on the *Sir Galahad* and one on the *Sir Lancelot.* The one on the *Galahad* was sitting in a comparatively easy access area. It was like a ghost ship on there. We had learned from the catastrophe of the *Antelope* that leaving the crew on board might not prove to be to clever, so they were asked to 'Foxtrot Oscar' (F Off) over to the *Intrepid.* I doubt any argued.

We gave FCDT3 some helicopter slings we had stolen and some other equipment and left them to it. The fuses on the bomb were in a right state, and after studying the path and battering the bomb had already taken, it was again decided to leave them well alone. They also decided to lift it up and over the side, being careful to keep it in the same plane. Just seven hours of solid work later, the bomb was ready to be transferred.

They didn't want to put the bomb on the bottom where it was because it was relatively shallow, and in what would be a busy part of the sound, so they lowered it into a Gemini, enabling them to take it off and sink it out of harm's way. It was a cold wet night, and to give the delicate bomb a soft ride, somehow they came up with the idea of lowering it onto huge boxes of cornflakes, which would take up the shape and plane. Luckily it wasn't an acoustic mine! It was another British-made 1,000-pound bomb. Tommo and Buster then towed it to where it was to rest in peace (until eventually being blown up). Tommo says they then slashed the Gemini and stood off to watch it sink. The Gemini was having none of it, though – it liked floating, even with no air in its tanks. Eventually they had to go back and, very gently, roll the very stubborn bomb over the side of the flat inflatable. All that gave away its position were thousands of cornflakes floating on the surface, like some kind of agricultural wreath. The next day on returning to find and blow up the bomb, the marker buoy had sunk below the surface and the bomb was lost (for now). Oops.

We hadn't seen or heard of an air attack all day. I was on the flight deck of *Intrepid* waiting to go over to *Argonaut* with Wilki and George Sharp. As far as I remember, there wasn't even an air raid warning. We were facing Ajax Bay (an abandoned meat packing facility) when three Skyhawks came from the southeast. I could see it all unfold as clear as you like. I guessed they had taken off from Stanley airport and stayed low so hadn't been reported or spotted. I watched them go over the group of buildings there and even saw the fall and trajectory of their bombs. They dropped what looked like about a dozen in all, large parachute-retarded bombs. The parachutes arrested the speed of their fall, hence allowing the small propellers at the tail fuse to unwind fully and arm the weapon properly. Had they got wind of what was going wrong with their fuses? I think so!

Four bombs exploded, some in the shed that was being used as a galley. What is it with galleys? Ashore or at sea, they seem mighty dangerous places in war. It was half an hour before scran so the place wasn't as packed as it might have been. They still killed six and injured around twenty more.

There was a field hospital with British and Argentinian casualties there, and right alongside it was 45 Commando's ammo dump. One bomb fell into the ammo dump and that one went off. So this was a full order with a bit extra added in! It was a colossal explosion, as you would expect. It carried on exploding all night. This was one sick drama we were watching. Phil Kearns told me:

> To be there that night was like a scene from *Apocalypse Now*. There were fires and spontaneous secondary explosions throwing all sorts of ordnance randomly around the devastated area. Utter chaos. The cries of the wounded intermingled with the dishevelled survivors, English and Argentinian, all wandering about like extras in some gruesome war movie. This was not a movie scene, though, it was very real and you had to pinch yourself from time to time to make sure you remembered that.

We watched from the *Intrepid* and wondered if that was indeed the field hospital that had just disappeared, taking God knows how many already suffering souls with it. It turned out three bombs had undeniably hit the field dressing station. Rex Turnbull, one of the lads from FCDT3, said one passed straight through the building, without stopping! One lodged itself in the roof and didn't go off and the third was also a dud and stuck in the building. Had all twelve gone off, 45 Commando might have lost hundreds of men, and we would have lost Fleet Team 3, who had only just pitched up there to be somewhere safer!

I've already mentioned listening to the BBC World Service – and we did listen whenever we could. You find out what is going on ashore politically and, more importantly, how your loved ones back home are hearing about the war. Are they making it sound how it is? You have to remember no one had mobiles back then. You couldn't even go to the radio shack and ask the RO to patch you through to home just to let Mummy know you're alright. Communications weren't that good or easy then.

If we're listening then we know others around the world are listening, including millions of Argentinians, because it was clear they knew their military junta did not tell the truth. They didn't tell the truth about the 'Disappeared' in Argentina and they wouldn't tell much truth about the Malvinas either.

Since 1976, the military junta that had seized control had been in charge of Argentina. They started a campaign to wipe out left-wing terrorism, but it soon spread to anyone and everyone including dissidents and innocent civilians. Depending on which report you believe or read, between 9,000 and 30,000 people disappeared in a terrifying period between 1976 and 1983. The army would snatch people off the streets or out of their beds in the middle of the night and they were never seen again. To this day, there is a weekly march in Argentina where mothers try to find out what happened to their sons, daughters, husbands and loved ones.

So imagine our dismay on hearing the BBC telling the world about the fuses on the bombs not being right. In fact dismay is not the right word, we were downright angry. How can they be doing this to us?

I don't really mean the whole task force was equally upset, I mean 'us' the divers, and the Royal Engineers who had to go and sit and work alongside these UXBs. Please don't tell them what they're doing wrong, they may put it right. I know the BBC endeavour to tell the truth, but information like that is helping the enemy. Had it helped the Argentinians, in that they now seemed to be dropping parachute-retarded bombs? It is very odd that the longer the war went on, the more bombs went off. I seem to remember Mick Fellows and the Boss getting a call through to Northwood and making their feelings known on more than one occasion.

Watching these explosions on Red Beach isn't the ideal preparation for going to *Argonaut* to work on a bomb, not for your nerves anyway, but at least it keeps you on your toes. It makes you give the ordnance you are working on an exorbitant amount of respect.

So now which team is in the safest place, us or FCDT3? Perhaps we'll stay here after all.

Day eight

Friday 28 May 1982 (DAY EIGHT)

Bomb out by about 05:00. You have never seen a more relieved ships company. We'd never been so popular, drinks all round, hand shakes from skipper, Jimmy, Commanders, signals from C in C etc.

08:00 Started to lift the smashed up Sea Cats and 40/60 Bofors shells. One of the Sea Cats war-heads had partially detonated, two others were missing. This was all caused by the bomb, some of the shells were reduced to 1/4 to 1/2 inch thick. All was smothered in diesel and oil, bits of war-head and HE were everywhere. I don't think the two guys had a hope.

Finished the job about 22:00. Black as Fuck. More drinkies from the wardroom, first touch of gin for 6 weeks. Nice stuff.

Got told the Paras have just taken Goose Green. The Pucaras had been bombing troops, but they were their own troops. They shot down one and left the other two because they were doing a good job. Bed about 01:00.

Mouth and neck swollen cause of this stupid tooth. I don't think diesel helps.

First thing in the morning the *Argonaut* bomb was out and sitting on the bottom.

The sense of relief from the ship's company was overwhelming, and some were emotional. They had lived with this objectionable and uninvited guest for seven days and nights. Think about living with that, think about what they had been through that week, air raids, being hit by bombs, the death of friends, near-misses. Think about watching the *Antelope's* destruction, knowing what you have in the belly of your home, and then having to sleep with it as a bedfellow. Think how every bang would make you jump, working and fighting your ship day after day. All this while sitting on a real live UXB. Earlier in the week they had had two on board. They all deserve a medal in my book, and I salute you all.

Hence there was a huge collective sigh. We were glad to see the back of it as well: it had been tying up some part of our team, day and night, since 22 May.

It wasn't quite over, though. Lester, Ian, Jan and I got into the magazine to finish up. There were still a lot of munitions in a precarious state from around and under where the bomb had lain. We had to leave the ship in a 'safe to fight' state. First we inspected all the easily movable shells. Then came the delicate manoeuvre of shifting three or four mangled Sea Cats, still in their fibreglass handling crates. We used the same rig used for the bomb and lifted them up and over the side.

It was on one of these ammo clearing days that we found one of the lads' wallets and handed it to the officer on watch. A sombre and thought-provoking moment.

It took about thirteen more hours to finish, and I remember we only stopped for 'action stations'. We grabbed something to eat then went back to work. We weren't badgered or pushed into it, we all wanted this over ASAP. This one had been too long. I wrote in my diary we finished about 22:00. I remember we sat in the wardroom filthy, drained but happy, then we sat in the senior rates' mess having a few beers, then another sailors' mess having a large gin and tonic with ice. It was heaven. 'Like an angel pissing down your throat,' said Jan. He was right.

Saturday 29 May 1982 (DAY NINE)

It seems a lot longer than 9 days. 05:15 Hands to action stations. Two jets dropped some bombs. We don't think they knew where they went (the bombs). It is the first time they've struck at night. Hope they don't make a habit of it. Back to bed at 06:00.

TOOTH!?**

Action stations a few times but planes believed to be attacking troops. Dinner, or 'Action Snacks' as they call them, has gone from a roll a tomato and a piece of corned beef, to just a roll, sometimes if we're good we can have butter with our roll. Tooth man Tooth!

Sunday 30 May 1982 (DAY TEN)

Went to sea in the middle of the night, woke up expecting to be in bomb alley. Gone to do a RAS (replenishment at sea) with RFAs and join up with Invincible and Exeter.

Nice to be away from bomb alley we thought, we'll get a restful night's sleep, we thought.

About one o'clock, I was half way up the vehicle ramp on my way to the helipad. Three rockets flew over head. They make a deafening noise. I and everyone else hit the deck. Waiting for the bang, it didn't come. Over the tannoy came 'We have just picked up a single sweep from a SUPER ETENDARD'S radar.' They are the horrors that carry Exocet.

The rockets we heard were ours, fired from the bridge, the theory is they explode in a pattern around us and drop millions of pieces of tin, silver paper. The Exocet is meant to go for them instead of us. I have my doubts about this theory. It was a false alarm but managed to get everyone else worrying about Exocet.

About 21:45 some of the ships company were watching 'Dirty Mary, Crazy Larry' on film. Those bloody rockets went off again. It worked again, everyone dived under tables etc. This time an Exocet had been fired, towards the three ships. When two miles away, this thing picks out its own target.

Action stations, anti flash, close all red openings etc. etc. One of us was to be hit. After the Etendard had fired its Exocet, the Exeter shot her down with sea dart. Then the Arrow opened up with her 4.5 inch guns on the missile and two more sea darts were fired from Exeter. One of them hit the Exocet, both claim it of course. All this was done by radar of course, of course of course! The two Skyhawks that escorted the Etendard were chased off by Harriers.

It's weird, sat waiting to hear either a bang or something over the tannoy. You can see fright in people. We've decided we prefer bomb alley, at least we know what to expect, and you can swim to the shore if need be. Exocet frightens me more I think. Out here at sea we have a sweep-stake on if it'll be Exocet or torpedo tonight?

Bomb alley in the morning! What a thing to look forward to.

On a big downer all day, tooth has stopped me from talking, to everyone else's delight I'm sure. Hacked off with it all and can see no quick end.

Home please!

Exocet!

What this planet needs is more mistletoe and less missile-talk.

The chaff rockets, as they are called, are loud, and the fact they are from your own bridge means they are close. They are also un-announced because you get them away first to stop the Exocet, then you make the announcement, along the lines of, 'Don't pan-ic, they were ours.' So the shock value is incredible. You would think they are 'incoming' because of the noise. I don't know how many people tried to make it under the same table during the film *Dirty Mary, Crazy Larry* on the *Intrepid* that night but you definitely all 'get down' together. About fifty per table is never going to work, is it? I know the projector went over because it was on a table and that needed getting under as soon as possi-ble. Are tables bullet- and bombproof? Maybe we should look at making warships out of what they make those tables out of, because the mystical shielding value of a table under fire has to be seen to be believed.

For me, when I realised we had been fired on by a Super Etendard, I didn't quite know what to do. The ship's company all have a part of the ship and a duty to perform in action stations. Their choice is taken away, they go to their gun, fire-fighting post, damage control party or whatever. Their place is set out.

We were passengers. We had nothing to do at action stations. So where do you go? Deep into the ship? Well, an Exocet heads for the middle of a ship. Nope, not there then. I think I'm right in saying the chefs were the branch that lost the most men because the galley was slap bang in the middle of every ship. What about the upper deck? Nope, not if you have ever seen that piece of film when HMS *Undaunted* (known in the Navy as the *Unwanted* because of what they did to her) is deliberately shot with an Exocet, fired by HMS *Norfolk*. It shows the Exocet hitting the ship's side in slow motion. Well, you wouldn't want to be up there. The stern, then? Well, if a skipper gets enough warning he may try and get the bow or stern end facing the attack to give a smaller target. The *Glamorgan* used this very tactic during the conflict, and the missile flew straight through the helicopter hangar and into, you guessed it, the galley. Thirteen were killed and twenty-two injured.

It was obviously discussed at great length by us. One night Wilki and I came up with the idea that just forward of the stern quarter was the place to be, and on the *Intrepid* you could go onto the upper deck there and see what was coming your way. One night, stood out there, the gunnery officer came by in full regalia, anti-flash tin hat etc. We put our theory to him that where we stood was the best place to be in an Exocet attack.

'Well, in theory, yes,' he said.

See! We said smugly too each other. We were right.

'BUT,' he said. 'Right here where you're standing is above the helicopter fuel tanks.' Then he shrugged his shoulders as if to say, 'Stand there if you like, deeps,' and hurried off.

Where then? I came to the conclusion it didn't really matter. If your time was up, you'd be in the wrong place. I don't think it's any more technical than that. I think later in the conflict I was proved right when I saw men terribly burned who were in no more dangerous a position than some of their colleagues. I generally went to the bridge when 'something was afoot'.

We just shuffled off to our newly appointed sea berths. Ah well, '*que sera sera*, whatever will be will be.' These berths they had found us were a bit basic, to put it mildly. They were alongside the floodable dock in the stern. Right above the fuel tanks. I remember you had to go through a hatch and down a vertical ladder to reach it. They were meant for embarked troops who would be there just until they could move off on one of the LCUs (the bigger landing craft). *Intrepid* had four in her dock.

It got you wondering about how to get out of there in the event of attack, fire, flooding, in the dark. When there were air raid warnings or chaff rockets fired we would all form an orderly queue at the bottom of the ladder and wait our turn to exit the 'coffin', as it became known. 'After you' ... 'No, you were before me, please, I insist' ... 'You're too kind ... Is this your boot?'... I'll leave you to make up your own mind how it really went.

After a couple of nights of this I went quietly back down to the vehicle deck and slept on my old camp bed (where I found Ian Milne and Saggy already ensconced in theirs). A knowing glance was all that was required, as in 'You too? Sod that for a game of soldiers/sailors!'

We never got undressed now. I would sleep fully booted and spurred, as we all did. Well, you don't want to be running around, 'tackle out', during an air raid looking for your trousers and shoes. Things like changing underwear or clean socks pale into insignificance at times like that. You just want to be ready. For what, you don't know, but you want to be ready at least for something!

I remember speaking to a girlfriend once about working almost non-stop, not washing and sleeping in your clothes and boots for weeks at a time. She said to me, 'Didn't you shower and brush your teeth? Urgh, I couldn't do that. If I couldn't wash my hair every day, I don't know what I'd do.' I couldn't be bothered to answer her. Those things weren't even worth considering. It comes down to priorities. Let's say you are as god made you, *au naturel* in the shower, when you are hit in an air raid. Can you try to imagine your injuries in the blast, or your flash burns with no clothes on, or running around naked trying to find an exit, or your boots? You probably stank, yes, but everyone stank. What was important was making sure you knew where your nearest exit was at all times, and you could get there quickly, and you had everything you needed (information and equipment) to make a hasty exit. You might have been in the dinner queue on an unfamiliar ship, but you knew where your quickest exit was, always.

<u>Monday 31 May 1982</u> (DAY ELEVEN)

Bank holiday, so what! Wish I was in a traffic
jam.

Wake up in bomb alley. It doesn't get light
until about 9 o'clock then gets dark about six.
The Argies this morning claimed the Invincible
was hit and ablaze because of an attack last
night. They couldn't have known the missile was
shot down until we said on the news today.

The quietest day yet. A couple of the old 'Air
raid warning reds' but saw nothing. Heard on the
news they're rolling bombs out of the back of
Hercules's. They've been using Hercs to refuel
their planes in the air we think. I never take
my clothes off when going to bed now, even sleep
with my boots on. Can hear my feet humming at
night.

Regrets

All my time in the South Atlantic I'd been harbouring a bit of
a regret. It will sound like nothing to most people but it was
bothering me at the time. Before we left the UK, we kept getting
24 hours' notice. 'Yep, definitely soon.' This went on for a couple
of weeks.

The task force had gone a long time ago so if we were going
to go it would be by air. As the diplomacy kept failing, we knew
we were in with a better chance of going. Early on, Mick Fellows
and the Boss had been summoned to see the big cheese of the
'Amphibious Task Group', Commodore Michael Clapp. He had
our destiny in his hands. It was up to him to say, 'I want them to
go,' or 'I don't.'

They came back within the hour and all hell broke loose. We were to pack everything and were definitely going soon. Well yeah we'd heard it all before – but now we had cancelled all other work we had planned, and we were packing. You know what it's like: when you pack, you know you're off. We just had a rough date after the weekend of 9 April.

With possibly just one more weekend off, the team scattered to the four corners of the UK to see loved ones. I went home to Lyme Regis to see my parents and my girlfriend, Marie. I seem to remember I had a good weekend, and then, on the Sunday I think it was, we got a call to rush back to Pompey. We were off. I loaded up my Datsun 120Y and kissed my mum, told her I loved her and I'd do the washing up when I got back (a standing family joke), and tried to remain matter-of-fact about it – an 'it might come to nothing' sort of mood.

My dad was the other side of the car and I just got in and drove off. I usually shook his hand, but I didn't do it this time. Why? I'm not certain. It was something to do with not wanting to be too dramatic, 'I'm off to war!' Something to do with me not wanting it to be like a final big important moment, you know, 'Now I'll say goodbye, maybe for the last time.' Maybe I thought it was bad luck. A bit of everything really.

I have always called him dad, but he is actually stepfather to my sister Kim and me. I call him that because he has been part of the family since I was about eight years old and has taken to looking after my mother as if he was born to it. You would think they were made for each other; they are true soul partners. I cannot do justice to what he has done for us all. Moreover, I have loved him like a father for that amount of time.

Down south it really bothered me. I should have shaken his hand. What if I didn't get the chance to do it again? A couple of times when I thought I might be a bit too close to my maker for comfort, I would think about it. I regret it to this day. Whether he even noticed my actions I don't know. I've never asked him.

Tuesday 1 June 1982 (DAY TWELVE)

43 days at sea!

A couple of air raid warnings during the day. One was a Hercules. Two Harriers attacked it, it was hit by a 'side-winder' missile and also cannon fire. Bet it went with a bang. We're hoping it was the tanker that was refuelling their jets. I mentioned previously that the other diving team had gone ashore. Some of them came on board today to bring more bomb disposal gear to us. They are having a rough time ashore.

They are living in red beach. The field hospital I said was bombed. Two hundred prisoners came in yesterday and two hundred today. They're keeping those in red beach there for a while. The team said some are very young and skinny.

They apparently are no trouble at all, just glad to be alive and want to go home. They were told, 'The British will shoot you if they catch you.'

Team dived on the Fearless today to blank a hole.

Going to Teal Inlet to pick up a small mine-sweeping team that we took there last night. Forgot to mention it. So it's back into Exocet country for a while.

Hope they found no mines. Another job for us if they have. Teal inlet is where the main attack is going to go in I believe. SHHH!

Wednesday 2 June 1982 (DAY THIRTEEN)

Going to sea for two days, to the maintenance place for a rest period. All the sailors on here are keeping what they call defence watches.

It is six hours on six hours off, constantly. They've been at it since we got in the danger area now. During the six hours off of course, there are meals to be had and washing etc. We are told we are out of Etendard range now.

Been busy and lost track of the days. Start again on the 5th.

Bluff Cove

<u>Saturday 5 June 1982</u>

Got picked for a good job, four lads and Mick and Ben left Intrepid, just as it was getting dark in a Sea King, the pilot was the Special Ops pilot (SAS). Six of us (divers) four Royal Engineers (for the land mines) and four SBS. There were also lots of Paras to protect us. We were complete with rucksacks, ration packs, and 'you can't see me' gear.

The pilot never went above 50 foot and ground-hopped 110 knots all the way. It was a spectacular ride – it took about 30 mins to cover the distance, through valleys over and around mountains. We landed at a place called Bluff Cove just as it was getting dark. It is a small settlement of only two families, they were English and would do anything to help us get the Argies out.

The old man from the settlement gave us a lift to the small estuary. We were to swim in search of mines. It was about midnight when we got there. Myself and Billy E. dived, searching for the mines. We cleared the estuary, the REs and SBS cleared the shore.

We finished diving around 4 a.m. and slept the night in a pigpen or sheep pen, both smell the same.

In the morning the families topped us up with tea and steak Sarnies. They flew a Union Jack that day, for the first time since the invasion. Our tanks and Paras appeared from all over the place that morning. The Argies have killed over 150 of their sheep and torn down over 4 miles of fences to burn.

The following day, nearly a thousand Royal Scots Guards will come in the Bluff Cove estuary and land at the site we dived. The families don't know that yet, for security reasons. She'll have some tea to make then!

Caught another chopper back about six the following day.

Sometime around midday on 4 June I was picked for a job ashore. Brilliant, I thought, I would hate to come all this way and not even land on the islands. You can't really say, 'Falklands? I've been there,' if you haven't landed, can you? Not until you've walked on the ground, anyway. As yet, my boots were un-muddied by the South Atlantic islands' peaty soil. However, it would appear, things were about to change.

Initially we were told nothing about the job, only to prep the rebreathers, mine-sweeping search gear, some detonators and PE packs in case we found mines, full camouflage gear and a sleeping bag. We were also told to pack ration packs, as they didn't know how long we would be away, that would depend on what we found. As yet, we still had no idea what the job was about, but it was getting more intriguing by the minute.

So I was pretty keyed up when we were summoned to a special briefing on HMS *Fearless*. Around 17:00 in the 'special ops' room, it soon became apparent that this mission was based around us, the divers. We were going to be required to search a small inlet called Bluff Cove for mines and underwater obstructions. No one I knew had ever heard of Bluff Cove, but of course only a couple of days after we searched the inlet, it became world famous for the tragic events that unfolded there on 8 June, involving *Sir Tristram* and *Sir Galahad.*

Everyone else was there to give us support. There would be four divers and two supervisors to make up the diving team, five members of SBS and some Royal Marines to provide protection, and some members of 59 Commando Royal Engineers, to do the land side of the mine clearing. They would sweep the footpaths to the coast and the beach itself, for all our safety, mainly looking for anti-personnel mines. All this was under the blackboard heading 'Clandestine Investigation Prior Amphibious Troop Landing', which meant at night and sneaky-beaky-styley, to coin a military phrase.

I remember my heart rate rising as the briefing ensued. Wow! I thought, this is going to be exciting! We were soon told we were only allowed to wear dogtags for ID. These dogtags, which I still have, are made of two different materials. One is a maroon colour and is fireproof, and the other one is green, and water- and liquid-proof. So! Shot, drowned, burned or whatever, they could still identify you. Nice, eh? All it has on mine is the only information you are required to give any captor by the Geneva Convention: name, rank and serial number. Mine reads: AP GROOM D153816M LSD (LSD standing for Leading Seaman Diver).

We were told to keep personal belongings down to an absolute minimum and were allowed to carry no other means of identification. The lecturer went to a great deal of trouble to point out all the points of interest, such as the Bluff Cove settlement, our helicopter landing zone, the boathouse, the track down to the beach, etc. We were also issued with passwords and dull red flashlights. Then, last but not least, we were told the last known enemy sightings in that area. Also, where to meet up, in the event of an ambush or counterattack. Crikey, I thought.

We would be flying in by Sea King under cover of darkness, and would be using one of the 846 Naval Air Squadron's choppers, earmarked for Special Forces insertion, complete with special ops pilots. This was getting more exciting by the minute. It was made clear we would be ground-hopping in the helicopter, which simply means hugging contours of the land.

Then, tapping the big map on the wall with his pace stick, the lecturer said, 'and this eastern bank, gentlemen, is still in enemy hands, so you must ... blah blah blah.'

'What did he just say? What was that?' I could see his lips still moving, but all I heard was 'still in enemy hands.'

Like Charlie Brown in the Peanuts cartoon, sitting in class daydreaming about pitching a baseball, and hearing nothing but 'blah blah blah' from the mouth of his teacher, all I heard after 'still in enemy hands' was blah blah blah.

Surely we can't go there if it's still in enemy hands. Can we? Oh well, we'll put our lives in the capable hands of the SBS and the bootnecks!

Of course, for the SBS and Marines, this was all taken in their stride. They moved away from the meeting chatting merrily. However, we were creatures of the sea, not the land, not at night, and not too close to the enemy! Would they give us guns again? Probably not.

All six of us headed off down to the vehicle deck to make up the diving sets. Some members of the team were hanging around, eager to find out what our mission was. Now was the perfect time to use the age-old phrase 'I could tell you, but I'd have to kill you,' or 'Sorry chaps, love to tell you but, you know, security and all that!'

We made final preparations to our rebreather sets, putting a fresh CO_2 absorbent (which will last twelve hours) into the canisters, checking all the connections and the contents of the O_2 cylinders, and a multitude of other tasks. We put our diving under-suits on under our combats, so we only had to take our top layer off, and put the dry suit on.

Billy went up to the gunner's mate and withdrew the PE packs and detonators we required. All our gear was then put into two hampers, and we were ready to go. We had time to watch the SBS down on the vehicle deck getting their gear and themselves ready. It certainly put my mind at rest. They were fully cammed up, and it looked to me like they carried enough ammo to take Port Stanley on their own.

Our ETD (estimated time of departure) was 19:00, but this was delayed until 19:45 due to heavy ground fog over the hills and enemy activity along the coast route.

At 19:35 we were prepped and stood just inside the hangar on *Fearless*'s flight deck, ready for the off. The matt black Sea King appeared out of the night with no navigation lights on, and landed on the helideck. We chucked our hampers on board, jumped in and were airborne within minutes. Now, this was like no other flight I had ever taken. There were no niceties, no 'Is your seatbelt fastened, sir?' or 'Here are the emergency exits, would you like a boiled sweet?' None of that. As soon as we were clear of HMS *Fearless*, the nose of the aircraft dropped, and we tore off just above the waves.

When we arrived at Bluff Cove we did the dive I have already described, on which I found the 'oil drum mine', and then we slept in the sheep shed.

Feeling British again

When I woke up in the sheep shed in the morning, the Paras had gone and I hadn't heard a thing, which was not like me. We were meant to be taking off back to *Fearless* at 12:00, but it was delayed until around 16:30. Walking over to the farmhouse, I noticed the farmer had the Union Jack flying. We had time to kill, so I somewhat accidentally fell into a conversation with him. Among other things, I asked him about the Union Jack flying at his flagpole. This in hindsight may have been a mistake. It was the symbol of everything that had gone on: it was Britain, he was British, English. He said this morning was the first time he'd felt confident enough to fly it. He said his gratitude to us Brits in general was overwhelming. He was trying to say, I think, that he felt a bit guilty about all the lives lost and that they had been lost for them, just a bunch of islanders. We were outside his house, we didn't even know each other, we never even exchanged names, yet we spoke candidly and from the heart. He was really struggling with his emotions, and if I'm truthful he lost that battle and let go, as I nearly did.

All I could say to him was that if one day I found myself living far away from home, in a little bit of 'Blighty', and I was invaded and my lifestyle threatened, I would hope someone would come and rescue me. I said I thought it was every Brit's right to expect help in times as dramatic as these. I felt quite sorry for them. This is also what I said when I was interviewed for BBC television in April 2007 as part of the 25-year Falklands anniversary, and I meant it.

As the morning wore on, more and more troops came through the settlement with their armoured personnel carriers and light tanks.

I, or should I say we all, saw an attractive young woman and her sheepdogs arrive at the settlement this morning. Some kind soldier, who I'm sure only had the interests of the girl at heart, and had no ulterior motives on his mind, had decked her out in a Navy foul-weather jacket and she was wearing a bright yellow civilian crash helmet. It was the first young woman any of us had seen for months, and the fields around just stopped and stared in silent admiration. Now would have been the Argentinians' perfect chance for a counterattack. We were all, to coin a phrase, gob-smacked. Some light tank commander had given her a lift to the settlement. She was sat on the front and throwing her head back, laughing as it bumped along through the boggy ground. It was the noise of her laughter that stopped every male in his tracks. Her dogs were running all around the tank barking and nearly being squashed. When her lift stopped, she jumped down giggling and took off the helmet and shook out her long fair hair, and I swear there was a huge collective sigh from all who witnessed it. It really made us all think of things that can only happen back home. Things that are quite important to a young man, things that this young man had forcibly kept at the back of his mind for a few months now. Move on, think about something else, 'that' could be months away yet.

Marie

'That' had been giving me a lot of anguish over the last few months. My girl, if you like, was keener on me and on that word that frightens most young men, marriage, than me. Marie was from Lyme Regis, where my parents had just bought a beautiful Tudor house, which had six letting flats inside it and still left us with a lounge the size and height of a squash court. Marie and I had a few bust-ups about how serious we were, or are, or whatever. Blokes generally find this all very confusing and think, 'Hey, we're having a laugh, everything's fine the way it is, why change it?' Women are always more complicated than that and want to know 'where things are going'. We had fallen out, again, just before I left the UK, but were writing to each other throughout the conflict. Boy would it be fun making up when we got back together! I eventually realised it was no more complicated than, I love her. I'm the one making it difficult. It did take me a few more years to figure it out though. Now my wife, Marie takes every opportunity possible to tell all and sundry how long it took me to (a) pop the question, and (b) actually do something about it. Thirteen years, if you must know. Ouch! It does look bad when you see it written down.

Back at Bluff Cove, the chopper duly arrived at around 16:30, this time a normal one with a normal pilot, with no catastrophes, and we were back on board Fearless by 17:00. It wasn't quite over, though, for we still had a detailed debriefing to go through. It was good to find out that two battalions of troops were subsequently landed in the cove on the night of 5/6 June.

Sunday 6 June 1982

It was 6th of June 1944, D Day really happened.

Yet here we were, 38 years later, fighting again. The Falklands campaign can in no way be compared to those dark days of the world's history. However, it was said after the First World War that it was so horrific it would never be forgotten; it was to be the 'War to End All Wars'. The French had their own saying for it, '*La der des ders*' (the last of the last). How soon we forget.

Only 21 years later of course was the Second World War. We humans have learned nothing. As I write these words, there are still men, women, and innocent civilians dying by their hundreds in the Middle East, in a war for what? What have all these wars cost? Not only the human cost – the financial waste of money must be astronomical. All spent so that some faceless leader somewhere can send his men off to fight and die.

In the eighteenth century, Benjamin Franklin wrote:

> What vast additions to the conveniences and comforts of living might mankind have acquired, if the money spent in wars had been employed in works of public utility; what an extension of agriculture even to the tops of our mountains; what rivers rendered navigable, or joined by canals; what bridges, aqueducts, new roads, and other public works, edifices, and improvements might not have been obtained by spending those millions in doing good, which in the last war have been spent in doing mischief?

Sea Dart

Monday 7 June 1982

I don't know what happened to the 7th of June. I don't think there was one.

Tuesday 8 June 1982 (DAY NINETEEN)

Bomb Alley!

It had only been light for a few hours. It was about midday, when ... 'Air Raid Warning Red Imminent'.

Two Canberras. I was stood on the flight deck, camera in hand, getting brave these days.

The Exeter fired her Sea Dart. She about a mile behind us in San Carlos Bay (all the ships at anchor). It was a very clear morning. The missile could be seen going up. It does twice the speed of sound, this thing. We all watched where it had gone, but could see no planes as

they were at 30+ thousand feet. A small puff of
smoke was seen after a few seconds, thousands of
feet up. It was confirmed a hit over the Tannoy.
Cheers accordingly. We could see it spinning
and glistening in the sun light as it came down.
The smoke train following it. It was the first
time they've tried it at such long ranges. No
doubt it's not the last. The high-level bombing
was a new theory of theirs. 'Not getting hit,
because we are too high.' (In Argentinian). Try
something else!

At sea tonight to pick up the landing craft that
dropped the Scots Guards off. OH NO!

Tooth okay, now. Think I'll wash my socks, just
for a laugh. They'll fall to pieces, it is the
dirt that's holding them together.

Goodnight!

WRONG!

It was a beautiful sunny day. I was standing on the back of the
Intrepid taking in the scenery, the sunshine and the ambience of
it all. As always, now, as soon as I heard the air raid warning, I
was up on deck with my camera. I was determined to get a good
picture of fighters coming across Bomb Alley. So I was panning
around looking for the first telltale sign – usually if you look towards the noise, you will find action – when the Sea Dart took
off from behind us. WOOOSH!

It was yet another of those moments that make you jump out
of your skin. As if our nerves weren't shredded enough. I wish
'our side' would stop trying to give us all heart attacks by firing
off weapons and missiles without warning the people around.

The *Exeter* had let loose one her first Sea Darts within the
confines of San Carlos Water. Now I could be wrong but I seem
to remember that the first one didn't fire properly, or the second
boosters didn't kick in, or something like that anyway. As far as

I'm aware no one had fired a Sea Dart from Bomb Alley before today. It was close and made a hell of a noise. It went straight up into a clear blue sky so fast, you couldn't actually see the missile. It takes a while to dawn on you that it's one of ours, going towards one of theirs, which is always good. You had to follow the smoke trail. Looking where the missile was heading we could see nothing. We thought it had missed, then there was a tiny puff of smoke

I wrote in my diary that it was at 30-odd thousand feet, but I really have no idea how high it was. Lots of matelots came out onto the back decks of the *Intrepid*, the *Fearless* and other anchored ships in Bomb Alley to see what was going on. We all stood for ages watching this glinting aircraft spinning as it came down towards the ground. It spun on its long terminal fall, which seemed to take an age. Every time it spun through one revolution it would catch the sun like a distant winking mirror. This time I was up and ready for an air raid warning red with my camera, and it was so high that it now looks on the photograph a bit like a scratch on the lens.

Eventually, it disappeared behind the hills of the Falklands. We assumed it came down out to sea, but it is now known that the remains of that aircraft, and its pilots, are on Pebble Island. Many more are out there somewhere to this day. We got the pipe that the *Exeter* had splashed one Canberra. I have to admit that a few cheers went around. It later turned out to have been a Learjet which was being used to lead the single-seat attack aircraft and do reconnaissance.

Wednesday 9 June 1982 (DAY TWENTY)

Attacked at about 17:30. Waves and waves of Mirages and Skyhawks.

After the attacks, the Plymouth came in just ahead of us. She was ablaze and listing badly. She asked for bomb disposal assistance. We all looked at each other, it's a sick feeling. Mick

Fellows myself and Billy E went over to her.

She had been hit by two 1000 lb bombs, plus cannon and rocket fire. The two bombs had gone in the port side and amazingly turned upwards and flew out of the deck around midships. The funnel was ripped apart. One of the cannon fire shots had hit a depth charge on the flight deck. It went off, nearly a full order. There was a hole ripped in the deck about 5 foot in diameter. That was above the POs' mess. The after end caught fire and swept forward. Again, brilliant Naval fire fighting saved the ship. When the bombs came in, they smashed two mortar bombs in half, in the mortar magazine. That's what we had to render safe. We eventually lowered them over the side.

Another air raid took place during job. It was not at us, but at Teal inlet, I mentioned it earlier, I believe. Tristram and Galahad were at Bluff Cove. Upon arrival back to Intrepid, we were hit with the news, Sir Tristram and Sir Galahad were ablaze and abandoned. Tristram took two 1000 lbs and Galahad three or four at Bluff Cove. The casualties were ferried to the Intrepid where a hospital was again set up in the dining room.

Crew and embarked forces were ferried to us from Tristram and Galahad. Some were burned beyond recognition. Many we knew well from four of five weeks on Tristram. It was clear lots had not been wearing anti flash. The blast or flash had caused most of the burns. Many had no skin on the exposed areas, their flesh was just black and swollen, most had no hair.

It was sick, disheartening and demoralising. The guys we knew from Tristram told us about it all.

They said she was exploding like mad as they
left. They don't know if she sunk. I hope not,
to put it mildly.

Lucky or unlucky

I've got pictures of HMS *Plymouth* coming back into San Carlos Water listing and on fire. When taking the pictures I thought, 'I wonder who will get that job.' Before she had even anchored, Billy Evernden, Mick Fellows and I were on our way over there in a Gemini. Of course, you don't know what you're going to be faced with until you get there. On approaching *Plymouth*'s port side we could see she'd been hit by two large bombs.

'Right,' I thought, 'we've got two unexploded bombs here!' I could also see she'd been hit by cannon fire, and I thought people had certainly been killed. She had been sitting just outside the entrance to San Carlos Water, the same place *Ardent* and *Antelope* had been attacked.

We arrived on board about 17:00 and commenced a survey of her damage. From what we could see two 1,000-pound bombs had gone through the port side aft, smashed two NC22 mortar bombs in the ready use handling room and caused a lot of structural damage to the compartments. Then they had inexplicably turned upwards and disappeared unexploded over the side. How lucky was the Plymouth? I shall try and do justice to how lucky she really was.

I know there were about five casualties on board, but none too serious. I spoke to a 'lucky' chief on board, who had been knelt down just outside the mortar room. He'd had a cup of soup in his hand. The bomb had passed no more than a few feet above his left shoulder, having smashed its way through the mortar room bulkhead. He'd spilled his soup all down his chin and had burnt his face. As he was telling me his story, he was still violently shaking, but other than that seemed quite in control considering he had nearly been decapitated.

It looked to me as if one plane had dropped the two bombs, as the entrance holes were about a wings-width apart. Bomb one (the furthest aft) had gone through what we call the garden wall, then had taken the corner of the mortar room off, hit and bent the centre barrel of the three mortar tubes, and disappeared off over the side.

Bomb two had gone in about 20 feet further forward and five feet lower (six feet above the water line), penetrated the mortar magazine, broken one mortar completely in two, without it going off. It did however manage to spill the explosives all around the deck and expose the proximity fuse wires and damage the tail unit of another mortar in the weapon hoist. The bomb had then turned upwards into the weapon handling room, through the second bulkhead (narrowly missing my chief, with his soup). For some inexplicable reason, it had then turned aft across the mortar well and continued upwards in order to go over the ship's side. Apart from the damage caused, there was no tail section, or any other evidence of what type of bomb it was.

But HMS *Plymouth* hadn't got away with 'just the two' 1,000-pound bombs hitting her, not exploding, not killing anyone, and just causing minor superficial soup burns. Oh no, Plymouth had more luck to come. She had also been strafed by rocket fire. I didn't count how many times she'd been hit, but I know she had one or two straight through her funnel. She had also taken a hit on her port aft Sea Cat missile system. Two of the Sea Cats had to be lifted and ditched over the side as they were in a precarious state.

She had also taken hits on the flight deck. The fact that two mark II depth charges were lying exactly where the cannon shells hit, and again no one was seriously hurt, was surely a sign that it was to be *Plymouth's* day! These two depth charges were lying innocently on the flight deck, waiting to be loaded into a helicopter. Not only were the depth charges hit by the cannon fire, but one had partially exploded, blowing a hole through the flight deck and setting fire to the compartment underneath. The second one had actually caught fire, and it was ditched overboard by the crew before the fire could spread to the torpedo magazine.

Whilst we were on board, there were more air raids taking place. This was day twenty under attack for us and we were all getting better at it – used to it, if you like. I do remember being knelt down next to the broken mortar chatting about how to sling it and lift it overboard. There was another loud bang and a roar of jet engines, not far away, and I remember us all just looking out through the bomb hole in *Plymouth's* port side to see where it had come from. As soon as we realised it was not going to affect us, we just carried on. What a picture that would have been, our three little faces peering out through a bomb entry hole, looking at an air raid!

You could argue that HMS *Plymouth* had more than her fair share of luck on that day. Two other ships, on the other hand, had less than their fair share.

Sir Tristram and *Sir Galahad*

My theory that surviving a war has more to do with luck than judgment or forethought was proven, to me at least, on this day.

Just 20 minutes after the planes attacked the *Plymouth* with their non-exploding bombs, and sprayed her with rockets to no real effect, five Skyhawks arrived at Fitzroy.

There they would find the two landing ships presenting themselves in the sunlight like sitting ducks, caught by the change in weather, unprotected by any warships and one of them full of guardsmen. It was the same type of bomb. Only this time the outcome was completely different. This time they exploded.

Who was to say I shouldn't still be on the *Sir Tristram* on this day firing my 40/60 Bofors?

It is not your decision whether you are offloaded first, second, today or tomorrow. As it turned out, the Rapier SAMs (Surface to Air Missile) teams and 16 Field Ambulance crew had gone ashore first from *Sir Galahad*, leaving a lot of the Welsh Guards cleaning weapons or playing cards in amongst all the vehicles and fuel down below.

The decision is by no means a clear or easy one. Get your SAMs ashore to give you some protection from air raids, so you can unload your troops and hardware with a bit more confidence? Or get your troops ashore as quickly as possible, taking the risk you may lose your SAM teams if you are hit whilst unloading? You have to get your field ambulance teams ashore, as they are no good to you stuck on board *Galahad*, and no good if they are hit. You could debate it forever.

My point is it's luck if you're on the *Sir Tristram* or the *Sir Galahad*. On one you have a better chance of surviving than on the other. But you don't know which is the right choice, and anyway it's not your decision. It is luck, whether you're at sea or on land. It is luck, if a bomb explodes or doesn't. It is luck, where you are standing and at what time. And if you are one of the Welsh Guards on the *Sir Galahad*, it is sheer luck whether you are among the 32 who died, or the many more who were terribly burned and injured, or one of those who walked away without a scratch.

It was undoubtedly a cock-up, all those men being left on board for around six hours, with no protection, in broad daylight, but then war is usually one cock-up after another. The choice for its decision makers is often between two bad paths; the art is to choose the least destructive and hope you guessed right.

By the end of the war I was totally convinced it didn't matter what you did or where you were. It had no bearing on whether you would survive or not. At times I found myself sat alongside a bomb of some description during an air raid and thinking, 'Oh well, whatever will be will be. I won't even know if it does go off, and if it doesn't go off I may still get hit by something else.' You could do nothing about it. So just get on with it.

I was out there as a diver and part of a bomb and mine disposal team. All our team came back, un-injured and physically un-scarred, and yet 30 or so chefs died in the Royal Navy. Which job would you pick for the safety aspect, chefs or bomb and mine disposal divers?

Arriving back at the *Intrepid*, we're told about the two ships. Shock is not the right word, devastated more like. Then immediately it occurred to all of us, what would loved ones back home be thinking? We had of course told everyone we were on the *Sir Tristram*. All our letters had been arriving there for weeks. We had only been off her a matter of days. We were sure the pictures of *Tristram* and *Galahad* exploding had been flashed around the world. The folks back home were probably more aware of the casualties than us. I remember worrying myself sick, as to what my parents and sister Kim and girlfriend Marie must have been going through.

When I finally arrived back home, my mother said this was the worst time for all of them. The families would generally watch all the news programmes, trying to pick up snippets of information. First of all they would watch the BBC news at nine o'clock. Then they would immediately flick over for the ITV news at ten. This was obviously a ritual that had been going on for weeks. Any news about your loved ones or their ships would result in phone calls all around the country to other equally worried parents, wives, girlfriends, etc.

On the night of 8 June 1982, I believe there was nothing on the BBC nine o'clock news, as it hadn't yet filtered through about the *Sir Tristram* and the *Sir Galahad*. There was nothing on the ten o'clock news either. Close to midnight, there was a news flash. 'Three British ships hit in Falklands, *Sir Tristram*, *Sir Galahad* and HMS *Plymouth*. No news yet on casualties.'

My sister Kim saw it, and my mother and father saw it, but

as it was late at night neither wanted to phone the other with the terrible news. Eventually my sister cracked and phoned our mother. They both had a good cry and panic over the phone together and had a pretty awful sleepless night. Meanwhile, back down in the South Atlantic, we knew this would be going on with all our families and friends, but there was nothing we could do about it. To give the MoD credit, they did manage to phone my mum about seven o'clock the following morning to tell them the Fleet Team had left *Tristram* a few days before. Other families aboard those two ships obviously were not greeted with such good news.

Burns

On arrival back at *Intrepid* we found that a number of the walking wounded, and some not walking, were arriving on board or passing through, and a makeshift hospital was again set up. Some of the images, smells and sensations I saw on these days will stay with me forever. We all have sympathy for anyone who has been seriously burned. Some of these lads were in agony. I saw one stretcher case on the flight deck of *Fearless*, I guess he was in transit to one of the hospital ships. At first I thought he was an African. He was unconscious, on a drip and had a big letter M on his stretcher, meaning he had been given morphine; it's usually put on a casualty's forehead, but he was too badly burned to write on. His skin was completely black, and his face was so swollen he couldn't have opened his eyes even if he were awake. The skin on his face was virtually gone. All he had on was the remains of a pair of boxer shorts and one boot. Bits of his uniform had been melted into his blackened skin by the searing heat of an explosion. I couldn't help look at these bits of material and think that it all had to come out, there isn't a nice way to do it. If being burned isn't bad enough, having material taken from your scorched flesh by tweezers must be the final punishment.

Both of his hands, which he held in a claw pose, had been put into clear plastic bags to prevent infection. It seemed that even in his drug-induced unconscious state he was still able to hold his hands up off of the stretcher to avoid them touching anything and causing more pain.

For a long time afterwards, walking around *Fearless* and *Intrepid*, there were men who had arguably been a bit luckier than their comrades. By that I mean they were alive, but they would not have considered themselves lucky. They would sit around dining tables and mess rooms trying to go about their daily life with plastic bags over their hands. These tormented souls could be seen shuffling about in the middle of the night, with ballooned faces, shaking their hands in some vain effort to try and cool the agony. They never seemed to rest, forever looking for a position or place where there was no pain. Burnt flesh doesn't stop burning just so you can get some sleep. These guys were just in transit; most had lost their ship, which was their home, and undoubtedly they had lost friends. Eventually the ones you saw or spoke to would disappear off to hospital ships or on their way home, but they were usually replaced by another group.

We knew the *Galahad* and *Tristram* were still afloat. The lads coming from there had told us they were both burning and exploding as they had left. At the back of our minds was the question, did they have UXBs on board?

We later found out that *Tristram* was salvageable, and in fact she was eventually shipped all the way back to England in a dry-dock ship to be refitted and re-commissioned. However, like the rest of our once proud Navy, she is now rotting in Portsmouth dockyard waiting to be scrapped, but not replaced.

The *Sir Galahad* was a more difficult proposition. Almost a fifth of the entire British forces casualties of the war were lost on that one day, on board *Sir Galahad*. Forty-eight soldiers and sailors died when she was engulfed in flames after being hit by two or maybe three bombs. Now the dilemma was this. She was still afloat in Fitzroy. Do you risk more men to go in and try and retrieve the bodies? Do you risk more men to go in and place charges in her? Even to keep fire fighting was a very hazardous operation due to possible unexploded bombs and a large amount of ammunition and fuel. The other problem was that she was morale-sapping, because she was sitting in full view of the troops passing through Fitzroy and Bluff Cove. All of the men watching every day knew that a large number of bodies, some close friends and comrades, were still on board.

A few days later we had heard rumours that someone had put charges on her, but seeing as it would have been us, or Fleet Team 3, that would have had the task of doing it, we were at a loss as to who could have done it. No one seemed to know. I spoke to the lads of FCDT3 about this. I know that Lieutenant Bernie Bruen (their boss) and one of the lads had been the only ones back on board after the initial abandonment. They had a look around and assessed her state but no charges were placed. Apparently, when they boarded her, she was still burning from stem to stern, and periodically letting off explosions as the ammunition cooked off. Some of the bodies of men who had so nearly escaped could be seen caught in doorways and stairwells.

As part of my research for this book, I found out that it was on 25 June 1982 that the crew of HM Submarine *Onyx* used torpedoes to sink what was left of the 6,000-ton *Sir Galahad*. She took with her thirty-two Welsh Guardsman, eleven other soldiers, and five merchant seamen, making her a substantial war grave.

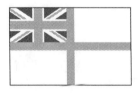

TG in CDBA. ▶

▼ To jump or not to jump?

▶

IED training with wheelbarrow
robot, wearing blast suit.

Deep work-up. L to R, standing:
Smudge, Tony, Dave, Tim, Shiner.
Kneeling: Ginge, Ian.
▼

◀ Navy 'bomb wagon' on the road.

▶

O$_2$ re-breathers. No bubbles. The driver has the swim board, his buddy would have the limpets.

Stay flexible. Dragging down a mine-lifting bag. CDBA rigged for deep diving.

▼

TG in Funafuti, air diving just for fun.

Our constant companions across the atoll.

Nick Hancock and TG, going local.

Our paradise island hostesses.

Arrival at San Carlos Water, 21 May 1982.
The first attack followed.

Sea Kings, the
workhorses of
the fleet.

◀ 42 Commando going
ashore on day one,
cammed up.

◀ Sheltering from an air raid in a landing craft, 24 May. Our friendly fire moment.

▶ Harrier 'running on fresh air' drops onto *Intrepid*'s deck.

◀ Leaving Bluff Cove 5 June. Divers and SBS.

▶ Morning at Bluff Cove. The Brits are coming!

▲ HMS *Plymouth* comes into Bomb Alley, on fire after being hit by two 1,000lb bombs and strafed by rockets. Who will get that job, I wonder?

▲
TG, post dive on HMS *Argonaut.*

▶
The 'lucky' *Plymouth*'s funnel, 8 June.

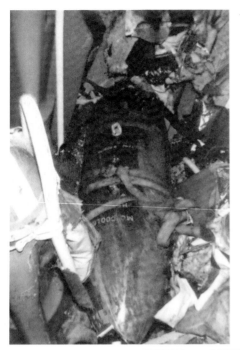

◄ 1,000lb British Mk 17 free-fall bomb, where it came to rest in *Argonaut*'s magazine. Smashed Sea Cat missiles all around.

The bomb, finally on the move, complete with PLEASE HANDLE WITH CARE, written on it by its British manufacturer.

▼

▶
After seven days and nights Stan and Dave ease the bomb through a hole cut in *Argonaut*'s hull, on its way to Davy Jones's Locker.

24 May: A final farewell to HMS *Antelope*.

▼

Dave, Ben and TG *en route* to *Argonaut*.

Main Street Port Stanley, the day after the surrender, still on fire.

Our new office in Port Stanley. George, Dave, TG, Billy.

TG with hundreds of prisoners on the town jetty.

After the Wireless Ridge booby-trap job. Happy to be out of 'the house'.

Stanley Police house, attacked by a Navy Lynx helicopter after intelligence reported it as the venue of a high-level Argentinian meeting.

TG with a small barracuda, Nigeria.

The *Seaforth Clansman*, 'The Diver's Navy'.

TG and 'John Boy' (Dave) Walton in sat waiting to dive, aboard DSV *Aquamarine*.

Where's Morris and TG, waiting for the tide. DSV *Sea Oyster*, minibell deep air diving.

◄ The 'flying bell' from the *Tharos*. The top atmospheric bell's large port hole is clearly visible.

TG entering the *Stephaniturm's* bell at over 600 feet.
▼

▲
Underwater welding.
(Photo: Longstreath.com)

◄ The standby diver, ready for anything, weather permitting!

A perfect sunset in the North Sea.

◀ More normal North Sea weather.

TG leaving the bell.

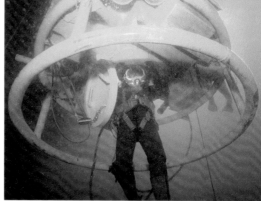

The *Tharos* bell – the pilot's view from inside. Grahame Murr on the outside.

Naval gunfire support

<u>Thursday 10 June 1982</u> (DAY TWENTY-ONE)

Attacked, but were all beaten off by Harriers.
Nice day.

<u>11 June 1982</u> (DAY TWENTY-TWO)

FRIDAY (I think)

Today was the day for the big attack on Stanley.
Naval gunfire, Harriers etc.

For some reason it was put off 24 hrs. They
won't give us any casualty numbers for some
reason. They were much more than expected.

<u>Saturday 12 June 1982</u> (DAY TWENTY-THREE)
<u>Sunday 13 June 1982</u> (DAY TWENTY-FOUR)

Big push forward ashore today. Two Para have
taken the two sisters and 45 commando have taken
Mount Longdon. In fact, all objectives have
been taken. We went to sea to Berkeley sound at
nightfall. It was to drop off one of the landing
craft the Intrepid carries and pick up four
others.

At about 1 a.m. there was an air raid warning.
Three waves of four. They were going overhead to
attack the troops ashore. They passed directly
overhead very low without seeing us.

We were 43 miles from Port Stanley. We could
see the flashes from the bombs, lighting up the
sky. One flash was in the sky, and shortly after
we could see a ball of flames come all the way
down until it went out in the sea. The warships
behind us were giving Naval gunfire support

around Stanley, when the attack came, and the
Cardiff got the one we saw with a Sea Dart.

We thought they were going to attack us on the
way back as they had to go over us anyway. We
heard the countdown, 10 miles ... 5 miles ...
1 mile! Again, they went over the top. We stayed
in a snow cloud and they didn't see us. Got to
bed about 04:00.

About 04:30 a.m. there was an Exocet warning.
So we were up again for a while. SLEEP? HA!

It is a waste of time trying to go to bed and have a proper sleep
when you're at sea on these night-time manoeuvres. Due to the
nature of what we were into, everyone was jittery. I don't mean
just us, I mean radar operators, sonar operators, radio operators,
everyone whose job it was to let the fleet know ASAP if something was amiss. Now you can't tell them not to do this, but it
does result in an awful lot of false alarms. If a radar operator
catches one blip on his screen, and then nothing, does he stay
quiet? No, he does not. It could be a Super Etendard just cruising
above the waves and poking its head up for a matter of seconds,
switching on his radar just for one sweep, trying to catch a radar
image of us, then, seeing where we are, instantly dropping back
down close to the sea hoping not to have been seen. Consequently, everything was reported all the time.

So to get an air raid warning at one o'clock in the morning
doesn't mean that it is an air raid, but it does mean you can't rest.
You can usually tell pretty quickly, by the amount of activity,
if it is a real raid or not. This was the cue for Dave Wilkinson,
Dave Southwell and me to take up our usual position, trying to
remain invisible up on *Intrepid*'s bridge, as this is where you're
going to find out what is really going on. I say in my diary entry
for 12 June that it was waves of planes. I have no idea how many
there were and I don't suppose there are any figures; after all, it
was one o'clock in the morning and dark. But I do remember the
countdown as they came directly over *Intrepid.*

The air raid warning would start with the traditional, horrible claxon (or possibly chaff), which would wake the dead. Even this late on in the war it made your heart skip a beat. Then the tannoy would pipe up, 'HANDS TO ACTION STATIONS, HANDS TO ACTION STATIONS, HANDS TO ACTION STATIONS, AIR RAID WARNING RED, IMMINENT, CLOSE ALL RED OPENINGS, CLOSE ALL WATERTIGHT DOORS, SPECIAL SEA DUTYMEN CLOSE UP!' I can't remember how the rest of the pipe would go, but it left you in no doubt that something serious was going on. It didn't matter if you were on duty or exhausted, or asleep, you were up and ready before the tannoy announcement had finished. By now everyone knew what to do and where to go, and I couldn't help thinking that really you could have just piped 'ACTION STATIONS ... NOW!'

Then came the countdown of how many miles away the fighters, or in our case fighter-bombers, were: 50 miles and closing from the west ... (then, only a few seconds later) 25 miles ... 15 miles ... 10 miles ... 5 miles ... 1 mile ... aircraft overhead ... Your head goes down, your heart rate climbs and you wait, hold your breath, maybe say a few words to yourself, pray if you so wish, this could be your last few seconds on earth ... 1 mile to the east ... moving away 5 miles ... Phew! You can exhale again.

You don't know if they're going to attack you, and if they are, with what. Everyone just loses themselves in their own thoughts, the only words spoken are those that need to be said. Your first thought is a somewhat selfish one, 'I hope they're not after us.' Then you realise they are going overhead and attacking troops ashore, and you think, poor sods!

The relief, however, was somewhat short-lived, as having dropped their ordnance on their targets ashore, and due to the constraints on them fuel-wise, they turned straight around and came back over our heads. I seem to remember the skipper of the *Intrepid* doing his damnedest to get the ship inside a snow cloud to help cloak us from the attacking aircraft's radar. Having managed it, we then had to endure the countdown and count up, until they were all away on their journey back to the Argentinian mainland.

After and during this bit of excitement, there was still a lot of other action going on, far too much to risk going to bed anyway, and this time it was close astern of us and an incredible spectacle. It was something I will never see again, and I doubt many more people will ever see it. For some reason we found ourselves leading a line of five ships. I say 'for some reason' because we lacked the one thing required to join in tonight's engagement, and that was a 'bang box', or a 4.5-inch Naval Gun.

There was us (*Intrepid*) the frigates HMS *Arrow*, HMS *Avenger* and HMS *Yarmouth*, also the destroyer HMS *Glamorgan*. We sailed up and down a 'gun line' about 20 miles out from Berkeley Sound. This was a decidedly dodgy place to be, as the Argentinians had already been using their battery of 155 mm howitzers (field guns). Nevertheless, with the ships being moving targets at night, and without proper fire control systems, they found it impossible to hit us, so far.

However, the Argentinians had been very ingenious. Their light frigate, the ARA *Guerrico*, had been badly shot up by the Marines at South Georgia. She had managed to make her way back to Argentina, but was in such a state she never left port again for the duration of the war. Despite this, the Argentinians stripped her Exocets from her and flew them to the islands. Using a great deal of improvisation, they put them on board lorry trailers, rigged up a launch system, and pointed them out to sea, not far from Berkeley Sound.

A gun line is a line drawn upon a chart, behind which a ship will stay to seaward. The job for all these ships was to provide NGS.

Naval Gunfire Support is a term you may never hear again. I say this because we have smaller ships, fewer of them, and smaller guns. NGS reached its zenith in the Second World War. Some of the bigger older ships were kept 'alive', if you like, expressly for this purpose. Some of the guns in those days were huge. Many of the old battleships carried numerous sixteen-inch guns that could throw a shell the weight of a Mini some 30 miles. Most of the cruisers had multiple six- and eight-inch guns. They were a little inaccurate, so the bombardments would sometimes go on for days or even weeks. But, if only to keep the enemies' heads down or to prepare for a landing, it was highly successful and put the fear of God into anyone who witnessed it.

Now if I say our guns are 'only' 4.5 inch it may not sound a lot until you see one of the shells, or if you see what one does, for instance, to a building. To be under one such explosion, if it didn't kill you, would make a lasting impression upon you.

The silence of a dark night was shattered when the first gun exploded into action. All the ships behind us had their targets set in the 4.5-inch guns, and when they start it's a shock if you're on this side of it. It makes you thank your lucky stars you are on the right side.

It started with the ship directly behind us. She fired one or two shells and you think, 'OK, they've got a small target, they'll take that out, and then it will be all over.' It went silent for a couple of minutes. I was thinking that was it. Then, listening in to the conversations on the bridge of *Intrepid*, we could tell something far larger was about to take place. On getting the OK that those shells fired were landing in the right place (and that must be coming from some poor soul on the shore spotting the fall of the shells), the ship behind us opened up again, but this time she didn't stop. Then all the ships behind her opened up, and they didn't stop either.

It is an awesome sight to see these guns firing. To see them firing at night with the flames coming out of the barrels against the black backdrop of the night, and the shock waves, is truly incredible. The flames would light up the frigate's superstructure, showing the gun at its angle into the sky. It was a bit surreal, in the vein of some strange, jittery colour movie being shown, with full sound effects, and what sound effects! We were a fair way out from the shore, so couldn't see where the shells were landing, but we could see whitish flashes coming from the land. At the end of our gun line run, I guess we must have fired around 150, maybe 200 shells. The shore where the shells were landing was now glowing above the dark horizon of the land. The *Intrepid* turned to starboard, and I thought it was all over. The ships behind followed in line astern. We made our way back to our gun line going in the opposite direction. Then the same again: the first ship, then the second, and the third, and the fourth all opened up with their 4.5-inch guns. More shells rained down on their targets. There might be the odd quiet spell, when I can only guess that the spotter ashore was telling the ships to elevate or adjust the range, then they would start again.

Now I can't say I got bored with this spectacle. I was captivated, but it certainly went on for hours. I spoke to one of the radio operators on the bridge, who had the task, either voluntarily or under orders, I was unsure, to count the shells fired. He was up to 750 rounds fired when I gave up and went to seek the relative quiet of the galley for some tea and Chinese wedding cake (rice pudding).

I could not imagine the feeling of being on the other end. I almost felt sorry for them. The glow I could see coming from the land was an Argentinian fuel dump that had been hit right next to the Falklands' very own racecourse.

After this bombardment was finished on the morning of the 12th, the Naval gunfire squadron was disbanded, and all ships went about their normal business. But the silence after the Navy guns did not last for long. Chaff was again launched from *Intrepid*, causing the usual panic. An Exocet warning immediately followed this. Never a dull moment on this night. Again, we were told one had been fired. All you can do is wait. Wait and see. We were the biggest ship there. If it was running, would it pick the biggest target, would it go for the chaff, did the firers ashore pick the biggest target?

HMS *Glamorgan*, after her brilliant night's work providing the NGS, was sent away to sea and safety. She went one way, we went the other. Chance again? Somehow she passed just too close to the shore, or they moved the Exocets on their trailers. Either way, one was fired and it picked out *Glamorgan*. Being an older ship, her radars failed to pick up the missile as it hurtled towards her just above the waves and against the background clutter of the shore.

The first person to see it was the officer of the watch, whose eagle eyes on the bridge must have only seen the glow of the rocket engines. He immediately ordered a sharp turn to starboard to present the smallest target to the missile's radar guidance system. That and another master stroke of luck, if you can call it that, undoubtedly saved the *Glamorgan* from a very different ending. The ship had not quite finished her violent turn to starboard when the missile struck. Instead of hitting bang amidships like the *Sheffield*, taking out the control centre and causing many casualties, this manoeuvre had the missile skid along the back deck before going through the helicopter hangar and into the galley.

The other stroke of luck she had? Well, this missile also failed to explode. Despite this, it still killed thirteen and injured twenty-two. Luck may not be the correct word, but they managed to fight the fires and the ship survived, eventually sailing 8,000 miles, under her own steam, all the way back to Portsmouth. She eventually arrived in port 10 July, blackened and scarred, looking truly like she had just been through a war, and her battered helicopter hangar shrouded from prying eyes by a tarpaulin.

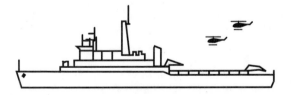

Would all those wishing to surrender, please form an orderly queue?

<u>Monday 14 June 1982</u> (DAY TWENTY-FIVE)

The push forward by troops went on all night with some resistance. This morning, the Argies had retreated again, further back. At 16:05 pipe came over that they had virtually surrendered. At 16:15 a White Flag was seen flying in Stanley. At bloody last!

At 11:30 tonight the peace treaty should be signed. This is only for the land forces, not the sea or air force.

At 11:30 a pipe from the commander said that we, the Intrepid will go to the West Falklands to secure that agreement and rescue the civvies etc.

West Falkland is still in Argentinian Hands, so it might be fun sailing into Port Howard. They may not wish or may not know, they are supposed to surrender!

It snowed heavily today. It's cold enough diving, but at least we can get into the warm afterwards. The lads on the hills and mountains mustn't half be cold at night.

Not at sea tonight, in bomb alley.

Pick up hundreds of prisoners. Been to Stanley. Seen the damage etc etc seen it, done it, read the book, seen the film, BLAH BLAH BLAH!

<u>23 June 1982</u>

Today is the 23rd of June, DAY?

```
Just been told we're going home on the Fearless
on Friday next. Don't know if it's poss, but
have to get mail away today.

It may all fall over, usually does.

Must go or I'll miss the next helo.

All my love, Tony

might even see summer?

Love to everyone

X X X X X
```

This was the last day's writing my diary for me, but it was far from the end for the team.

At 23:30 that surrender night, on 14 June, everything changed. A huge weight had been lifted off our shoulders. No more UXBs, no more bloody air raids, no more working 20-plus hours a day. There would be no more chaff rockets in the middle of the night. Well actually we didn't know that yet, as it was unclear if the AAF had surrendered along with the land forces. So air raids were just 'on hold' for now. We thought we could, maybe, get ashore, have a look around and take it easy for a while. That was of course until we could hitch a lift home. The thing that made it all a bit uncomfortable for us was that we were still homeless and essentially relying on other people's hospitality.

The surrender day itself was a wonderful feeling. For the first time in ages, I actually allowed myself to think about going home, to see family and loved ones. There was, however, a great deal of work to do.

We, the *Intrepid*, went over to Port Howard and picked up about 700 POWs. This may sound like a lot but in the big picture it was nothing. There were around 11,000 Argentinian prisoners to be taken care of, and eventually taken home. I remember going in there; it was freezing and blowing a proper South Atlantic gale, with plenty of snow thrown in for good measure.

The prisoners looked like conscripts. They looked like they didn't want to be there – on the islands, I mean, not on *Intrepid*'s vehicle deck. Down there in the warm and constantly eating or asking for food, they seemed perfectly happy to me. Happy to the extent that when you said to them 'home' or '*casa*' and put your thumbs up, they would smile elatedly, all nodding. As far as I saw, there were no triumphant feelings, nor hard feelings towards them, and certainly no ill treatment. When you saw them up close, you could see they were no match for our volunteer troops. The saying 'One volunteer is better than ten pressed men' seemed to fit the bill exactly here. They smelt terrible, like they had been living on top of a smoking peat fire for weeks, which I guess they had.

Diego Maradona's controversial 'Hand of God' goal in the 1986 World Cup probably turned more Brits against Argentina than the war. Even then it was a simple reaction to the cheating, rather than because of his nationality. Ossie Ardiles, an Argentinian player plying his trade in England, helped Spurs beat Leicester City 2–0 only a day after the invasion to no ill effect – though he did subsequently leave the UK for around a year, of his own volition.

We'll soon be on our way home as well, we thought. Or so we presumed. These thoughts were soon put to rest, for us at least, when the next assignment came in.

The day after the surrender we were tasked again with some fun jobs: 'Give us the all-clear for Port Stanley harbour, i.e. no mines or obstructions.' Hopefully there would be no mines. 'Oh, and have a look at some houses that may be booby-trapped!'

Put the homeward-bound thoughts to one side for the moment, I thought. This could still get ugly, and there was still a good chance of one of us getting seriously hurt.

Now we couldn't do all this from the *Intrepid*. She was too big to be coming into Port Stanley, and with the air war not officially over she would be a juicy target for any pilot. She had to stay in San Carlos under the safety of the Rapier missile systems. So, guess what? We were on the move again. This time to the RFA *Sir Bedivere*, I think it was. She would be going alongside the Falkland Islands Company jetty. Having the word 'diver' in her name would surely bring us luck? I say I think we stayed on the *Sir Bedivere* because my diary was winging its way home and I have no record of where we made camp. I have asked about seven members of the team the same question, and had seven different answers. I've had the tug, RMS *Typhoon*, the mining shed at Navy Point, the suspect booby house at Wireless Ridge and a few more suggestions to boot. I think we were all exhausted and a bit shell-shocked, and it didn't matter where we stayed. We didn't worry about comfort or mattresses or cold, we just passed out where we could, wherever it was quiet and safe.

This could be entertaining. A good booby trap is almost impossible to spot, and arguably more dangerous than the bombs we had been disposing of. The bombs could go off while you were working on them (*Antelope*), but they weren't, as far as we could tell anyway, set up to go off if you tampered with the fuses.

During World War II the Germans used to regularly slip booby-trapped bombs in amongst a load of normal ones. The idea was not only to catch out, and if possible kill, the bomb disposal expert (fine if it did). It also tied up a huge amount of resources and a large area: if it was in the docks, say, it would be a no-go zone for the duration of the disposal operation.

The German general bombardment bombs in WWII were the most commonly used HE bombs, and were generally fitted with an electric fuse. The armer of the bomb had a choice of how it would explode: he could choose instant (i.e. normal, or direct action, as it was known) or short delay, from about ten seconds to around 168 hours, or sometimes even longer. Or he could choose to arm it with a booby-trap fuse under a fuse, one that would only detonate when you attempted to move or remove the first fuse. The outward appearance of all three of these different fuses was exactly the same.

Whilst at DEODS they taught us how to dispose of bombs

and mines. There were also quite a few weeks on IEDs. An IED is just military parlance for letter or parcel bomb. 'Improvised' as in home-made, using things that weren't designed for the purpose. A hand grenade can make a perfect booby trap, but the bang bit, the grenade, isn't improvised, it was made to explode and do as much damage to the human form as possible. A totally improvised device might have an alarm clock or a trip wire to set it off, and home-made or possibly stolen explosives.

Coming into Port Stanley the day after the surrender was a new experience. None of us had been there before. As we came into harbour there were still fires burning but apart from that there didn't appear to be much outwardly visible damage. As we came alongside the jetty, however, we got a closer view and could see the squalor left behind, after a hurried surrender. There were tin hats, clothes and weapons everywhere. All along the jetty there was excrement.

It was a sorry, stinking mess up close. There were even two dead Argentinian solders still lying in the road along the sea front. Along by the pier there was an enormous warehouse with its door open. Inside there was food piled up to the ceiling, so why the Argie POWs seemed so hungry was amazing. There must have been hundreds of huge round cheeses, cases and cases of wine, and luxury meats. A strange mix of food, when all that was really needed was thousands of easily made-up and nutritious ration packs. From this room alone, one could see how this military junta was thinking. These were the victuals for the officer contingent and not the conscripts, who from what I could see had to fend largely for themselves. The ones who had been near the town had eaten, but the ones that came in from the far-flung reaches of the islands were in a state. Even the ones around the town who were lookouts had to make their shelter from what they were able to scrounge and steal.

Ashore on the day after the surrender, I made my way to the post office in Port Stanley. On the way I passed hundreds and hundreds of prisoners. They were all sat along the jetty waiting to be moved onto ships or to camps. They stank of bonfire smoke. They were being guarded by immaculate Paras and Marines who looked like they had just come from their normal barracks. It was a stark reminder of the difference in quality between our forces and theirs.

I joined the unlikeliest looking queue in the post office you would ever see. Everyone, including us, was in various stages of battle dress. Paras, SAS, Marines, and us – all, I'm sure, having looked better in our lives. Billy Smart, Nobby Noble, Nigel, Dave Barrett and I were wearing dry suits, with camouflage jackets to keep the wind off. We all tried to book phone calls from the phone booths, but the waiting list was too long. I stood in the queue as only the British know how, and posted the whole diary, all 51 pages, home to my mum and dad. They of course had virtually no idea what I'd been doing all the time down there. Then one day towards the end of June they receive this fat envelope with fifty pages detailing my whole war experience in full graphic detail. The one you've just read. It was quite a shock for my mother, who had spent the whole time listening to my father telling her I'd be fine and probably not doing a lot.

Booby traps

On 16 June we made our way to a jetty directly opposite Port Stanley. We then walked very carefully, not on the path in case of mines, towards a house just south of Wireless Ridge, which we had to investigate for booby traps.

Only two nights previously, 2 Para had been involved in a fierce battle for control of Wireless Ridge, losing three men in the process. Helped by 3 Troop of the Blues and Royals, who brought two Scimitars and two Scorpion light tanks with them, they brought down a devastating rain of fire on the enemy. Using the tanks, artillery, mortars, Naval gunfire, GPMGs, and at one stage two Scout helicopters, the Paras and Argentinians fought all night, with the Paras pushing their enemy back to win all their objectives by 14 June. Out of the 500 Argentines estimated to be occupying Wireless Ridge, about 100 were killed. The rest were either taken prisoner or fled.

Why that particular house was suspected of being booby-trapped, above all others, I never found out. But it was a very uncomfortable few hours just getting into the house, never mind about clearing it and its outbuildings. Uncomfortable in the sense that you do not know where to step or move, what to touch, or whether to sit or stand. It's squeaky bum time, mentally exhausting, and generally not a nice experience.

We made an extensive search round the edge of the front door with torches, looking for trip wires or anything untoward, then eventually went in through an outward-opening window, after opening it with that age-old booby-trap safety detector, string! From a safe distance that is. If ever you find yourself anywhere dodgy in the world, or confronted with any package you are not sure about, always remember string. Tie it to the package, briefcase, gizzit or whatever it is you're not happy with, retire to a safe distance and give it a pull. If it goes off and blows your house up, well you're insured. If you move it and it goes off and you lose your hands, sight or wedding tackle, don't say I didn't tell you about string.

When we eventually effected our safe entry into the main building, it was evident that this was a high-ranking mess. Definitely officers' quarters. They had left in an almighty hurry. There were half-eaten meals on the table, personal belongings everywhere. Mind you, if you have the combined fire power I described and it all starts with a 'noisy phase' assault (as opposed to silent and sneaky), including 6,000 rounds from the 105 mm field pieces, and Naval gunfire, you could maybe see why they hadn't had time to pack.

There were pretties or gizzits (as in 'give-us-it') lying about all over the place. By that, I mean things an occupying force may find attractive. For instance, on a chair was a shiny, chromed bayonet with the 'Argentina Armada' crest stamped on it. You think it may look a nice thing to have, to show the grandkids in years to come. That is exactly the sort of thing to trap your enemy with: attach one end with fishing line to a grenade, or set up a crude pressure switch underneath it and ...

A civilian woman in Port Stanley found her five-year-old daughter's doll booby-trapped with a wire to a hand grenade in her own house after a group of officers had been driven out. That was a deliberate attempt to target a young girl who hadn't seen her toys for a while. Sick.

For these reasons, reasons of temptation, among others, the Israelis don't even bother to clear house to house. If it is suspected of being trapped, they will just bulldoze it. But this was not really an option in the Falklands.

We cleared a few houses in Port Stanley as well. Many were full of excrement mines, as we dubbed them. Well, it was a shorter word, but we all knew what it meant. 'Watch out, there's a live one over here on the window sill!' Why they felt the need to do this all over the place, indoors, in people's houses they really had no beef with, I could never quite understand. Maybe they started when they knew they were beaten, as a sort of dirty protest. I know I heaved a few times.

Islands of the condemned

Whilst on one of these clearing jobs, I found something I haven't seen anywhere else, before or since. Something I thought only the Nazis were into in a big way.

Something called PSYOPS, Psychological Operations. It can of course also be tagged as Psychological Warfare, PSYWAR, but that doesn't sound so Politically Correct, does it? Whichever tag you want to give it, PSYOPS or PSYWAR, it is a technique used by military and police forces to try to influence someone's behaviour or emotions. The British have dabbled in the more friendly PSYOPS, especially in WWII. There were famous campaigns such as 'Loose lips sink ships,' and 'The walls have ears.'

OK, the Argentinian junta were a bit desperate. They had already proved they would use all sorts of unsavoury measures, such as kidnap, murder and torture, on their own people. So possibly they might try a radio campaign – but we wouldn't be listening anyway, would we? What about us, then? Surely we wouldn't get into all that, would we?

Certainly not, according to the Ministry of Defence (MoD) Psychological Operations group website anyway. It says, and I quote:

The Falklands Campaign (Op CORPORATE) 1982

A limited British PSYOPS campaign was developed during the brief Argentine occupation and subsequent liberation of the Falkland Islands. A radio station was set up on the Ascension Island, known as '*Radio Atlantico del Sur*' and broadcast to Argentine troops and included music, news and sport. Printed literature including Safe Conduct Passes, were developed but never deployed due to the UK's inability to air-drop leaflets at this time.

Well, I'm afraid that's not quite the truth. In fact I know it to be a lie. You see, I have one of those air-dropped leaflets. I found it whilst searching a house that had been closed down, for the safety of our troops, because of suspected booby traps. It had, though, been occupied by Argentine officers. I took it to a friend of a friend who is a Spanish teacher and this is how it reads. On the front, in red, it says:

¡¡ ISLAS DE CONDENADOS!!

ISLANDS OF THE CONDEMNED!!

Under that bold capital heading are grey, basic recognition pictures of various British war machinery, the sort of thing pilots would have to ID British military hardware – Harrier, destroyer, aircraft carrier, Sea King helicopters, etc. Over those, again in red, is a small rough drawing of the Falklands (Malvinas) surrounded by wooden fence posts, all joined by barbed wire. Suggesting of course that they (the Argentine solders) were trapped. This is what caught my eye, this is what made me pick it up. We wouldn't have ID pictures of our own fleet, and this was written in Spanish. Turn the leaflet over, and on the back the red text reads:

SOLDADOS DE LAS FUERZAS ARGENTINAS ...

Translated from the Spanish it reads:

SOLDIERS OF THE ARGENTINE FORCES:

You are completely alone. There is no hope of relief or help from your motherland. You are condemned to the sad fate of defending a remote island. Soon there will fall upon you all the rigours of a cruel and merciless winter and the Argentine Navy is in no condition to supply you with the reinforcements or provisions that you so desperately need. Your families live with the terrible fear of never seeing you again. You well know that all of this is the honest truth.

¿ CUALES SON LAS RAZONES POR LAS CUALES SE ENCUENTRAN VDS. EN ESTA SITUATION TAN CALAMITOSA?

WHAT ARE THE REASONS THAT YOU FIND YOURSELVES IN SUCH A CALAMITOUS SITUATION?

Those responsible are the egotists who have named themselves the leaders of Argentina without taking into consideration the wishes of the Argentine people, and who have sent you on a ridiculous adventure, knowing there is no hope of any kind for an end to it. Now, these same leaders look for a way to disguise their stupid incompetence.

¡¡ SOLDADOS!! HAN CUMPLIDO VDS. CON TODO QUE LA PATRIA LES PUEDE EXIGIR.

SOLDIERS!! YOU HAVE DONE ALL YOUR COUNTRY CAN ASK OF YOU.

UNICAMENTE SON LOS GENERALES QUE EXIGEN MAS.

ONLY THE GENERALS STILL ASK FOR MORE.

IT IS NOT FAIR THAT YOU SHOULD FORFEIT YOUR LIVES TO FULFIL THE AMBITIONS OF THOSE RESPONSIBLE FOR THIS CRAZY ADVENTURE THAT THE WHOLE WORLD SEES AS WRONG.

Not really very 'British', is it? So who dropped the one I've got? A Harrier, a chopper? And why bother putting on the website that they didn't deliver any? A conspiracy, a slight smudging of the facts? How much more PSYWAR went on that we don't know anything about?

¡¡ISLAS DE CONDENADOS!!

SOLDADOS DE LAS FUERZAS ARGENTINAS:

Están Vds. completamente a solas. Desde su patria no hay esperanza de relevo o ayuda. Están Vds. condenados a la triste tarea de defender una isla remota. Prontamente caerá sobre Vds. todos los rigores de un invierno cruel y despiadado y la armada argentina no está en condiciones de suministrarles los víveres o refuerzos que Vds. tanto necesitan. Sus familias viven con el tremendo terror que nunca los volverán a ver. Todo esto, como Vds. bien saben, es la purísima verdad.

¿CUALES SON LAS RAZONES POR LAS CUALES SE ENCUENTRAN VDS. EN ESTA SITUATION TAN CALAMITOSA?

Los responsables son los egoistas que se han nombrados a sí mismo como dirigentes de la Argentina sin tomar en consideración la voluntad del pueblo argentino, y quisieron embarcaron a Vds. en una absurda aventura, sabiendo que no existía esperanza de éxito alguno. Ahora, detrás del reconocido coraje del soldado argentino, los mismos dirigentes buscan esconder su torpe incompetencia.

¡¡ SOLDADOS!! HAN CUMPLIDO VDS. CON TODO QUE LA PATRIA LES PUEDE EXIGIR.

UNICAMENTE SON LOS GENERALES QUE EXIGEN MAS.

NO ES JUSTO QUE CON SUS VIDAS PAGUEN VDS. LAS TORTUOSAS AMBICIONES DE LOS RESPONSABLES DE ESTA LOCA AVENTURA MAL VISTA POR EL MUNDO ENTERO.

Fearless on our way home

We survived the booby-trap days. It wasn't nice, but we were very careful, and methodical, so came out in one piece. They are butterfly, sick-in-the-stomach memories, so I won't dwell on them any longer for my own peace of mind.

I had no idea when we would be going home, but I thought it would be weeks away, if not months. There was work everywhere we looked. Mines on land and at sea. There were Argentinian (sorry, British) bombs all over the place. The one we dumped over the side of the *Argonaut* was sitting smack bang in the middle of San Carlos Water. The two that passed through the *Plymouth* were lying on the bottom somewhere just outside Bomb Alley, along with the ones that hit and missed all the other ships. One thing that made all these jobs fairly urgent was that they all had fuses in them and were, in a sense, ready to go bang. How long was all that going to take? There were also wrecks to be dived on to remove sensitive secret equipment. We were in for the long haul.

Then, out of the blue, 'Move ship again, lads.' Before we could moan about our sixth move too much, they told us we were going home on the *Fearless*, tomorrow. Yeha! That'll do nicely, thank you very much.

When we moved on board and had a bed, of sorts, you could actually get undressed, take a shower, and go to bed like normal people do, with no boots on, without fear of a rude awakening by a chaff rocket, quickly followed by an Exocet warning, or an air raid warning red. I think that when we eventually sailed from the Falklands, we were all mentally and physically exhausted. I have no idea what I did for the first few days on board the *Fearless*. We were crammed into one of those horrible troop-carrying messes again, but at least it was somewhere we could relax and make our own for the long journey home.

I'm not going to drone on about this, but there were a lot

of sleepless nights. Rest did not come easily. Not just for me, for many of the lads. We should have slept like the dead, but we were all very nervous, on edge, and highly strung still. One or two were having nightmares every night. One in particular would wake up surrounded by boots and training shoes and pillows, which had been thrown at him all through the night in a futile attempt to shut him up. 'Was I dreaming last night then?' he would say, when he woke up thinking he was in Clarks shoe department. Another one of the lads was still sleeping down on the vehicle deck, on a camp bed. Any loud bang would make us jump – hardly surprising really.

I have a few faint memories of wandering the ship. I seem to remember there was a lot of stolen property on board. Well, it wasn't stolen: we were the conquerors, the winners, and the unwritten rules of war say you can take what a defeated army used to own. On board, we had an Argentinian helicopter, tanks, armoured personnel carriers and even some of their howitzers. Mind you, I was wearing Argentinian boots that were American-made and far better than the ones I was issued with. Don't ask!

Eight days into the long journey home, with little or no warning, a Chinook landed on the back deck. I didn't even know the flight deck of the *Fearless* was big enough to take a Chinook. Someone back in Pompey was thinking of us after all. The Chinook was looking for the Fleet Clearance Diving Team, and it was going to take us to Ascension Island, some 200 miles further north, where rumour had it there would be a VC10 waiting to take us all the way home! Things were looking up indeed. I seem to remember we had fifteen minutes to pack one rucksack each. I did mine in five. Some of the lads were still bleary-eyed, as we climbed into the chopper, and it took off.

Two and a bit hours later, we landed in Ascension, where we were met by some sort of Navy regulator. The Navy don't have MPs as such, just wannabe policemen that we used to call 'Reggies'. This one was no different to any other I had met, in that he was a jumped-up little know-it-all, and was wholly full of his own self-importance. He completely misjudged the situation and how best to handle it. He proceeded to give us a long speech, along the lines of, 'If any of you bubble heads think you're getting on the flight drunk, I have news for you. In fact, I think it best if you don't drink at all. You are not the only ones on this VC10 flight. In fact you're lucky to be on it at all. There are some high-ranking RAF, Army and Navy officers, and if I find out you have been drinking, there will be no ifs, no buts, you will not get on that flight. Do I make myself clear, gentlemen?' He was met with a steely silence and about eighteen fixed stares. 'Now, you have about five hours before your flight. You can get tea, and something to eat down at Lunar Camp, there are some spare tents down there. I suggest you get your heads down. I shall see you again, SOBER, at check-in time. Goodbye gentlemen.'

Did he really think that we gave a shit what he might do to us if we got a little exuberant after a drink or two? Did he really think he could stop us from getting on that flight? After what we had just been through, there was nothing he could say or do to affect the way we were feeling. We'd survived, now let's celebrate the fact!

It was the first day of July 1982, and it was the first time I could see an end to all this. We were actually going home, this was the last leg. So taking on board what our little Hitler had just finished telling us, we went looking for a bar. Not necessarily a proper bar, anywhere we could find alcohol would do. Before you finish an experience like we had just been through, you should have a party – no, that's not right, you NEED a party. A party puts closure on the whole episode. Is there a bar on Ascension Island? Well, we found one.

Wherever the Americans go, they take a little bit of home with them, and we found their home. It was the American PX bar, which is a bit like our NAAFI, but better. With a little pleading, a lot of cajoling and stories of having 'just been to war', they foolishly let us in. 'OK, but don't go mad,' I think they said. Go mad? We went ballistic. There were about two dozen American servicemen sitting quietly having a Bud, when we walked in. I don't know what we must have looked like, but we weren't on our best behaviour.

We started off just drinking, as you do, then some bright spark had the idea to do some 'Tequila suicides'. It may have been me. What you do is put the salt on the back of your hand as normal and prepare your drink and your lemon. Unfortunately this is where it differs slightly. You 'do a line', as in snort the salt up your nose, drink the tequila, then squeeze the lemon in your eye. It brings a tear to the eye of the participant, and often to the eyes of any observers.

Then we played spoons.

Spoons

Spoons deserves a few paragraphs of its own. If you've never witnessed it, you should start a game at the next opportunity. You require two, preferably large, dessert spoons and a ladle. You will also require two suitable combatants, one who is familiar with the rules and one who is not. This is where our American friends stepped in. You turn two chairs around so that their backs are facing each other. The two combatants must sit astride the chair, facing one another. You must then explain the rules clearly and quite seriously to each entrant. Each 'spoon jouster' must clench the dessert spoon between his front teeth, and must at all times keep his hands behind his back. The jouster can only hit his fellow jouster on the crown of the head. The jousting can only take place in strict turns, and at the word of the umpire. The idea is to hit your opponent on the crown with a spoon clenched in your teeth, as hard as you can. Once you have done this you must bend your head forwards and offer your head to be hit. Each opponent is effectively looking at the ground when he is being hit, so cannot see the technique of his fellow jouster. One hit each, turn after turn, until someone gives in, or there is blood, though the blooded may elect to carry on, at the umpire's discretion.

If at first it is difficult to find yourself a suitable opponent, as any onlooker won't know the game, you can set up a game amongst parties that know the rules to show potential victims that it doesn't really hurt, to entice them in, so to speak. As soon as you can see an interested party, who you think may want a go – if possible, someone from the gathered audience – one of the jousters quickly gives in, rubbing his head to the applause of everyone else. It is also a good idea to have one of the jousters as a champion, who never loses. 'Right, last game, as you always win, George. Anyone else brave enough to take on the champ?'

Once you have the novice and your own man, the champ, sat down and ready to go, you start the game. 'Jousters are you ready?' Your champ goes first and 'spoons' the novice on the head. Then the champ bends down and the novice 'spoons' the champ on the head. As you may have gathered it is impossible to hurt someone, hitting him on the head with the dessert spoon, using only your teeth. So, the next time your novice bends his head forward, the champ leans over him with his spoon in his teeth but doesn't actually make contact, he just makes the movement. What actually happens is you, or one of the champ's friends, hit the novice properly with a ladle from behind his sitting position. He just thinks the other guy is good at spoons. The audience ooohs the same when the novice gets clouted as when the champ gets one. Even if you've never seen it before, as in this case with the Americans at the PX, and it's your friend that is getting whacked with the ladle, it is funny. Your mate is being done up like a kipper, as you would say in London.

Your champ, if he is good, does a bit of 'Ohhh, that bloody well hurt, are you sure you've never played before?' The novice thinks he is hurting the champ as much as it is hurting him.

I once saw a squaddie getting walloped over the swede with a ladle so hard I had to turn away (to laugh). There was a lump on the back of his head with a little split in it and the 'ladler' was skilfully increasing the amount of punishment he was ladling out, with each hit. It got so bad he had to move areas, because of the blood, and start a new lump.

Now this may all sound a little brutal, and it is, but after a few beers it is highly amusing. The Americans, to give them credit, took it all in good faith and laughed along with us as one of their seemingly unpopular airmen took a right beating. Yes he bled profusely at the end, but he was quite convinced he had hurt Dave Barrett just as much. By the time he found out the true nature of the game from his hysterical friends, we were going up the stairs of a VC10.

Was I drunk at the end? Well yes, we all were, and I think we deserved to be. I have a faint recollection of our own personal regulator being at the steps of the plane as we boarded and Jan Sewell grabbing him by the ears and giving him a kiss on the lips and just saying, 'Goodbye and thank you, you sad, sad little man!'

Jan was never scared of anyone and always seemed to be supporting some sort of modification to his face. We were in Largs once, on the west coast of Scotland, and had gone into a little club for a late drink. Being the only Sassenachs in there, our accents made us stand out a mile. Jan had asked a girl to dance. That can be tantamount to declaring war in Scotland. Without any warning, one of the locals walked up behind him and smacked him right in the mouth. The bouncers then came running over and threw *us* out, which is fair! I think their theory was, 'If ye hadne a been here, it couldne have happened.' Jan, as I recall, saw no justice in this act at all, and went back to seek clarification as to why he had been punched, then ejected. There were two huge bouncers on the door, and Jan kept saying to them that he knew who'd done it, and he just wanted to ask him why. The bouncer said the one who'd hit Jan was his younger brother.

'Well just get him out here so I can ask him why he hit me, that's all, please. I just want to talk to him.' Eventually the bouncer's young brother came to the front of the club and gave his reasons. 'Ye asked my girl te dance,' he said. 'Well I didn't know she was your girl, did I? Let's just shake hands on it and we'll go, OK?' said Jan. The young lad, feeling safe in between the two bouncers, stretched his hand out to shake Jan's. Jan took his hand, pulled him forwards, and punched him straight on the nose. Jan immediately disappeared under a hail of blows and bodies again. When we eventually dragged him outside, he was still laughing and shouting back at them, 'Welcome to Bonnie Scotland eh? Some welcome this is!'

Apart from the kiss on the steps, I have absolutely no recollection of the flight home. Wilki tells me we were asleep on the floor under the chairs. Don't forget this is a military flight, you don't have to be buckled up – well, we weren't anyway. Wilki apparently woke up in Dakar on the westernmost tip of Africa and went for a walk around under the aircraft and took in a bit of sun while we refuelled. A week or so later, when we all got back together, he told us this and everyone else said he was mad. There was no way we had landed in Dakar, we had flown straight home. It took him many weeks to convince us, and unfortunately he was right.

Brize Norton

So we wake up at Brize Norton, the RAF base near Oxford. Bleary-eyed and looking pretty terrible, we grab our one rucksack each, and get on the RAF bus to the terminal building. We were then expecting another bus all the way back to HMS *Vernon*. As we walked into the arrivals hall, pandemonium broke out. Nearly all the parents, wives or girlfriends, brothers and sisters, grand-parents, the lot, were there to meet us. We were gob-smacked.

My mother and my sister ran up to me and we embraced. They were both in floods of tears, and I had to swallow hard.

My mother kept repeating over and over again, 'Don't you ever do that to me again, don't you ever do that again!' It was very emotional for us all. For long periods, especially when the *Sir Tristram* was bombed, they had no idea if I was alive or dead, terribly injured, or burnt. They didn't know if they would ever see me again. It all came flooding out in those few minutes.

When I managed to extricate myself from and their vice-like grips, I went and righted a wrong. I shook my father's hand. Everything would be okay now.

Mum

She had, shall we say, a 'difficult' sister. I say 'had' – she may as well be not on this planet, for I doubt they will ever speak again. One of my earliest memories as a nipper is of going to my mum's sister's on Christmas Eve. It was perfection. We were poor, she was rich; we had nothing, she had everything. She had a huge house with a white Christmas tree, white decorations and presents that were the size of houses – well I was only five or six, so they seemed that big to me. They had bowls of sweets, real little presents on the tree, a singing moving reindeer, real cream, all the trimmings. All things we never had. My mum and she had a row about nothing serious, and we were sent packing. On Christmas Eve, with two babes, in the snow, with nothing at home, and all three of us crying, we had to pack up our Mini and drive the long haul home to an empty cold house, leaving our presents behind. Does that make her a bad person, or just misunderstood? She did, the following year, buy my sister and me a real portable record player and some records, which would have been very expensive at the time – but it wasn't money she was lacking.

She would take Kim and me swimming, very nice. Once, I remember watching her afterwards, in the café, eating a knickerbocker glory. She sat with us and worked her way through it, the cream and the fruit. Can you imagine the look on our faces? It was torture. I personally couldn't do that to a child.

My mum had what's known as a 'miserable early life'. Two young children, a husband in hospital, for what seemed like ever, and a sizable mortgage to keep up. She held down three jobs and always had a migraine. I would hear her cry herself to sleep every night for many years until my now father, John, appeared like a bridge over troubled waters. Were it not for him, I don't know how it would have turned out.

She had all the mother's typical wisdom. Before I ever went out she was always telling me, 'Don't you go getting any girls into trouble.' For years I thought she meant with the police.

Nibby Nobble, Nobby Noble

In Brize Norton arrivals, Nobby Noble (or Nibby Nobble as he was affectionately known because of his dyslexia) disappeared under two sisters, his grandmother, his mother, his girlfriend and what seemed like a swarm of females.

We were once at DEODS doing a mine radiography course (yes, you can X-ray a mine to see what's inside it – you may want to see how it works, and how it is triggered). We were invited into the sergeants' mess for a few bevies, along with a CD1 course. We were invited in because it was Trafalgar Night, always a big night in the Navy because of our, and indeed my, greatest ever hero, Lord Horatio Nelson. Trafalgar Night always managed to include drinking a copious amount of rum or grog. Grog is rum and water and was first introduced in 1756 for two reasons: to stop the sailor getting as drunk as he would on his neat rum, and to stop him hoarding it.

Eventually it all got just a little bit out of hand when we started the 'Trafalgar Olympics'. We played a few of our games, then they came up with a game they played in their mess, called the 'Cresta Run'. I'd never heard of it, apart from of course the winter games, which involves tearing down an ice course on something that resembles a tea tray.

In the mess they had a long polished antique-looking table that would probably seat 30 diners or more. They placed a soft blanket on the table and explained the idea behind the competition. What you had to do was take as long a run-up as you liked and, hurtling down the mess, launch yourself into the air and land on the blanket, skidding as far as you could along the table. Hence the Cresta Run. Whoever can slide the furthest is the winner. There are of course all sorts of variables that can affect your glide distance, including some you find out the hard way – like if you jump too high, you come down too hard and don't travel the maximum distance; if you are heavy, you have greater momentum; if you are light, greater agility and acceleration. Also, I discovered, the smaller area you had in contact with the table, the less friction, the better glide you enjoyed. They gave us the opportunity to practise. Being all pretty fit, we saw this as right up our street. Fully grown men, running full tilt and flying through the air onto a blanket? Who invents such games?

Each distance is measured by a glass on the side of the table, until it is beaten, and the furthest having a bottle of rum as the future prize and encouragement to all the competitors to ever greater endeavours. Ned Kelly, one of the divers, was winning at the time with a fantastically long leap. Ned was a lovely bloke who later died in a tragic diving accident at Horsea Island.

Nobby, during all of this, was quietly getting drunk, and was standing by the side of the table with a bit of a wobble on. The sergeant of the mess, a huge barrel-chested man, was determined to beat Ned's record distance. He came tearing down the hall and took off on his leap of faith.

Nobby then pulled his master stroke. Whilst the sergeant was in mid air, he grabbed the blanket and whipped it out of the way like a matador, shouting *'Olé!'*

The sergeant of course now had no soft blanket to land on

and nothing to slide on. His buttons scratched a deep groove in the ancient table and his face slammed him to a halt, ripping the skin off of his bottom lip and bloodying his nose. It made a noise not unlike a short skid from a car's tyres, but this was human flesh on varnished oak. Nobby told me he just thought, 'Oh dear, he looks angry.' Well, he was angry. He rolled off the table and, even with his injuries, sought justice, and went in search of the matador. He took a swing at Nobby, who even in his drunken stupor saw it coming and did what anyone would do with enough warning – he ducked. The force of the sergeant's momentum carried him right through his now prone target and he hit another chief diver, Terry Settle, who was stood behind Nobby, square in the face. Terry, a quite innocent bystander, took umbrage at being hit by a man he had recently been passing pleasantries with, and hit him back. It soon developed into a typical bar-room brawl, only it was Army versus Navy.

I wonder if Nelson ever had such an incident after celebrating some distant battle: celebrate a battle, with a battle.

Home to Lymers

I sat in the car with my mum, dad and sister as we drove home, and they would innocently say things such as, 'What was it like?' or 'What was the worst bit?'

How can you answer that? I tried to bumble through my experiences, leaving out the worst bits, so making it sound boring. Something was not right with me. I can't put my finger on it even now but I was uncomfortable around people, even my own family. That night at home in Uplyme, Lyme Regis, we went to the local pub, the New Inn, to sort of welcome me home. We got there and mum and Kim went in, then dad, and as I stood outside alone, I nearly didn't make it into the pub. I think it was the noise of the people in there. My heart was racing, I was sweating. Something about them not knowing what had gone on, not being a part of what I knew. It's hard to explain and it stayed with me for a while.

I had a quick temper and drank far too much, for far too long. I was outside the Cobb pub on the sea front in Lyme only a few days after my return, and some jack the lad told me a pathetic joke about Exocet being a contraceptive, by killing seamen, or something. I just punched him square in the face and walked home. I even tried to take on the village nutter. The lads I was with in the Standard pub by the beach kept warning me, 'Don't start on him, he's the sort that if you do beat him up, he would come round your house later and shoot you, he collects guns and swords!' But he kept looking at me so I kept goading him. Even in front of his friends, though, he backed down, and I'm not the biggest man in the world. I must have been giving out some kind of signal. Not that I was tough or anything, but maybe that I didn't care.

But I got on with Marie like a house on fire, and I think our relationship turned a corner when I got back. She never asked awkward questions. I was lucky back then, I knew no one in Lyme Regis except six women. Marie and her sister Julie; Kim, Julie and Jane Thomas (Julie worked in Marie's hairdressers); and Caroline. I had met them with my buddy Jock Lindsay at the local 'hop' in Seaton just before the war and we had a ball together. We would go clubbing, drinking, windsurfing, you name it. I'm sure the local lads were wondering what was going on. In short, nothing was at the time, we were all on the same wavelength, that's all. However, something was simmering between Marie and me. We just found it hard to get it together. Well, to tell the truth, I found it hard. We just laughed all the time, you can't say fairer than that.

On one occasion I took Marie, the two Julies, Kim and Caroline over to a night club in Honiton. I had a few beers first then (Marie says) I drank thirteen double gin and tonics, then drove them all home. Six of us in a Datsun 120Y. We didn't go straight home, though. I did a little detour first, and drove around the Cobb wall with my lights off. If you don't know the Cobb at all, watch the film *The French Lieutenant's Woman* with Meryl Streep. A year earlier, the girls and I blagged our way into her end-of-filming party in Lyme. I went to the private party, in the private house, walked up to the door, and said, 'We're on the catering side.' And because I had five beautiful girls with me, we got in. Meryl served us drinks and said what great catering we had provided. One of the producers knew we were gate-crashing and followed us around all night asking awkward questions. It was a brilliant night, though. Cheers, Meryl!

Marie's uncle Cecil asked me to do a talk on the Falklands to the Lyme Regis Rotary Club at the Buena Vista Hotel. I reluctantly said yes as I had never done any after-dinner speaking before. I wrote down a rough outline of a speech and tried it out on Marie's mum and dad, Margaret and Snowy Cubberley. I looked up after reading it and Snowy said, 'No! Don't do it like that. Just be yourself, speak your mind and let it all come naturally.' He was right. I just threw it in the bin. I would wing it. At their request I wore full number one uniform complete with brag rags, and turned up there not knowing what to expect. I walked in and just said, 'Fire away, any questions, what do you want to know?' It went well considering how nervous I was. By the end it was a free, easygoing discussion on the whole affair. I was asked to relate any funny stories I heard and one popped into my head that I haven't mentioned here yet.

After the surrender, I was sat outside in Port Stanley one day talking to bunch of lads from 42 Commando. They were telling me about the yomping across the islands. Yomp is the Marines' word for a long walk with all your kit. The rest of the Army use the acronym TAB, which comes from Tactical Advance to Battle. The guy I was shooting the shit with (another nice military expression for you there) said he had the radio and was at the back of the snaked-out column of troops (just like the famous photo with the union jack on the aerial). He said he received the warning 'Air raid warning red!' Nothing unusual: this would obviously happen a lot on their long yomp to Stanley. The usual routine was to get away from each other (so as not to give a big target for a bomb or strafing) and take cover as best you could. The message is then passed forward and usually everyone can be seen swiftly taking off in different directions. This time he saw half the column take cover, then from the middle onwards they just stayed where they were, and at the far front end they were seen jumping up and down and hugging each other. He says he couldn't figure it out, and after the all clear he caught up with one of the front lads to see what all the fuss was about.

It turned out to be a typical 'Chinese whisper'. That is, a series of cumulative errors from mishearing the last trooper. So 'Air raid warning red!' had passed down the line and mysteriously changed into 'Galtieri's dead!' hence all the hugging and jumping up and down and celebrating. (General Leopoldo Galtieri was the *de facto* President of Argentina from 22 December 1981 to 18 June 1982, during the conflict.)

Too young to die

'One of the main reasons that it is so easy to march men off to war,
is that each of them feels sorry for the man next to him, who will die.'
Annie Dillard

She is right. It was not going to happen to me. 'Others yes, maybe, but not me, I'm different, I can't die, I've got too many things to do yet to die now!'

War is a time to grow up quickly. People come out with clichés like 'He went away a boy, and came back a man.' Well I don't know if that happened to me. I had already lived a fair bit compared to people I went to school with. I'd been around the world and seen some weird shit already.

Then, I was a 23-year-old lad who could not be hurt by anything or anyone. I thought I would be this age forever, I would never be 40, that was sooo far ahead it wasn't even worth considering. Now I'm a 48-year-old with a 12-year-old son. My ramblings are just those of an old fart who went on a short war, which didn't even have the decency to be called a war. It was a 'conflict'. Why? Because, apparently, nobody actually declared 'war' on anyone. A conflict sounds like something you might have with a neighbour about fixing a fence, or noisy kids. A conflict of interest, about a group of islands that, I would warrant, less than one per cent of the world's population had even heard of before 2 April 1982.

I remember a roving reporter doing a TV piece going around a shopping centre somewhere asking people where the Falklands were. 'Near the Shetlands, I think,' was one famous reply. A close friend of mine, after seeing me on the BBC, was astonished when I told her the Falklands were 8,000 miles away, and this was in 2007!

Nevertheless it was still a conflict of interest that resulted in the deaths of almost a thousand young men.

UK	ARGENTINA
258 killed	649 killed
777 wounded	1,068 wounded
59 taken prisoner	11,313 taken prisoner

It was a 'conflict' that everyone's forgotten now. Or will do soon. Well, I haven't forgotten it.

I haven't forgotten the look on the prisoners' faces.

I haven't forgotten the sound, and feeling, of HMS *Antelope* blowing up a bit too near me. Or having to endure her burning, melting and creaking as the slow inevitability of her demise was played out to the thousands of British onlookers over the next 24 hours.

I haven't forgotten the burnt man on the helideck I thought was an African, or the smell of his cooked flesh. That image is forever burnt on my retina.

I haven't forgotten the invasion of my senses on the first day as the fighters roared over my head, and the futility of my WWII pop gun firing in the general direction of a recently passed jet.

The noise. I'll never forget the noise.

I haven't forgotten my night on board HMS *Coventry*, two months before the conflict was even in our minds.

I haven't forgotten the farmer's tears at Bluff Cove as he apologised – to me! – for the men we'd lost to save 'them'.

I haven't forgotten the gut-wrenching wait for the incoming Exocet to hit my ship, and indeed I haven't forgotten that, for some, that was the very last 'wait' of their lives.

Whenever I smell a wood bonfire, I think of the stink of the prisoners, then comes the smell of shit.

War doesn't prove who's right ... only who's left.

Brag-rags

Personally, I could not give a monkey's about receiving a gong. We all got one for being down there, a basic Falklands Campaign medal. But then so did the guys 200 miles out from the islands on a water tanker, tug or whatever. The same one as us. I haven't got a problem with that.

Mick Fellows got the Distinguished Service Cross (DSC). Mick deserved it and more. He ran the team, the jobs, the lot. He was everywhere, doing his job, and sometimes other people's too. The Boss, Brian Dutton, got one higher, the Distinguished Service Order (DSO). That is the third-highest order you can get:

only the George Cross stands between it and the Victoria Cross.

But why didn't any one of us get something? When the Boss was dealing with the UXB on the *Argonaut* Dave Southwell and Stan Bowles were beside him the whole time. Dave, being the senior Kilick (lead diver) on the team, and Stan, being built like an all-in wrestler, between them did most of it in fact. Other men at other times. But the exploits of the guys on *Argonaut*, and with Mick on *Antrim* and *Plymouth*, and on the covert operation at Bluff Cove, went unrecognised. I have no idea if I or any of our team were recommended for anything (I'm told not). Nobody ever said we were recommended, so we got nothing.

No wonder the team were not mentioned in any of the official conflict history documents, or even represented on the war memorial at Port Stanley until this year, 2007, 25 years late! Nobody knew we existed. Jan Sewell, who wrote the piece about HMS *Antrim*, told me once, 'I didn't even think about medals. When I got back, though, I did just once wonder, "Which one I will get?" Not "I wonder if I'll get one."' Some of the *Antrim*'s crew that helped Jan, Nigel and Mick, I believe, got mentioned in dispatches. Good luck to them. We just got our Commendation. It looks a bit like a child's swimming certificate. Mine is so valuable, I don't even know where it is.

Medals are usually dished out for things done 'beyond the call of duty'. Rightly so. None of us had done anything remotely near 'How to remove a new bomb from a working warship during an air raid.' We'd never been trained to do it. We were divers.

It grated on some more than others, and why not? Not long after we got back to *Vernon* after our week's leave, we had an official photo taken of the team. The photo was really to show the Boss's new medal. Well, we didn't have a great deal to show for our efforts. So we made some. Stan had a stroke of brilliance when he suggested we make our own and surreptitiously stick them on just before the shutter went 'click'. I and most made some sort of fancy medal. Stan went right overboard and hung what looked like a huge German Third Reich eagle on his chest.

Wilki had made a sort of 'Military Order of the Bath' like Nelson had. The photographer got us ready and said 'say cheese', which was our cue to 'up medals'. The photographer did look up from his camera when he saw the twelve simultaneous moves, like some bizarre military salute, as all our arms went across our chests to stick on our home-mades – but he took some photos without saying a word.

Then our devious plan was uncovered. Wilki's Order of the Bath gave up its tenuous grip on his tunic and floated off in the breeze. Of all the places it could have gone out there on the edge of the sea and the heliport, it landed at the Boss's feet. He bent down to pick it up, looked at it and then looked behind as the remainder of us frantically tried to remove our unearned decorations. We were rumbled, and the grown-ups were not amused. We then had an official photo taken, minus the home-mades, and that was the one that was circulated. But I had a word with my mate, the photo-tech. He got me copies of the unofficial photo, which still makes me laugh to this day. The smug looks are everywhere, like naughty little boys who have just got away with stealing a tot of Daddy's whisky.

Life back at the Fleet Team just carried on like nothing had

A more relaxed photo of the whole team, taken at Ascension.
Back row, standing: Ben Gunnell, Bill Bauckham, George Sharp, Lester Geoffreys, Stan Bowles. Dave Barrett, Mick Fellows, Nigel Pullen, Billy Evernden, Brian Dutton.
Front row: Dave Southwell, Tony Groom, Nobby Noble, Ian Milne, Billy Smart, Wilki Wilkinson, Jan Sewell.

happened. We were all a little bit 'stir-crazy' for a while, and to give Mick Fellows his due he did cut a number of the lads a lot of slack. Drinking, fighting, drunk-driving, AWOL, all came his way over the next year. Two months after our return we were up in Rothesay on the Isle of Bute raising merry hell again.

Ding ding round 2

'First they ignore you, then they laugh at you, then they fight you, then you win!' – Mahatma Gandhi

When you put in for a draft you can put in 'preferred' places or 'places to avoid'. Under the 'avoid' heading I put Scotland, for no other reason than it is about as far as you can get from my home (I had just bought my first house, in Beatrice Road, Southsea, Portsmouth). Drafty, having a sense of humour, sent me from the Fleet Team in Portsmouth to Faslane on the west coast of Scotland again. I didn't want to be there, and to top it all, Skip was there again.

At the time I was a windsurfing fanatic, and had bought myself a VW camper van. I elected to drive my camper up there with all my toys on board. 'He who dies with the most toys, wins!' My dad used to love that saying. The amount of virgin lochs and deserted beaches I would come across would be worth the slow drive. I had a canoe, three windsurfers, half a dozen sails, masts, booms, the lot on the roof. With a fridge and sink, a double bed, a sleeping bag and a radio on the inside, I was self-sufficient. I left Pompey wearing shorts, but by the time I reached the Shap Summit, some 1,350 feet above sea level in Cumbria, I had a rude reminder that the weather in Scotland is considerably colder than Portsmouth.

In my eight months there I would spend nearly all of my private time on my own. I lived in my van, in car parks or in the diving section. I would use the shower in the section if I was there, or swimming pools when I was touring Scotland at the weekends. With a bit of ingenuity and forethought you could 'work' your weekends to sometimes go from Thursday night to Monday, or even Tuesday. So I went everywhere, on my tod, sailing, white-water canoeing, and even diving on my own. Now that is a no-no, but I used to do it. It was a time I needed, for me, it was 'Tony' time, and it helped me big style to sort my head out after the madness of the previous few months. Scotland is cold, but I found some spots to sleep in my van that would take your breath away. It undoubtedly has some stunningly beautiful scenery, but it did sometimes, only sometimes mind, give me a somewhat melancholy mood. I soon realised it was partly because of the similarities with the Falklands. The grey, windy, wet weather, the rocky mountains, even the colour of the sea in the lochs was very similar.

I went everywhere, even up to the northernmost tips of the British mainland, including Wick, John O'Groats and Thurso. I had read about the surf they have at Thurso, but to be honest I wasn't really expecting much. I have read somewhere that it is the northernmost surf in the world. I turned onto the seafront, and was amazed by what I saw. These weren't piddly little waves, so close together you couldn't do much with them, these waves had no place being here. They were huge, eight to ten feet, and with a perfect green right-to-left breaking crest. The peaks were a long way apart so you had time to recover between sets, it was all faultless. I sat for an hour watching the breaks, in total awe of the serenity of it all. It was Saturday lunchtime, the sun was out (but as was the norm in Scotland, there was no heat in it) and I was the only one on the water. First of all I broke out my surfboard, and it was vicious out there, cold enough to give you a headache even with a surf cap on. Then, feeling brave, I came in and rigged up my short wave jumping board. It was blowing a perfect easterly along the waves about a force six. Within half an hour, I was wave jumping and wave riding the best waves I have ever seen, and there was absolutely no one there to see it. I came in about five o'clock, just before it got dark, and I was exhausted but beaming and brimming with life.

I would regularly have to sleep in my old flying jacket, just to keep warm. That night I slept right next to Thurso Castle in my camper and listened to the waves crashing up the beach all night. You know its cold when you wake up with ice on the inside of your windows. I woke up in Thurso that morning to find the few bits of washing-up I had left in soapy water frozen solid in the stainless sink.

Unfortunately, things would never get that good for me in Scotland again. I was a loner up there, and kept myself to myself. I would do my work, diving, retrieving mines from fishermen's nets, treating bends cases, whatever came our way during the week, then I was off, usually on my own, every weekend. I do concede that I didn't exactly endear myself to the other divers on the team there.

Dave (John Boy) Walton was one of the few that was on my wavelength and we had some laughs together. Maybe it was because he had been 'down south' himself on Fleet Team 3. He would even come away with me some weekends and stay in my van. He's a good-looking bastard and would 'trap' women just by walking into a bar or club. Attractive women would come up to me and I would think, 'Hello, what's going on here then?' and they would say, 'Who's your gorgeous friend?' Git!

One Monday morning he came into work all full of himself and proceeded to tell us the story of his weekend. He had met a nice Scottish girl who was a bit of a stunner. They had been out for the evening somewhere around Helensburgh near the base. He had gone back to her flat, where she lived with her sister and one of their friends. When he got in, the friend was still up and they all had a drink in the communal kitchen. Out of earshot of JB's girl, the friend said to JB, 'If you need a light in the middle of the night, just come up to my room on the middle floor next to the loo.' He thanked her, but seeing as he didn't smoke, he didn't think it would be necessary to take up her kind offer. He went to bed and did what boyfriend and girlfriend do.

In the middle of the night he got up and went to the toilet. When he came out, there was the friend at her door. 'Come fe a light, have yeh?' she whispered, and ushered him into her boudoir. JB, powerless to resist, went in, and what went on was only between him, me and the other earwigging divers in the rest room at the time. Well, having had no sleep at all, the poor soul, and not wanting to get caught in the wrong bed, he crept out onto the landing and into the kitchen to make a brew and revive his flagging energy levels. Now you're not going to believe who should wander in. Yes, believe it or not, the girlfriend's sister. JB, being JB, soon worked his charm. He didn't really know he was doing it, a sort of mischievous innocence that made the women melt. He then was forced to go to bed with her, to keep the peace ... and to get his hat trick.

Feeling rather disgusted with himself, he felt the only way to cleanse his soul was to tell us and seek forgiveness from his peers. Boys being boys, we all forgave him and called him a dirty, lucky, bastard, among other things.

Now, by Wednesday, things had changed a bit. JB was not such a happy man. He was having problems with his pee thingy to such an extent he had to go to sick bay and get some penicillin to make it work properly again. Apart from that, he now had a dilemma or three. Did he get the dose from girl one, two or three? If it was from girl one, number two and three may now have it. Even if it was from the last girl, he had to tell her. He was mortified at the thought of having to call all three and tell them they had something very embarrassing and he didn't know if he'd given it to them, or them to him. Well, we felt dreadful for him, and showed our concern by continuously laughing and begging to be allowed to listen to the telephone conversation, if he ever plucked up courage to make it. He made the calls, and the relationship, which had so much potential, was over as quickly as it had begun.

Ten years after Faslane, JB and I would find ourselves doing many months of deep saturation work in the North Sea and Denmark together.

Not long after I got to the team I put in a request to go on a saturation course. I wanted to leave, which didn't go down too well. I thought it may well get me out of there before my year was up.

The now promoted Skip had basically gone from bad to worse. We did a pretty good job of avoiding each other wherever possible, and when we had to converse a grunt would usually suffice. This time I was back as a CD2 and so was not at his beck and call to bully as he wished. I was also still a bit 'unpredictable' myself after my recent experiences. About two months in, Skip and I were two of only a few left in the diving section for a while so couldn't avoid working together blanking an inlet on a nuclear submarine alongside the Naval base. The morning went fine, but the afternoon was a different affair altogether.

Myself, JB and the other divers went back to the diving section for lunch. Skip disappeared aboard the submarine. Come one o'clock, we all got ready to dive again, when Skip arrived, shall we say a little the worse for wear after too good a time on board the sub. He was barely able to string a sentence together so, not wanting to drop him in it, and wanting the dive to go ahead safely, I took charge myself. I told Skip, in no uncertain terms, to sit down in the boat and keep quiet and I would do it. Amazingly he did, and I got the two divers in the water. When they were in, he started on all of us. Asking irrelevant and stupid questions a power-hungry teacher might ask a pupil. Only this time I wasn't playing his games. 'What's the capacity of a twin mixture bottle?' was the sort of question he was coming out with, not just to me but to the other divers in the boat.

'Who's the top goal scorer in division one?' I would retort. He just gave me a blank look. 'Well, if you want to learn meaningless statistics like that, fill your boots, I am more interested in football and windsurfing. Ask me something on those?' I could tell he wasn't happy.

There were civilian scientists working on the sub's bows in

white coats, complete with note pads and 'gadgets', and one of them was an attractive-looking female. Skip got up and decided to take a leak over the side of the Gemini in full view of everyone concerned. All I could muster was, 'Skip, that's not a good idea!' He was wobbling about all over the place and clearly drunk. I felt embarrassed more than anything.

We finished the dive and went back to the diving section having escaped unscathed. The lads sat down in the rest room and had a brew, and I went out the back to the lockers, which were situated in a long corridor connecting us to the rest of the building. I was putting my stuff in my locker when in walked Skip. I knew it wasn't to say thank you for running the dive and getting me out of the shit, or sorry for being such a twat and asking all those stupid questions. Or even, sorry for getting drunk whilst running a dive, it's unforgivable and it won't happen again. Oh no. He walked up to me and said, 'Give me your hands.'

I said 'Fuck off, Skip, you're pissed. Leave it, and we'll talk tomorrow.'

'Give me your hands!' he shouted, holding his out in front of him, with his fingers splayed out, like I'd seen all those years ago, but this time I knew what was coming.

He stood there, hands out, giving me that cocky 'I'm gonna make you squirm and beg' look. I interlocked my fingers with his, and saw his intentions as clear as daylight as he thought, 'Yes, I've got him.' I resisted his finger bending for a second as I felt him trying it, then quickly wrenched him towards me, but this time I was holding *his* hands, and I butted him hard on the bridge of the nose.

He collapsed onto the floor. I considered going in again and taking out eight years of frustration on this bully, but he was finished. He threw up on the floor, so I went back to my locker to finish getting changed. No more than a minute later the door at the end of the long corridor burst open and in walked two MPs. Don't forget this is a nuclear submarine base and they take breaches of security or protocol very seriously. Greenpeace and

CND were permanently camped outside the main gates and would love any story like this to feed to the press. They strode purposefully up the corridor and said to me, 'Diver Skip, where is he?' I just nodded to the heap on the floor. 'We've had a report he was in charge of a dive on the jetty, he may have been drinking, and urinating in front of civilian workers.'

'I don't know about that,' I said, 'but that's him there.' They then picked him up, one under each arm, and off he was marched.

I went into the rest room again and someone said, 'Where's Skip?'

'He's just been arrested. Apparently someone saw him pissing over the side down at the jetty.' Nobody seemed surprised, interested or bothered. We on the team never saw him again. He went over the wall to DQs (Detention Quarters, Navy prison) for 60 days I believe. I've not seen him since.

Not long after this unseemly episode, out of the blue came a draft for the *Seaforth Clansman*, the Navy's deep diving saturation boat. Magic, get me outta here.

Remember, when someone annoys you, that it takes 42 muscles to frown, but it only takes four muscles to extend your arm and whack him in the head.

He looks like me

One day whilst going back to my little three-bed terrace in Pompey, I was putting my key in the door when I got that feeling I was being watched. As I went in the door I looked across the road and I thought, 'That bloke looks like me,' then I went in. After I'd shut the door I thought, 'Hang on, he really does look like me, a lot!' It was my estranged dad, Harry. He had driven down to Portsmouth to see if he could just see me, from a distance I think.

Despite not having seen him since I was seven or eight (I was then 25) I knew who he was. I opened the door and he was trying to make good his escape. I went over and introduced myself. Now that is a weird experience. I don't want to go into what went on when I was young, I barely remember it anyway, but I invited him in and we had our first cup of tea together. Life has a way of throwing up these quirky little scenarios every now and then. That was one of mine.

When you're saturated, are you just really wet?

'Anyone who cannot cope with mathematics is not fully human. At best he is a tolerable sub-human who has learned to wear shoes, bathe and not make messes in the house.' – Robert Heinlein

As soon as my draft date arrived, I was off, tear-arsing my way back to Portsmouth in my bus, sometimes approaching speeds of over 55 miles an hour! I knew there would be a course to do to get my saturation ticket, but I thought it would be mostly wet, in the water. It turned out that there was quite a bit of diving, but before I got anywhere near a bell or decompression chamber I had to get through the theory.

Maths and I are on different planets. I don't know if it is possible to be dyslexic in one subject; if it is, I am. You can sit with me for an hour and explain a mathematical problem, the easy way to conquer it, show me some examples and work through the whole quandary. The next morning, I haven't got a clue. This would drive my fellow potential sat diver mate Phil Kearns mad. It would be as if we had never met and discussed this alien subject. It has driven many a teacher wild in the past. 'What do you mean, you've forgotten? We only did it yesterday!'

What made the theory even harder for me was having a naturally gifted, mathematically minded officer as our teacher. Lieutenant Kearns his name was – another Kearns. One day, he even explained to us how the famous philosopher Robert Boyle, as in 'Boyle's Law' (the most fundamental diving law) had got his law wrong! He did this with the prodigious use of blackboard after blackboard of figures, diagrams and graphs. Before we get into that, let me try and explain what 'saturation diving' is.

Why bother with sat?

Say you have a long, complicated job at around 100 metres, lots of intricate work. To do it conventionally, with air (too deep – remember nitrogen narcosis, narcs?) or even with oxy-helium (heliox), it would take you years and you would need hundreds of divers. Why? Well for a start your bottom time would be so short, say five minutes, and your decompression stops so long, that it would be completely impractical. Not to mention the danger from the bends, and the sheer distances involved, and being at the mercy of the weather during decompression stops.

Even with a conveyor-belt system of divers you would soon run out and there would be no continuity of work. Everything under water takes longer. Except getting tired, and cold. Well, not everything, then. Any work, I should say, takes longer. To find our job in poor vis, and it probably won't be great at 100 metres, would be hard enough, so it's time-consuming, which is exactly the element you don't have. Even if you have a line going to the job in hand, it will take you time to orientate yourself with what is going on, where you are, where the tools are. Too late, time's up, leave bottom.

Rushing when you are deep is a no-no also, a lesson you learn very quickly because once you are panting you can rarely get your breath back without stopping completely and resting. Now if you are breathing an oxy-helium mix and in a rush because you have a short bottom time, you will quickly become exhausted. Your time in the water and your gas (helium) works out very expensive, so you are always under pressure to get a move on. On top of that you have the need for long, in-water, weather-dependent decompression stops. You may argue you could do them in a bell, but how may bells can you get on a ship? Usually two comfortably, and if they are being used to convey divers up and down your conveyor-belt system has already broken down. It won't work, honest!

How can you not decompress, then? Well you can't, but you can save up all the decompression and do it all just the once, at the end.

Bobby Boyle's law

I am no expert at all this, I just do it, but this is how I remember the laws. As you sit reading this, you are saturated. Your tissues are saturated with the nitrogen at the current partial pressure (PP), that is at atmospheric pressure (one bar). That is the weight of air above us. This is measured in weight per area, usually 'pounds per square inch' (PSI). If you travel up from the earth, the pressure decreases because there is less weight of air pressing down on you. So take a balloon up a mountain and it will get bigger, less PSI on it, and as there is less air you will find it harder to breathe.

Back at sea level you cannot absorb any more nitrogen unless you increase your depth (PP) or increase the percentage of nitrogen you are breathing.

So take your balloon and drag it under water with you. It will get smaller. Water is approximately a thousand times denser (heavier) than air at the sea's surface. So, look up at the sky and it takes all that height to give us the weight of one bar, one atmosphere. Go beneath the surface of the water and it only takes a depth of 33 feet (10 metres) to give us our next one bar of pressure.

Now exchange your balloon for something else that is full of air/gas, the diver's lungs. At only 10 metres you have twice the normal atmospheric pressure and twice the amount of gas in the diver's lungs. Assuming that the lungs are the same size as we keep breathing but the gas is compressed, you have double the amount. Go down to 20 metres and you have another atmosphere of weight and pressure in your lungs and you now hold three times as much as you did on the surface. At 30 metres (third atmosphere), a diver's lungs hold four times the amount of gas, and so on. The deeper you go, the more you hold, the longer it will take to 'fizz off' on your long slow ascent back to the surface.

That is Boyle's Law. Bobby said, roughly, that under a constant temperature, gas will compress as pressure is applied. And if the amount of gas is fixed, its volume is inversely proportional to the total amount of pressure applied. If the pressure doubles, the volume shrinks to half.

Bob Boyle's law for idiots basically means: If you increase the pressure on a flexible gas-filled object (balloon or lungs), it will get smaller; if you decrease the pressure on it, it will get bigger.

In the bin

Saturation diving: long periods of boredom, interspaced with short periods of abject terror.

If you are not diver types you will still be wondering about the practicality of staying in the water for all these hours, nay days, to get saturated. Then the days to decompress and fizz off all the bubbles in your blood. Well, you don't have to stay in the water.

Imagine you drive to the garage and you put one bar of pressure in your tyre. You know that because it tells you on the gauge. You haven't gone underwater, but you have the same effect. Inside your tyre you have one bar or an equivalent of 10 metres water depth in your tyre. If you took it down in the ocean to 10 metres and opened the valve, nothing would come out. The two pressures are equal.

So put your divers into a decompression chamber (usually on board a ship, but sometimes on a rig) and blow it down to the equivalent depth of the seabed (using a heliox mix) to say 100 metres (or where you want to work). They are 'at depth' and they haven't even got wet.

These chambers will be the divers' home for as long as the dive takes, usually a maximum of 28 days. As it is your home it has to have everything you require. Now you cannot take 28 days' worth of meals in and cook for yourself. Apart from a range of hazards such as fire, it would not be very practical. So in every chamber you have a medical lock. Through a series of very thick metal doors and valves that isolate the medical lock from the chamber and the outside world, it is possible to pass food, medicines, washing, hot drinks, diving equipment, rubbish etc in and out of the living chamber.

Inside the chamber, it's not pretty, and you had better not be claustrophobic. They are all decorated in the same shade of putrid, monkey-sick, fire-retardant, hospital green. I have lived for months in chambers that have six or eight divers inside and it's no bigger than a rounded garden shed about fifteen feet long. You usually have two bunks on either side, which just about leaves enough room to walk between them, and maybe two at one end. Some have tables, some do not; there is usually a separate toilet and shower compartment, but not always! You can become quite close to your fellow plungers' personal habits and routines in the more primitive of these systems. The chambers are small because helium is expensive and because they are under a great deal of pressure from the inside. Everything inside is built of either heavy-gauge steel or aluminium. The smell in

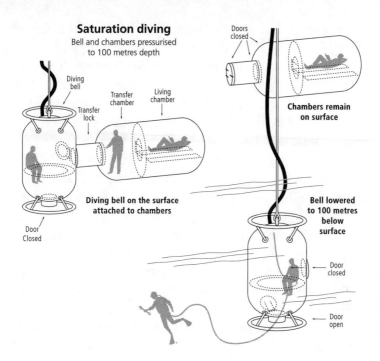

Saturation diving
Bell and chambers pressurised
to 100 metres depth

Diving
bell

Transfer
chamber

Living
chamber

Transfer
lock

Diving bell on the surface
attached to chambers

Door
Closed

Doors
closed

Chambers remain
on surface

Bell lowered
to 100 metres
below
surface

Door
closed

Door
open

the chambers is of other men, and in the bell and wet pot, of wet rusting steel.

Nature's strongest shape is round. The diving bell itself is round, the chambers are cylindrically rounded, a submarine's pressure hull is round, and the space shuttle is round inside. It is the only shape to take such pressures.

So for simplicity and cost's sake let's say we will put in four teams of three divers, in two interconnecting chambers, so we have a 24-hour diving capability. You will pack everything you need for the month, which will not include cigarettes and alcohol, but will include personal diving gear, toilet bag, light clothes, lots of music and books.

On getting the go-ahead to get into your new home, the Life Support Technicians (LST) will shut the three-inch-thick round metal door and that is you for a month. The only time you can get out is when you go diving or in a month's time. Yes, it can be a depressing thought. What keeps the doors from leaking out gas?

One 10 mm rubber 'O' seal between the door and the chamber. If that goes, it's good night Vienna.

In the Navy we would all LST for each other, which is good training to see both sides of how it all works. In the North Sea and around the world, the LSTs are professionals and do that job only. They will pump the gas on board, mix it, check the gas you breathe, then check it is right, then check it again, then again before you get it. They figure out the depths and the gas mixtures required, get the meals and the diving gear, look after your personal wellbeing, and a great deal more besides. It is a full-on job, with a lot of responsibility, and other people's lives in you hands. Get it wrong once, and you may easily kill someone. It has happened on many occasions. As I write this I have just heard of one LST in hospital, having been hit in the shoulder by a medical lock door as it blew open when he tried to open it with pressure still in the system.

You have to think about everything you do in the chamber, and so do the LSTs. One lad called Danny Webster was in what he thought was a pretty safe place in the chamber. He was sat on the loo. Whilst doing his paper work, if you know what I mean, he asked for a 'shitter flush'. The LSTs will then come round to your chamber and open a series of valves so the pressure inside blows the waste away and into a holding tank. You also have to open a valve on your side for this to work. Double valves at least, all the time, everywhere. On this occasion, though, Danny was still sat down, and his valve was already open. Can you see where this is heading? The LST came around and opened his valves and the waste was sucked out of the bowl. The only thing was, Danny was almost a perfect shape to form a seal over the loo. It sucked out his large intestines. He did live, but ...

When you are locked in and they start to squeeze in the gas, you talk like Donald Duck immediately – and that is your voice for the next month. If you go really deep, say over 200 metres, the depth and the helium acting on your voice can make it almost impossible to understand each other. During the blow-down, you check that all airtight containers (tomato sauce bottles, shampoo, mayonnaise) are slightly open, because if you miss one it will implode (explode on the way up) under the pressure – and what a mess.

Let's say you blow down the diving bell with your heliox gas at the same time as the chambers to 100 metres. If you were then to lower it down near the seabed and stop it at 100 metres and open the bottom door, what would happen? What would happen to the water on the outside? Well, nothing: the pressures would be equalised; it would not come rushing in as so many people seem to think it should. If you were to raise the bell with your now open door, the gas in the bell would bleed off out into the water. If you were to lower it, the water would come in, but you could just keep it out by opening the 'blow down valve' with the right breathing mix in it to keep the water at bay. Make sense? I hope so.

Right, you are blown down to your depth of 100 metres and the LSTs lock in a 'pot-o-hot'. With your hot water you make your tea or coffee and have a chat. If you are first team away, you may have to dive straightaway; if not you may try and get some sleep. You are now to all intents and purposes in sat, but your body wont yet be saturated with the gas you are breathing. During these first few hours your joints are a bit clicky because all your cartilage is squashed.

The first team away will be given an hour's notice to dive. If you've been in for a few weeks, or you're asleep when you get the call, you will be fed first. You then prep your personal gear and with about ten minutes to go you go into the 'wet pot'. Usually the wet chamber has the heads and shower in it, and it is generally the chamber that will also have the entrance to the bell. You change into your hot water suit, put on your harness, and wait for the supervisors to 'give you the bell'. By that I mean they will bring the diving bell to your depth – either they blow it down to you or, if there is a team coming back, you wait for them to vacate the wet pot, then you go in and go on up, or along, to the bell.

Now all this talk of depths often confuses people into thinking we are under water again. Remember, though, that this is all happening in the dry, on the surface, usually on board a ship. The depths are all obtained only by changing the pressure in the relevant chambers. The underwater depths don't 'happen' until the bell goes into the water.

There is good reason not to have all six men from both teams in the wet pot having a chat about the job in hand. One of the most dangerous times in sat is the locking on and off of the bell. Why? Well try to imagine the pressure on the huge clamping system (and the tiny 'O' seal) that locks the bell onto the chamber (wet pot). That clamp is a potential weak spot. When you crawl over or past the join, on your way in or out of the bell, that little gap is there. If it goes, you die. So you have as few men as possible in any one area when the doors are open to the bell and the system.

In 1983, aboard the Byford Dolphin, a drilling rig in the North Sea's Frigg Field, four divers and one tending diver were killed when precisely that happened. The bell had just returned from a successful dive and they were all expecting to be waiting for weather as the forecast was not good. The word is, the guy on the outside was told the transfer tunnel was on the surface, i.e. with no gas in it, so safe to un-mate the bell. In fact the trunking was still at 100 metres. With that pressure still inside, it was obviously very difficult to un-mate. The problem that led to the deaths of five men was that this clamp had stuck before with no pressure on it and being of such a heavy construction had often had to be whacked with something to get it moving. The poor lad outside tried to un-mate the bell. Had the four lads in the chamber had the door to the trunking and/or the wet pot closed, they would probably have survived, but they didn't, maybe because this had never happened before. The clamp came off and resulted in the explosive decompression of the system. The clamp hit the tender so hard that the first people on the scene couldn't even find him. For a while a man overboard search was started. The divers in the chamber died instantly of explosive decompression. It's a sad fact that someone usually has to die in the diving business in order for a serious safety flaw to be brought to the attention of the relevant bodies. So, we have a safe-ish industry now, thanks largely to the 58 deaths of divers in the North Sea alone since the early 1970s.

Now, if you are in a sat chamber, nobody ever leaves the door to the wet pot open. The door to the bell is always closed ASAP. Usually the bellman goes in first and does bell checks on his own. That is, he will check the position of every single valve in the bell, of which there are around 50, and whilst he is doing this, one of his companions who is not in sat will check every single valve on the outside.

Also the bellman has to check that every piece of equipment works and is where it should be. Bell checks are done via the communications with the sat supervisor. He reads out to the bellman every position of every valve, e.g. 'Onboard gas to the bell closed.' The bellman spots, and usually touches, the valve and says, 'Closed.'

'Hot water dump valve open,' etc.

This is repeated for every valve, every dive, every time. It is all recorded so if you lock your diver out with no gas or hot water, he will be very cross and, worse, he will have proof!

Once the bellman is happy with 'his' bell the two divers will join him. The general rule is, you will be bellman one day, then diver one, then diver two, then back to bellman. So you have two days diving and one day bellman/standby diver.

All three of you lock yourselves into the tiny sphere, pushing the door closed from inside the bell and locking and clipping it. The door from the chamber has the same treatment. Then the short tunnel space in between is vented to the surface. Now the bell is a separate entity from the sat chambers, but you know that they are still both at the required depth (pressure) on the inside. Using hydraulic power, the heavy mating clamp is undone, then the bell is moved away from the system that joins it to the chambers and over a moon pool, usually in the centre of the ship. If you have a two-bell ship it will be slightly to the bow or stern. You can then lower the bell into the water.

All the bell's systems are supplied through a six-inch-thick umbilical, down which comes power for the lights and heaters, communications, cameras, gas, hot water and more. Going the other way it carries the used helium, depth measurements, gas monitoring etc.

On the outside of the bell itself, in huge bottles, you will have enough gas (oxygen and helium) to keep you going for hours if by some catastrophe you are separated from the ship. You will also carry onboard battery power, to run atmosphere scrubbers and through-water comms, if need be. You will have a multitude of spares for every eventuality, even warm survival suits. You can also cut the main lift wire and main umbilical from the inside of the bell (via hand pump guillotines) and you can ditch weights from the bell to make it float up to the surface. If you have to do any of these tasks, your whole world has caved in around you and you are in a world of shit.

Got it? On a better day, on the other hand, all you need do

when you get to the bottom in your bell is open the bottom door (because the pressure on the inside and the outside are – ? Equal, that's right) and put on your helmet. The bellman then switches the hot water to your suit, and you drop out the bottom and away into the deep blue, or dark black, depending on your whereabouts. All your gas, hot water, hat light, camera feed, now comes down the bell umbilical, into the bell, then on to you. The bottles on your back are for emergency use only. If you lose surface gas, the bellman can put you on bell gas. If you are cut off from the bell by an accident or something landing on your umbilical (which once happened to me), you could in theory switch to the bailout bottles on your back and cut your umbilical to go back to the sanctuary of the bell. You had better be quick, though, because with no hot water your time, in the North Sea at least, is going to be very short.

Now, I hope you understand why the water won't come in. But you can pop out for about six hours (that's the usual working time used in the UK) and have a walk/swim about and do some work. This bell is now your life, it is not merely a lift to work as many seem to think. I don't care what sort of trouble you get into on the bottom, you can't go up to the surface. You must go back to the bell. If you cut your hand off, and there is a disproportionate amount of divers missing digits and limbs, you have to go to the bell, and back to the chamber, then worry about it. There have been explosions, entrapments, amputations, and divers drawn into propellers. Divers dragged to the surface, stuck on the bottom, dragged off the job and stuck on the job. There's no doubt it is a dangerous business, but tens of thousands of hours go by every month with men in the water all over the world, in some ridiculously dodgy situations, and I think, for what we do, our safety figures are good – disproportionately good.

Say three or four hours to blow down and get on a bell run, and finally you are doing some work. We're at 100 metres, we said, didn't we, on a mixture of say 20% oxygen and the rest helium? Whilst down there you will eventually reach a point where your tissues can absorb no more of your inspired gas (typically it takes at least twelve hours, but let's not split hairs). At this point your tissues are 'saturated', they can take on no more of what you are breathing (oxy-helium). If you start your decompression now or in four weeks' time, it will make no difference to your decompression time. Once you are saturated with this gas at this depth, it will take you about three days to safely reach the surface. The deeper you go, the longer the decompression journey back to atmospheric pressure. If you were to come up any quicker the inspired gas in your blood and in your lungs would expand too quickly, a bit like opening a coke bottle. Result, the bends, or burst lungs, and death. Of course your lungs aren't the only cavities in your body that are subject to compression during descent, or expansion during ascent (barotrauma). There are also the sinuses, middle ear, and intestines, to name but a few more delicate spots.

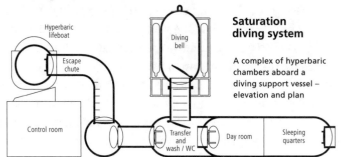

Saturation diving system

A complex of hyperbaric chambers aboard a diving support vessel – elevation and plan

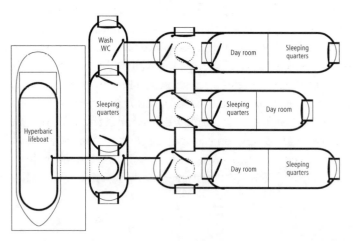

Something else to think about whilst you are saturated. You have to depend on a lot of people doing their job to the best of their ability. Not just your LSTs, but your supervisors, deck crewmen, chefs, engineers, stewards, everyone. How can the chef affect me? Well, he has to get hot meals to you, obviously – but everyone on board has a responsibility to the sat divers, in that they cannot easily come out. You cannot just open the doors to the chambers if there is a serious galley fire, for instance, or if you have a collision, or run aground. That's your lot; you are at everyone else's mercy. They'd better be good at what they do, or you are in trouble.

All sat systems (in this country, at least) now have a 'hyperbaric lifeboat'. This is an 'if all else fails' route to take, and I for one would not fancy my chances in one in a howling gale, in huge seas, at night. It is basically a decompression chamber, attached to the ship's sat system, and kept at the diver's depth, squeezed into a lifeboat along with all the gas and life monitoring equipment required. It has to be capable of taking all the divers in sat into the floating chamber and away from the ship, to a distance of 100 metres away, within fifteen minutes.

I say I don't fancy it, but let's think about the alternative for a minute. You are in sat, the ship is sinking in a gale, and you have no hyperbaric lifeboat. They can't just let you out (the gas in your blood would fizz off like our coke bottle); you need three days at least to come up. So you would have to stay put. You would have to watch the last LST leave through the tiny portholes. You would then have to watch the water coming down the stairs and filling up the ship. The lights would go out, the life support systems would fail and then eventually you would make your way, aboard the sinking ship, to the seabed. You would no doubt survive this descent. Until, that is, you reach the depth that you are stored at, we said 100 metres. If the seabed is 120 metres, the doors would pop open as you arrived there and equalised with the water depth. Shall I go on?

DB29

This unfortunately has happened, during 'Typhoon Fred' in the South China Sea on 15 August 1991. Four divers were in sat and had been diving at around 380 feet (115 metres) on the McDermott barge the *DB29*. Because of the storm warning, emergency decompression had been started, and by time the barge went down the divers were only a tantalising 35 feet from the surface and safety. This was a huge barge, some 128 metres long, with a colossal crew of 195 men. Because of its size and construction, it had been labelled 'unsinkable', which history tells us is not a clever tag to attach to any ship. During the typhoon the barge took a battering and started to take on water after its ballast tanks were ruptured. To compound this already difficult situation, a ten-ton anchor buoy and pump broke loose on deck and rolled about, smashing holes in the pump room. The crew discovered eighteen feet of water in the ballast tank at one time, but the distress call was still not given.

The supervisors, realising the gravity of the situation and getting ready to abandon ship, opened the main vent valves, and the divers shut theirs, thus giving the guys on the inside control over their destiny. Three of the divers made an attempt to escape by venting off and exiting the trunking to where the bell should have been (it was off for maintenance) but unfortunately drowned. The other was still in his bunk bed when the subsequent sat dive was done on the barge, two months later.

Every sat diver has times to think about disasters that are out of his control. The *Seaforth Clansman*, after I had left her, ran aground in the Kyle of Lochalsh and all the divers in sat had to climb up into the long cold tunnel that leads to the lifeboat. They all squeezed themselves into the lifeboat chamber, the doors were closed, and the boat was actually launched and sailed around the loch for a few hours until the *Clansman* was re-floated.

In the North Sea once, I was in sat doing two-man lockouts

with John Boy Walton (the same man I'd been in the Navy with). We were aboard the *Aquamarine*, an ageing dive support vessel (DSV), and I was over on the jacket of the oil rig when the bell lost all power. Luckily the supervisor could still speak to me, and I could hear him. I went back to the bell and got myself back inside the now dark sphere. There was then a somewhat long, slow, juddery journey up to the surface as the surface crew recovered the bell with emergency air power. We thought, 'OK, they've had a power failure, no big deal, they can still lift us and lock us onto the system.' We got up to the moon pool and spent half an hour or so stuck at the air–sea interface, then another half an hour locking on to the system, an operation that usually takes a few minutes. Eventually we climbed down into the wet pot and I started having a shower, as it was pretty clear the dive had come to a premature end. JB went into our living chamber and was getting nowhere trying to order a pot-o-hot. Whilst showering, I had the feeling something was amiss. The water was not pouring straight down, and it was all gathering in one corner of the wet pot. JB could see out into the sat control area where all the gauges and valves work the system, and there were people running about all over the place looking very worried. Listening hard over the communications phone, JB heard Muddy Walters, the LST, saying, 'Do the divers know we've hit the jacket and are taking on water, though? Should I tell them?' Shit, we were listing because there was a hole in the side of the ship. We had to go all the way into Germany and dry dock. These are the uncomfortable times that you think a little too hard about while in sat.

The Merchant Royal Navy

Indecision is the key to flexibility.

Eventually I just scraped through my saturation mathematical, nightmarish exams with 71% out of a required 70. Thank God for cheating. I was then sent to join the Navy's only dedicated saturation diving ship to finish the diving part of the course. When I say it was the Navy's that's not exactly true. It wasn't like being in the Navy at all, and for good reason. The *Seaforth Clansman* was a civilian ship that the Navy hired, which was great for us. It wasn't painted grey, we had only one Naval diving officer on board, a few grown-ups, as in chiefs and POs, and between twelve and fifteen leading divers. Perfect! We had absolutely no Navy rules. The rest of the crew were civilian and worked for Seaforth. We had no seamanship duties other than looking after the diving system, we had stewards to serve us our meals, and we took the meaning of pirate rig to new levels. In short we never wore uniform. We did have Navy blue overalls, but we saw them as 'optional'.

I thoroughly enjoyed the rest of my sat course. It puts an entirely different slant on diving and it re-ignited my enthusiasm for getting wet, which had been waning somewhat over the years. You don't of course go straight into a deep saturation dive. By far the best way to learn is to do lots of short, shallow-water air lockouts. One lockout means leaving the bell to do a dive, hopefully accomplishing the task you have been set, coming back in again, and locking the bell back on to the system. Whilst doing these shallow bell dives, the course aims to put you through every single situation that might arise. If you were bellman, for instance, both divers would go out to the very end of their umbilicals and pretend to lose consciousness or get trapped. Your job would be to swim out and recover them both into the bell, get the bottom door closed and recover the bell, hopefully without losing too many men. This is not as easy as it may sound. To lift a man back into the bell wearing twin diving bailout bottles, weights and hard hat would be impossible without a pulley system to hoist him out of the water and into the bell. It would be made more difficult of course by your fellow divers tying a round turn and two half hitches in the umbilical so as to make your task twice as difficult as need be. Tim Horner's favourite trick.

Don't be a pleb

Good from afar, but far from good

When you have completed your sat course, every few months a new course would come along and have to do their lockouts to qualify for their sat tickets. To break the monotony of this, there are a few tricks you can play to liven up your day. One of our favourites was played on the supervisors. One of the POs was affectionately known as 'Pleb'. Pleb had a BO problem like no other. Now you get this in all walks of life, and unfortunately for most people they go through life not knowing that they stink. This was certainly not the case with Pleb. He was told, in no uncertain terms, by just about everyone, 'Pleb, you stink,' but he chose not to do anything about it. It could easily have been remedied with a shower and change of clothes but no, he was happy with the way he was. He would go to bed stinking and wake up stinking.

To lie festering in your own flea-ridden pit all night might be fine in your own eyes, but it is not fine to the man who has to come and give you your daily shake. To avoid going too near Pleb, some wag made a Pleb shake stick. This consisted of a very long broom handle. On one end was a diver's nose clip and a dust mask and on the other end were taped three aerosol cans, one can of deodorant, one can of air freshener, and one can of fly spray.

The idea being you put on the mask, put the nose clip over your nose and opened the door to his cabin, thus avoiding smelling his room. You then poked him vigorously around the ribcage area until all three of the aerosol cans went off, thus nullifying most of the nastiness. Even this embarrassing wake-up call was not enough to force him to wash. The aroma in his cabin was said to resemble 'skunk fart gorilla dog shit breath'.

I don't know if it was because of this treatment, but despite knowing everything there was to know about saturation, he was also a very nervous character, which would make him worry and sweat more and make his BO problem worse. In the forces, if you have a weakness you had best do your damnedest to keep it to yourself. If your peers find out what it is, it will be used against you relentlessly. As I said, Pleb was good at his job but he was easily rattled. The most nervous time for the supervisors like Pleb is when you open a new box of divers and they are doing their first shallow lockouts. Let's say Pleb puts in three divers, Tony (yours truly) as bellman, and two trainee divers – let's call them Tom and Dick. The trick would be to launch the bell and get both divers out under the ship somewhere working on a job. Tom would then secretly come up into the moon pool, take all his gear off and swap with another diver, Jack, who would then get into the water and finish Tom's dive. You can of course only do this when doing shallow lockouts, say down to ten metres. Then Dick would swap with Harry, who would finish the dive, until told to go back into the bell. All going well, eventually they would go back to Pleb to sign off their dive and he would have the wrong people standing in front of him. The dilemma on Pleb's face was always fascinating to watch. Pleb would look at me, Jack and Harry, all wet and just finished their dives, because he would invariably watch us exit the bell. He would be looking at his dive log stating that Tony, Tom and Dick had entered the water, but Tony, Jack and Harry had clearly finished the dive. Now he would have to decide quickly whether to say something or not. Sometimes he would, and everyone knew to look at him incredulously as if to say, 'Are you mad, what are you talking about? You've just seen us exit the bell.' On other occasions he could be seen rubbing furiously at all his official Navy diving documentation changing all the names. Sometimes we even changed the bellman. That would really test him.

The moon pool is basically a hole in the centre of the ship where the bell, ROVs (remotely operated vehicles) or anything can be launched. It is always situated higher than the ship's water line so you look down quite a way to the water. The area round the moon pool usually has a roof and is known as the bell hangar. The beauty of it is that you are in the safety and warmth of the ship no matter what the weather is doing outside. Some have covers and some don't, and in rough seas the water will come up over the sides of the MP and soak everyone trying to launch or recover the bell. The 'suck and blow' effect in heavy seas creates quite an air pressure. Around the hatchways it is quite formidable and can take your hard hat off.

Other jolly japes would involve opening a scuba bottle behind his main dive panel to pretend he had a serious gas leak. Another very cruel one was to attach a small air bottle to the bell depth gauge and pretend the bell was plummeting to the seabed as his gauge climbed from 30 to 50 to 70 metres. This was made all the more realistic by getting the bell team to scream and have them breathe a helium mixture to simulate a great depth, and the wrong gas.

We did sometimes have to do some work as well. Some of the work was training, as I've said, but occasionally a hot one would come in. Like the tragic loss of a Sikorsky S-61 helicopter just off of the Scilly Isles on 16 July 1983. The *Clansman* was tasked to recover the bodies (20 in all) and lift the helicopter. These people clearly had absolutely no warning of their impending disaster, as most were still wearing their seat belts when recovered. Only six survived, including the two pilots.

Phil Kearns was one of the divers, in his first ever sat outside of training. What a first dive it would turn out to be. Most divers will try to make light of doing stressful dives like this. Phil is a straight-up sort of bloke, you know where you are with him, he tells the truth. This is how he relates it:

It was the first time I had listened to the pre-dive bellman's checks outside of my training to be a saturation diver.

'Diver is dressed. His bailout is open on both bottles, closed at the hat, and his gauge shows 205 bars. He is breathing off the panel, upstream 14 bar, downstream 12 bar. His 18 is secured with the spider and the fittings have been checked. His umbilical is attached to the harness and he is wearing a knife. He's on reclaim, he has hot water and is ready to go.'

That was the signal that all was clear and I could enter the water via the open hatch in the bottom of the bell. At that point there was a mixture of excitement and trepidation. We were looking for a civilian helicopter with around 20 persons still believed to be onboard. It was my first sat dive and we were working in two-man teams, meaning that one diver would remain behind in the bell, to monitor life support systems and act as a standby diver in the event of an emergency.

On coming out of the diving bell I was relieved to see that the visibility was pretty good at maybe ten or fifteen metres. I was holding a hand-held locator which was tuned in to the frequency of the lost aircraft transponder fitted to the helicopter. The locator resembled an oversized hairdryer and at the back was a red light which flicked on and off. As the lost aircraft signal grew stronger, the light would stay on for longer until, when it was locked on, the light would be solid.

I looked around the area of the diving bell but could see nothing and so ventured out the forty metres to the end of my umbilical. The visibility being good, I was puzzled to see that as I walked about the seabed, the red light was beginning to flash more frequently, until suddenly, it turned to a solid red light. This confused me as I could see ahead and to my left and right but no wreckage could be seen. I turned round to check my umbilical and make sure it was leading directly towards the bell when, there it was! In all its horrific glory. Lying on its side and only a couple of metres away, with my diver's umbilical running hard up against it. I am not able to fully convey the shock I felt at that instant. Even though I knew what I was looking for and having only the year before come back from the Falklands conflict, where I had seen my share of dead bodies. At the best of times, there is something unnerving about seeing an aircraft or even a car lying on the seabed. It shouldn't be there – it doesn't look right!

At that point my breathing became so hard, I was hyperventilating, and consequently started to suck water in via the face seal. At the time I did not realise that this was the problem and so presumed the hat had failed in some way. The reason for the panic was partly due to the strong tide which was firmly pushing me towards the helicopter, which just at that moment, without being able to assess the situation, was the last place I wanted to be pushed up against.

I quickly started to make my way back to the bell as I was having a problem dealing with the amount of sea water I was taking in. On entering the bell and taking off my hat I thought 'We need another diver!' Unfortunately that was not to be. On checking the hat and finding nothing wrong with it, I was asked, well told, to go back out again with a hand-held video camera and survey the wreckage. On carrying out this task the first item I came across was a child's shoe lying on the seabed. This was not boding well. Unfortunately my umbilical was not long enough to survey completely around the wreckage, as in those days we were working on a four point anchorage mooring system. Moving the vessel and the bell closer to the location was going to take some time.

A couple of dives later it was decided that we would pick up the helicopter using the ship's crane. A chain was wrapped around what was left of the main rotor (the strongest point) and the wreckage would be lifted inboard. Prior to lifting the helicopter, the other diver and myself had to secure any openings to the wreckage using cargo nets and rope in order to prevent anything, or anyone, from falling out. That was not a pleasant task as several of the victims were in full view during this process. The Sikorsky was successfully raised and placed on the ship's deck, where the real work began.

Phil Kearns

We picked up two Sea King helicopters that year as well that had crashed into each other whilst on exercise from HMS *Ark Royal* in the fog, and a lot more jobs to boot. As a diver involved in all these recoveries, you can see why my trust in choppers is not the same as in fixed-wing aircraft.

On board, Tim and I had our windsurfers, canoes and water-based toys. Phil Kearns and Mac McNally had their dirt bikes, and wherever we went into harbour, the toys would come out. There was also a gym on board with weights and a running machine for us to keep fit. Unfortunately there was an emergency cut-off valve to the running machine just inside the door. The game was to wait till your buddy was running flat out on his final sprint, then reach around the door and hit the button. If your timing was spot on he would run full speed into the metal bulkhead as the treadmill did an emergency stop. Funny, yet painful, Tim!

You get paid extra to be a diver, and extra when you pass all your subsequent courses. Unfortunately, back then in 1983, we only got an extra £100 per day for being in sat. We were pretty well off compared to normal sailors, and were even better paid than junior officers.

One day the *Clansman* was alongside two destroyers at Fountain Lake jetty, in the dockyard at Portsmouth. Ginge Lincoln and I were loading up our short wave riding windsurf boards onto the roof of his brand new black 2.8 Capri, the car to have back then. An officer from one of the destroyers had been watching us as he loaded up his old battered Vauxhall Viva. He then said, 'Are you men in the Navy or what?'

'Yes sir,' I assured him as I climbed into the passenger seat of Ginge's car.

'What rank are you?'

'Leading Divers, sir.' We could see him considering this as he compared vehicles.

'Don't you ever wear uniforms?'

'Oh yes sir ... for weddings ... funerals ... things like that!' Clunk! In Ginge got and off we went, leaving the poor lieutenant staring back at the *Clansman*, which looked a bit like a Club 18–30 holiday boat, no doubt wondering where he had gone wrong.

Officer Darling

'I refuse to have a battle of wits with an unarmed person.'

Around this time, whilst doing my sat course, I was out having a drink with a few buddies. Tim Horner, a good friend of mine and fellow windsurfing fanatic, was in the Apsley pub in Portsmouth with us. All of a sudden he came running over all excited and says, 'Hey! Big T, guess who's over there!'

'I give up, who?'

'You'll never guess.'

'Right, I won't try then.'

'It's your mate, Officer Darling!'

I'd forgotten all about him over the years. Since leaving the *Kirkliston* all those years ago, my Navy reports had gone from Satisfactory (SAT) under him to Very Good Superior (VGS) ever since. Tim was positively revelling in the opportunity to see us 'have a chat', but I wasn't interested.

'Oh go on, just go and say hello!' No way.

I carried on having a drink with my back to where Tim said he was and forgot about it. Then there was a tap on my shoulder. I turned round and there was Tim, grinning like a Cheshire cat who's just won the lottery, with Darling at his side. Apparently he'd gone over to him and told him some cock and bull story about there being someone who used to serve under him, and had been influenced by him, couldn't wait to see him again, but was too shy ...

There was a stony silence as we just looked at each other. Tim looked back and forth at us both and realised this was a bit more serious than he thought.

'Aaargh ... Groom,' he eventually managed. Well at least he hadn't forgotten me, which was nice.

'Hello, Mummy,' I said. He visibly flinched at the nickname that he probably hoped had been long forgotten (Mummy

Darling). There was no way I could call him Sir, was there? He still didn't have my respect, you see. Even Tim was embarrassed now. He'll deny it, but it was one of the few times I ever saw him blush.

'What are you doing now?' he eventually asked.

'I'm on sat course.' Going OK now, Tim thought, they're getting on.

'And you?' I asked, not really interested.

'I'm in the mine warfare section,' he said. Then I heard myself say, 'Well – that's good, because you never were any good at diving, were you?'

Then it got silly, a slanging match, all very childish. I don't think he could work out if I was still in the Navy or not so I got away with murder. In the end Tim had to step in all embarrassed and break up our little 'tête-à-tête', as people were watching and moving away.

The end of the Andrew

The *Clansman* is about as good as it gets in the Andrew (Andrew comes from a particularly over-zealous press gang officer by the name of Andrew Miller). Like many other divers, I put in my eighteen months' notice to leave not long after I passed my sat course. I left the Navy on April Fools' Day 1985. Marie was staying with me at my house in Southsea the day I left. I had no idea how long it would take to leave or what the routine would be. I went into HMS *Nelson* at 08:30, handed in a few bits, like gas mask etc. and they said goodbye, you can go now. That was it, I was a free man. I went home to Marie and she was still in bed as it was only about 09:30. I stood at the end of the bed in my No. 8 uniform and said, 'That's it, I'm Mr Groom from now on,' then I ripped open my shirt à la Incredible Hulk, and jumped back into bed. Then it dawned on me I would have to find a job.

A few weeks later I took my old VW camper van all the way to Aberdeen with me, but this time I was without toys. This time I had a suit and three mates with me. For the first time in my life I went job hunting. It was a hideous experience and I wouldn't wish it on my worst enemy. Rejection is a tough one. Getting past the 'battleaxes' that ran the front desks was hard enough, then you could look forward to the rejection of the next defender of the company, the offshore personnel manager. Tim Horner and I got through the first line of defence once at one company's headquarters in Aberdeen. We then made it to the divers personnel head honcho, the hirer and firer. The man who could send you offshore or not. We stood patiently in front of him in our suits, with our CVs, and waited, and waited. Nothing. He didn't even look up. Eventually I coughed and said 'Errrr excuse me, we were sent up to see you, we're both ex-Navy and have our sat tickets and are looking for work. Have you got anything?' Nothing. He still didn't look up.

Eventually he said, 'Leave 'em there,' and tapped his desk. We put our CVs there, and waited, then turned and left. Demoralising is not the word for it.

About ten years later this ignorant git lost his job and I met him whilst flying out on a chopper. He had fallen to the level of security guard at the helicopter check-in. Tim and I walked over and had a word in his ear. Not gloating, you understand, just a reminder. He didn't recognise us of course, because he had never had the decency to look up. The Lord does work in mysterious ways, and I believe brought us together so that we could have this chat, and I could point out the error of his being so rude to one so young and impressionable. I also have a very long memory.

It was not what you knew, but who you knew, and it's the same now. If your name fits, you'll work. Most divers have a name to remember. Like Wiggy, Diggers, Cheesy, Piggy Trotter, Buster Crabb, Knobby, Creature Foot, Biffa, Basher, Dusty, Ginge, Crazy Craig, Reckless Eric, Pincher, Shady Lane, Ned Kelly, Smudga, Back Draft, Thrush (irritating c***!). I could go on.

Hardly anyone is called David or Peter. Or Tarquin.

Well, we knew people, divers that had been out a while and could help you get your foot in the door. We bumped into Jock (Alan) Stewart, the ex-CD2 bike squasher, whilst up there and he took us around Aberdeen and introduced us to the people to know.

The next day (thanks to Jock) we were in past the witch at the Oceaneering desk, and the following week we were on our way to Madagascar (via Mombassa, where we were forced to wait for two weeks for the jack-up rig to be towed nearby), for two months' diving in the infamous Madagascan straits. I say infamous because that's where they filmed *Blue Water White Death*; it's one of the world's best breeding grounds for great white sharks.

Our first day on board the rig support boat brought us down to earth. I was leaning over the front of the bridge and looking down into the hold where all sorts of drilling equipment was being unloaded to go up to the rig. One of the crew was stood between a fork lift truck and the ship's steel bulkhead. He attached the crane to the lifting straps, and gave the 'come up' signal to the crane driver. The problem was that the crane was not directly above the forklift truck, it was over at an angle. When the forklift truck came off the deck, gravity made it swing underneath the overhanging crane, which just happened to be where the crewman was stood. It only moved about two feet, but right under our gaze it squashed the life out of the poor man. We hadn't even been on board a day and already we'd had our first death. The following day the chief engineer was flown off after losing four fingers in a fan. This was the sort of place where one had to look after oneself.

Nigeria! Oh you must go there!

Not long after Madagascar, I unfortunately ended up in Nigeria. Wow! What a place. If you've been there, you don't need to hear any of what I am about to say. If you haven't, well I would say you haven't lived, but then that would be suggesting you should go there, and I wouldn't want you to do that. No offence to the Nigerians meant. I met some nice people while I was there, but the country itself is mad. I don't know how I found myself out there really, by accident I guess.

I was lucky in that I spent a lot of my time living offshore. We used to have a rota, where each of the divers would have one week ashore, out of his two months offshore. You would look forward to your week ashore for the beer, and the change, but you also knew you were taking your life in your hands.

The night fighters (hookers) were something else. They did not know the meaning of 'No' or 'Just leave me alone' or 'Bugger off I'm not interested!' You could be stood at the bar ordering a beer, and one would come up behind you and thrust her hands around your waist and straight down the front of your underpants. You have not paid her, or even made eye contact with her. The idea being to get you going, if you catch my drift, then get some naira off of you, and finish the entertainment with a bang!

One of the divers who died out there, so shall remain nameless, used to be able to keep a straight face while these night fighters would stroke his manhood and he would look to all intents and purposes like he was ignoring them; he could even manage to look bored. His game would be to 'go off' without paying, and the girls would go ballistic. All he would say while they were hitting him was, 'I didn't ask you to do it.' I had a different ploy.

Ray Padderson, a supervisor out there, and I would pretend to be gay. I don't mean kissing and holding hands, or even acting up gay. We would just try to convince the wildest ones that we were together, an item, if you like. I found if you could make them laugh, they were generally alright with you. We would make up long stories about being in love and our flat in Kensington, our dog called Liberace and how we would take it in turns to be the boy and the girl.

'Mr Tony, then you say dat you chop de hammer?' [eat the hammer: give felatio]

'We are in love,' I would say.

They would roll about laughing, knowing full well we were lying, but eventually they would leave us alone and find some other Wyeebo (white monkey) to attack.

Another one of the staff there couldn't get enough of these crazy women. I would walk into the heavily defended staff house and he would be in the shower with two or three of them. He was like a manic kid with a new toy. I would listen to him go through the bartering with them and wonder what on earth for. He would not pay them for sex first, or to have a shower with him, or a hand shandy, because, he explained, if you gave them the money they would do a runner. They, on the other hand, would not want to go to bed with a client in case they didn't get paid. These negotiations would go on most of the evening, and he loved it. He had their lingo off to a tee. 'I will balance you 50 naira.' Which, depending on which side you were on, was always too much, or not enough.

It was a pastime to be savoured and enjoyed by him. One of his games was to try and pay them without giving them any money. One of his favourites was a famous brand shampoo (Timotei). Yes, he would try to buy women with shampoo, and on some occasions he would get away with it. Hence why he always seemed to be in the shower with one, on a bad night, and a few if he'd been more successful. He would have one stroking his long hair, which he would just use conditioner on, and tell them his hair used to be a tight Afro curl like theirs. They, too, could have long soft, straight hair like him, if they just used this miracle shampoo. 'Oh yes, all the models in England use this shampoo, it costs £100 a bottle.' He used to call it something like 'hot semen shampoo'.

They would often reply, 'You are a cunny man.' A trickster, a cunning man. If that didn't work, he would have a bag full of the cheapest Casio watches in his suitcase. It would take him an hour to show them everything that they did, alarm clock, light, timer, etc. Most of them would be convinced by the end of his display that they were buying (with the use of their bodies) one of the finest watches in the world. He should have been a salesman.

Lots of them have been there too long and get used to how dangerous it is. We were in an expats' watering hole in Warri once called 'Auntie's Kitchen' and one diver who worked for a rival company started taking the mick out of one of the night fighters. Not really a good idea: they are streetwise beyond anything we know. I was unfortunately stood with this nutcase when he sort of made a pretend lunge at her, as if to hit her.

'If you do that again, I am going to beat you!' she said in a matter-of-fact way.

He didn't heed her warning and thought it was a laugh, so made to hit her over the head with his bottle. She threw him to the floor, and in one swift movement disarmed him and smashed the bottle of Star beer on the wall and had it pressed to his temple, before he even had a chance to look up. We all stepped back, then forwards as we tried to calm her. She could have killed him and he wouldn't have had an inkling what had happened. The thing that amazed me was that he went home with her afterwards. Another one gone bush. There are a lot of men out there that never make it home. If they do, it's too late.

On the same night we got a lift with one of the Bristow's (helicopter providers to the oil industry) pilots to the BP compound. Our taxi driver ordered us to 'Climb that moto!' (get in the car). We would have one driver all night, as the stories were rife of getting a taxi and being taken for a ride in more ways than one. They would take you home, but via some of their mates, who would by all accounts accompany you to your dwelling, then relieve you of all your valuables. All the expats live in these huge high-walled compounds protected by armed guards and dogs. On the way over there the pilot was telling us how they were always down on numbers. He told us they had started getting pilots in from Canada as they couldn't get enough from the UK. One pilot who had only been in Nigeria a week had already been 'casivaced' back home to Canada. Foolishly I asked why, thinking it would be malaria or some such ailment. 'He was wearing a bimetal Rolex in a cab home one night and as he stopped at a junction someone ran up and machete'd off his hand and ran off with hand and watch.' Our driver had been listening to this and immediately ordered us to 'Roll up de glass!' (close the window).

I did two months on and a month off for a couple of years in Nigeria and considered myself a seasoned traveller by the end of it. I thought I was unshockable, I'd seen it all. You have never seen it all out there, something will make you say 'NO!' Like public hangings, which, being public, you could take a picnic to and watch if you so wished. I never saw the value in going to see someone die, but I spoke to expats there who had stumbled upon a public hanging.

I was reading the Warri local rag one day and read about a couple who were sentenced to death in northern Nigeria under the Sharia or Islamic law, which considers sex out of wedlock a crime punishable by death. They had both admitted the offence, so were sentenced to death – by stoning. The courts can, and do, also order amputations. One man in the paper had exactly that punishment dished out, for stealing a cow.

The art to travelling, I found, was to look like a student trekker with not a bean or anything worth stealing, never to look lost or confused, always to look confident, and to say no to everyone. I was once in Lagos airport waiting for that little bit of England (a British Caledonian 600-seater Jumbo) to take me home on my well-deserved month off. All these seats would always be taken; they were referred to as 'cattle class'. It was not unheard of to take six hours to get through the mind-boggling bureaucracy and queues in the airport. I had only been there an hour so hadn't even broken through the first barrier of checking in. The check-in hall was a myriad of confusion, bartering, arguing, fighting and fending off sellers of everything from yams to car tyres. The heat? Well, the heat would be bad enough on its own, but throw in all those bodies and it was sometimes unbearable.

I would carry no hold luggage any more, not only to save time, but also because it would invariably get ransacked on the way into the country, and for good measure on the way out as well. I now travelled with just a rucksack on my back that had my bare essentials in it, dive log, change of clothes, bottled water, toilet paper (not provided anywhere) and a few dash items. 'Dash' is a word you soon get used to in Nigeria. It is said that one of the few medals they have in the Olympics, is the 100 Naira Dash. It basically means 'bribe me.' This could be any thing from fishing hooks to money, to shampoo!

It was around 7 p.m. as I stood in the never-ending check-in queue, when the already dim fluorescent lighting flickered, then gave up, and went out. It started as a murmur of discontent, then moved to panic, then quickly built into a cacophony of screams and shouting. It wasn't just dim, it was dark, very dark. I shuffled my way along to the nearest wall, took my rucksack off and sat on it with my hands out in front of me. At least that way my bag and my back were protected. Slowly my eyes became accustomed to the darkness and I chose to just ride this one out and sit and take in the entertainment. I could make out the procession I had just left, where many Nigerians, on their way to London, were unwilling to give up their place in this long queue just to save their lives or their bags. All the oil workers, like myself, chose self-preservation and life first, and took off.

This was a perfect opportunity for all the dodgy sellers, robbers and vagabonds who permanently patrolled the airport to ply their trade. I saw one body jump over the check-in desk, grab a suitcase off the now stationary carousel and be gone out the front of the airport in seconds. This seemed to be the cue for a few more to have a go at something.

By now there was a bit of dull light from the road outside

creeping its way into the interior of the departure hall. I watched another man who looked like a taxi driver, an opportunist who had seen what was going on from the outside, run in and try to grab a very old wealthy-looking Nigerian lady's hand luggage. She was having none of it. She thrashed him around the head with her bag and whenever he put his arm up to protect himself, she hit him with her other hand, all the time screaming at the top of her voice. Eventually the Army, who were responsible for the airport's non-existent security, came to her aid. I could just see the taxi driver as he tried to make good his escape, without the lady's bag, back to his cab. He was running towards the doors when one of the Army guys opened fire. The noise and flash of a gunshot inside the packed terminal instantly stopped all the screaming and shouting, as people seemingly well versed in the art of gunfire and self-preservation threw themselves to the floor. There was a moment's silence, then the noise resumed, at an even greater decibel level. The taxi man escaped outside, but when he got there his cab wasn't where he had left it – he had been robbed. I saw him look quickly up and down the road, but it had gone, so he took off on foot.

I was wondering about the wisdom of opening fire inside a crowded terminal building when the lights came on. Instead of bringing calm, this caused a whole new set of alarms and accusations. People had used this unexpected opportunity to queue-jump, steal boarding passes, and even place their bags on the carousel behind the desks without having them checked in. The two soldiers who had fired the shot came back into the terminal building and tried to trace where the bullet had gone. There was a man sitting on the window ledge with blood coming from his hand. It would appear that the stray bullet had taken this young man's middle finger clean off. The two soldiers asked him some very accusing questions and then arrested him. The poor bloke from what I could see had been nowhere near the attempted bag snatch, but he was guilty – of being shot, at least!

When we eventually tried to board the plane there were a lot more than 600 people at the departures gate. The bright spark who had stolen the boarding passes had been selling them all around the airport. There were at least 800, maybe even 1,000 people trying to board the plane. It was utter pandemonium.

The first gin and tonic with ice and lemon when you're safely aboard in your air-conditioned seat is utter heaven. The stewardesses are very forgiving when you first board; they can see, from the sweating and stressed passengers, and know from first-hand experience, what you have just been through. I had a drink with one of the Jumbo pilots once in the hotel the night before departure and asked him about Jumbos. We were both legless at the time, so most of his stories escape me now. I do remember asking him about what would happen if he lost an engine or two on our flight home tomorrow. One, or even two, he could manage, apparently.

'What about all four then?' I said.

'With no engines,' he said, shaking his head, 'the Boeing 747 has the gliding characteristics of a safe ... hic ... with an anvil tied to it!'

Well – that put my mind at rest, flying in a safe with a pilot that had been at the bar till 4 a.m with me. They don't do that now, of course.

Arguably the scariest flights are the internal ones. I was almost arrested at Warri once waiting for one such flight, for taking pictures of secret air force buildings. It was a derelict wooden shack outside the airport with 'Warri International Hilton Hotel' written in huge letters above what looked like a double garage that had an annex of a garden shed nailed to the side. I don't think it was a part of the Hilton chain at all really. I thought it would be a good photo to tell my Mum that I'd stayed at the Hilton. The security officer, sporting an ancient bolt-action rifle of sorts, wasn't happy until I pulled out my film to expose it to light, obviously making it useless. He couldn't see the offending image (having not been developed) so insisted on keeping it and promised to get it developed, and if there were no national secrets on it, I could have it back when I returned. Really he was after my camera.

Warri airport was littered with old Russian 1950s Mig fighter jets, all in various states of disrepair. Most had either bits missing or bullet holes in them. The internal flights were usually little twin-engined passenger planes that couldn't get a licence to fly anywhere else in the world. After my brush with Mister Sensitive, we boarded flight 'one' to Lagos and were each given our meal of a boiled sweet, with the sugar missing, complete with the attitude 'suck on that!' There was no door between passengers and cockpit so we could see all that was going on. All I could see was a white arm in the pilot's seat and a black arm in the co-pilot's seat. The captain, if you could call him that, would move all the switches and tell the co-pilot what he was doing.

'My god, this is on the job training!' I thought. We revved up and tore off up the runway. We just about got airborne when the co-pilot reached over to flick a switch. The pilot smacked his hand, just like a naughty child gets a slap, as if to say, 'Don't touch that!' or 'Not that one stupid!' Then they both fell about laughing. I, on the other hand, was worried for my life again. This seemed to happen most days when ashore in Nigeria.

Offshore, the diving was pretty simple, really. We lived on a Nigerian oil tanker, with Nigerian crew, run by the Italians, with English divers working for the French diving company, Comex. Never mind the diving, the fishing was just incredible. There were groupers under the floating oil buoys the size and weight of a fully grown fat man, but we would let them be. They were like old men of the sea and they gave you a look when diving in amongst them that said, 'Leave me alone, and I'll let you live.' We would fish nearly every day for barracuda, red snapper and dorado. We would then gut and clean them, freeze them, and sell them to the provisions boat that came out to the oil fields once a week. This money was really only used as beer funds.

Whenever we saw fishing boats out at sea we would take a boat out and barter with them. We would swap cigarettes and porn for baiting fish on the passing boats. It was all one big swapping session between people at sea for long periods.

When the rumour got around that one of us was going home you would accumulate friends at an alarming rate on board the tanker and the oil rigs.

'Mr Tony, my friend, how is you today?'

'Fine. Sorry, who are you?'

'Ha ha Mr Tony you are my friend. Ah wus wonderin Mr Tony if you could bring for me somting from England.'

'What?'

'Ah need four tyres for my caa, and some football boots size of meh please!'

'Car tyres?'

'Yes please, tank you Mr Tony, ah dat would be most kand of you if you could bring dem to meh.'

'What car is it?'

'It was a green one'

'Was a green one?

'Yes'

'OK. And what size boots are you?'

'White boots, the size of meh please.'

'OK, white boots, but what size?'

'Dis is my size [pointing to feet]. Ah need two.'

'Yeh, I know you need two mate, I would need the monies first.'

'But Mr Tony, ah don't have any moneies, ah haf a sik mudda and two wives and many childrens.'

'So, to recap, you want four tyres for a car that was green, its colour now undetermined, and two white football boots, the size of you, and you want me to carry all this back for you, but you don't want to give me any money for this?'

'Yes'

'NO!'

This would happen even at the airport. People you had never seen before would ask you to bring them an English bank account when you come back, or perhaps an English job!

When I got ashore I would always have between 20 and 30 thousand naira (about £130) spare on me but, because the currency is in such huge demand around the world (not), you are not allowed to take much of it out of the country. So I found a good cause for mine.

There was a beggar not far from the Comex house called Kehinde (meaning, the one who lagged behind). He was about ten years old and got around on a piece of flat wood that had what looked like a supermarket trolley wheel on each corner. He would drag himself around the roads with his knarled, hard-skinned knuckles, begging for change from all the cars 'caught in the go slow', the never-ending traffic jams, or at the never-working traffic lights. He must have had one of the hardest lives of anyone I've ever met, but he was always smiling and happy whenever I saw him. His face would light up when he saw me because I would go to great lengths to take him 'stuff'. If I saw him on my week ashore I would give him what I could. This was not like giving money to a bloke outside your local supermarket, then seeing him later on drunk on cheap wine or beer. This lad needed the money to live. His clothes were in tatters, there were always sores on the stumps where his legs should have been, he was always hungry, and he seemed to live permanently under an old roadside newspaper barrow.

I once took my life in my hands and went to a birthday bash at the Shell Oil compound. Going through the streets of Warri in a taxi that night, as always, there were lots of neighbourhood watch schemes in evidence. Not the 'hood watch' you would see in, say, Knightsbridge or Chichester, where just a sign will do. These neighbours would put up road blocks and search every car, saying they were looking for robbers. That was OK I guess, but the machetes and World War 1 bolt-action weapons on show made me twitchy. We were coming home about 1 a.m. and I looked out for Kehinde. One of the Nigerian staff had been in the car with me and told me off because I 'dash him too much dat one', as he put it – I had given him too much. He was convinced that he was really a crook and ripping me off, but there he was, under his barrow. He was sound asleep under a pile of old newspapers and boxes, with an excuse for a dog on top of him.

One time whilst going offshore along 'his' road, I noticed a dead body in the central reservation. My driver told me that no one would claim or report these bodies because you would then be responsible for it and have to pay. On my way home two months later, what was left of it was still there in the same place.

I would always have a chat with Kehinde and give him T shirts, fruit, toys, even antibiotics, and most importantly food.

'Mr Tony, Mr Tony, you have been swimmin unda da sea again eh? Mr Tony, you go home to England yes?'

He always asked that for good reason. If I was on my way to the airport to go home I would give him all the naira I had made out of my fishing and bartering escapades, plus a bit more. I would tell him to make it last because I wouldn't see him for a month or sometimes three if I missed him on my way back. I was always amazed when he was still alive. He would scoot between cars and taxis, and even under lorries and buses. Having no legs, his spine would bend at an impossible angle, enabling him to 'go low'. When I left for the last time, I gave him my rucksack and every goody I had accumulated over my two years there. I often wonder if he made it to teenager and beyond.

It don't come cheap sonny

Q: You're a diver? Wow! What do you dive for?
A: Money.

After my time in Nigeria I came home and tried to add some normality to my life and convince myself and others I hadn't 'gone bush'. I got myself a job in the North Sea doing deep air work.

Hmmm, not good, that. It's not good for your body, certainly not your joints. After a month of deep stuff my knees would be painful and clicking like mad. It was time to get some sat. The money was better and believe it or not it is better for you. With the deep air 'minibell' system you were decompressing every day. With sat, you decompress once, nice and slowly, right at the end. Oh, and the money was better.

I worked for a company called Ocean Technical Services doing these deep air dips. There were something like fifteen divers on each shift, two shifts on board and two shifts at home. The boat would have to come into port every two weeks or so for a crew change, which was an excuse for a 'run ashore'. There were some great lads on there and some crazy ones. There was an Irish lad called Eamon Masterson, a real gent, and we would laugh all through our night shift, usually at other people's expense. He would say 'To be sure Tony, you're a fonny man, so ya are, a fonny man!' There was Phil Floppy Bottom, Biffa, Barry Porter and his baby daughter, Where's Morris, and many more, known collectively as Fairfield's Fuckwits. Mike Fairfield was known as Grumpy, being the superintendent. He was grumpy, though. He once ran me off the boat for drinking offshore! I mean, how grumpy is that?

Phil Roberts was a funny man. You should have one like him on every team for the things to go wrong to. If someone lost a camera, it would be him; if someone missed the ship, it would be him. He had some great stories of the catastrophes that he had somehow survived.

Whilst working for OTS in the yard, he had to load up a flatbed lorry with two brand new 120-metre air umbilicals. Driving down the road he noticed a few drivers flashing him and wondered what was wrong with them. He started to slow down on the motorway and a huge eighteen-wheeler went screaming by. The lorry had picked up an unwanted protuberance round its rear wheel. As it overtook him, Phil noticed that the speeding lorry had a newish-looking umbilical wrapping itself around its axle. It looked remarkably like an older version of the one he had just coiled up on the back of his truck. When he eventually stopped on the hard shoulder he couldn't even safely get out of the cab because of the speed the umbilical was unravelling itself off his truck. When he arrived at the dive boat, it was not what the supervisors were expecting when they saw the state of the 'new' umbilical.

Another time he flew into London from a holiday in Spain, loaded up his car with his girlfriend and shot off to a party that night in London somewhere. Whilst there, he needed something from his briefcase but couldn't find it. Then that horrible feeling washed over him, that feeling that he had left it at the airport. He drove furiously back to Gatwick and couldn't find where he'd come in, so went to information. 'I flew in earlier this evening from Malaga and I think I left my briefcase here somewhere. Where would I have come through?' The assistant tapped away on her computer console and said, 'Well not here, sir, all the flights from Malaga come into Heathrow.' Panic again. He had gone back to the wrong airport. Then the long drive over to the busiest airport in the world. Upon arrival at arrivals, he couldn't get anywhere near where he had loaded his car up. There were Police and Army all over the place. He parked up and took the long walk of shame up to an Army bomb disposal man looking at a briefcase though binoculars and in the process of directing a mechanised tracked bomb disposal robot. He then had to walk out the hundreds of metres on his own and pick it up. 'Yeah, ... it's mine ... sorry!'

If you want to get out of 'air' and into saturation it's going to cost you a few bob (unless, like me, you got the Navy to pay you extra to do it). You would need to have done your air course first, cheap at around the 5–7 grand mark. The sat course itself back in the late 1980s would probably cost you around £10,000. The thing is, you have no guarantee of getting any work after completing it. You're caught in the typical catch-22. The diving companies and clients want experienced saturation divers, you can't get experience until you get in the bin, and you can't get in the bin until you have more experience.

On top of your sat course you would also need your underwater inspection engineer's ticket. This went by the catchy name of CSWIP (Certification Scheme for Welding and Inspection Personnel). Or as the widely worn T shirt says, 'Complete Swindle With Inflated Prices'. It would cost you around £4,000 even back then to get to the mother of all qualifications, the coveted 3.2.U (after having first done the 3.1.U).

They were never quite finished with you, though. Unlike a driving test, or almost any qualification you may gain throughout your life, the CSWIP was different in that every two and a half years you would miraculously forget everything you had learnt. The governing body then would relieve you of around £900 for a day, to remind you of everything you had learnt those few short months before. I remember going to Fort Bovisand in Plymouth one year for my two-and-a half-year review, feeling quite sorry for myself that it was going to cost me the best part of a grand including digs, to relearn something I already knew inside out. But I began to feel a lot better when I learned of the plight of two Australians over for their examinations. These two Aussies had travelled from the other side of the world to do their refresher and it was foggy. That's it, it was too foggy to go out for the short diving side of the test. It was just tough that they had return flights booked the next day. They would still have to pay their £900. I remember leaving the office as the exchange became quite heated.

You would also need an offshore survival course, and again that's about a grand. And a diver medic's ticket, which would probably cost you a little more than £1,000. This was a pretty intensive ten-day course and one of the few where you felt you'd really got your money's worth. You would, and still do, stand in on real operations in theatre, stitch patients, stand in on autopsies etc. My first day in hospital training, I helped stitch a lad's face back together after he'd been slashed across the temple and cheek with a Stanley knife (box cutter). This was in Liverpool's Fazakerley Hospital, where above the accident and emergency corridor it read 'ELM STREET', as in Nightmare on. The thing about this poor lad's injuries was that his attacker had put two blades in the knife, and jammed a penny between the two razor-sharp edges, so as to cause a tramline-effect cut that was almost impossible to make a neat job of. There are some nice people out there.

So it is quite possible to spend 20-odd thousand pounds on diving courses and certificates and never get any work. Even then, you may do it and find you can't stand being locked up with eight strangers you wouldn't choose to spend the day with, never mind a month. For these reasons I don't think the North Sea will ever be inundated with divers.

Piper Alpha

I was offshore on the *Sea Oyster* at the time of the Piper Alpha incident, alongside a busy oil and gas producing platform just like the PA. Work didn't even slow down to take in what had happened. The oil industry is like that. Nothing gets in the way of getting the black stuff out of the ground. Nothing.

As I've said before in these pages, your safety as a diver depends on lots of other people doing their job. This is not only true for divers, of course, as proved that fateful day when 167 men lost their lives. I only identify sat divers as a special case because of their inability to help themselves. Had they been under the Piper that night with the *Tharos* alongside and she caught fire, or had the bell been in the water, they could not take the choice to jump over the side, or abandon ship. They would have to take what was dealt out to them, sinking, fire, or, in the case of the bell occupants, probably dying of hypothermia on the seabed. Whatever fate may have dealt them, they could have done nothing about it. All because someone with nothing whatsoever to do with them, someone on a different platform, indeed, failed in their duty to act safely. The Piper disaster, and it was a disaster in the true sense of the word, was caused by bad practice. Basically, someone removed a relief valve from a compressor, and didn't tell the right people not to use it. That in turn brought out all the flaws in the old-fashioned equipment and unsafe working practices that had accumulated on there over the years.

Another thing that exacerbated the problems on the Piper Alpha that day was that the fire pumps were set to manual, not automatic. Usually on oil rigs the pumps are only set to manual when the divers are diving near to them, because of the danger of divers getting sucked into the massive intakes underwater. The Piper Alpha's routine was whenever diving was taking place anywhere, the fire pumps were set to manual, no matter that the diving could be well away from the intakes.

The personnel on the Piper were trained to collect at designated lifeboat stations in the event of any disaster, but the fire prevented many of them doing so. So many men did the next best thing in their eyes, and that was to collect in the fire-proofed accommodation block. The smoke was quickly so bad it prevented any landings of helicopters, and started to fill the personnel block with black acrid smoke.

Around this time, two brave men donned their fire-fighting equipment and tried to reach the diesel pump machinery room below to activate the fire-fighting system. They didn't make it and were never seen again.

When the Piper Alpha exploded on 6 July 1988, there was an air diving team from the company 2W (Wharton Williams) down below the main decks, and they had a man actually in the water. It took them approximately three minutes to get him back to the surface. When the poor man arrived on the surface there were flames licking all around the 68-foot level. The first explosion shook the dive shack so hard, the dive supervisor was knocked off his chair, the shelves emptied, and the ceiling came down.

I think it's fair to say that most days in the summer there was a team of divers in sat and diving on either the Piper Alpha or the Claymore platforms. At about 21:50 on 6 July, by pure chance, there were men in sat on the *Tharos*, but not in the bell, and the semi-sub was about 100 metres away when the first explosion shook everyone out of their normal, somewhat casual routines.

The *Tharos* was a massive 29,000-ton semi-submersible multi-task vessel. It looked more like an oil rig than a dive support vessel. It sat on eight huge legs that disappeared below the surface, and they in turn were connected to two colossal underwater buoyancy chambers, which, as the name suggests, could be filled either with water, to lower it, or with air, to raise it. She had her own propulsion system in the way of four large thrusters controlled by 'dynamic positioning' computers, so she could manoeuvre anywhere, in any weather, albeit at a ladylike and sedate pace. She also carried very powerful, multiple fire-fighting water cannons, and hotel accommodation for an extra 225 men, on top of the average 80 crew. The *Tharos* could raise herself up and drop a bridge across to the Piper and men could walk across and use her accommodation or cinemas and 22-bed hospital. Whenever any serious amount of work was happening on the overcrowded and somewhat out-of-date Piper Alpha, this was where the overflow of men would live.

The saturation system on there in 1988 was the Rolls Royce of diving, it was the place to be. The bell was like no other. It was, in effect, two bells, stuck one on top of each other. It didn't just dangle under its mother ship as all other systems did at the time, and indeed do now. This was a flying bell. The top sphere was at atmospheric pressure and sported a large Perspex dome through which the pilot and co-pilot would drive and 'fly' the bell around the North Sea using its powerful thrusters. Underneath this was a conventional bell with sat divers in, who would wait for the pilots to fly the bell under the Piper and then use its powerful grab claw to clamp onto either one of the legs or a purpose-made 'totem pole'. Once secure, the divers could exit the bell and go to work, making full use of the bell's onboard hydraulics for tools, and her brilliant floodlights etc. Perfect luxury diving that was way ahead of its time.

A good friend of mine, Grahame Murr, had just left the Navy at the time and had stumbled into the job of co-pilot on the *Tharos*. This was his first job out of the mob, and little did he know it would never get any better. This is what he told me about that night.

> Having been on days, 6 a.m. to 6 p.m., I was just crawling into my bunk at about 21:50 when I heard the first explosion. It sounded like someone had dropped a heavy load on deck as the *Tharos* vibrated and shook. I barely had time to utter, 'What the?' when every alarm on board went off.
>
> As me and the other off-duty divers arrived on deck, the *Tharos* was moving in closer to try and bring her massive fire-fighting cannons to bear on what was a huge fire. There was already black smoke billowing out of the centre of the platform. Even at this early stage we could see people jumping from the deck of the Piper, which was around 200ft above the waves.
>
> The superintendent gathered us all together and said something along the lines of 'Look lads, I know the stewards are meant to be the main first-aiders on board, but it looks like there could be a few fatalities. I would like you lot to take charge of any bodies there might be and take them up to the sick bay and the cabins along that deck.'

The *Lowland Cavalier*, a typical rig support vessel, had been involved in pipeline trenching duties and was about 25 metres away at the time of the first explosion. Unsurprisingly, she was the first to report the explosions. She and other boats like the *Silver Pit* launched their smaller Fast Rescue Craft to pick up the jumpers, dead or alive, and take them to the *Tharos*. Two of their crew were later killed during one of the explosions whilst looking for survivors.

Well, the bodies did indeed start to arrive, first two or three and then the trickle turned into a flood. Pretty soon the sick bay was full and we had to start putting them into people's cabins five at a time. Lots of men that survived the first explosion and the jumping were now swimming across to the *Tharos* and climbing the stairs up the huge legs. At one time while we were talking about what to do on deck, a dishevelled-looking, wet young lad in T shirt and jogging bottoms walked over to us.

'Where have you come from?' I asked.

'Oh, I've just swum from over there!' he said, pointing to the Piper.

A lot of these survivors had all sorts of injuries, not just burns, but lots of broken limbs and other injuries associated with hitting the water from such a great height.

We were quite close to the Piper by now but couldn't get too close because of the huge fireballs that kept coming at us from the centre of the rig.

One thing I'll never forget as long as I live, is when I was looking up at the Piper and could see men climbing the two huge drilling towers to get away from the heat. Maybe they just couldn't bring themselves to jump from such a height, I don't know. It was probably around 20 minutes to half an hour after the first explosion, and we were looking up at these men, when the biggest explosion of all took place, accompanied by a massive fireball. We on the *Tharos* were 75 metres or so away and we all had to run for cover. When the fireball cleared and we could look back, my eyes were drawn to the drilling towers and there was nobody left, they had all just, gone!

The fire and the noise was now incredible. The high-pressure gas was making the noise and it was being fed by the now burst oil pipelines.

I remember one time making my way to the bottom of the leg on the *Tharos*, keeping an eye out for any more that had made the swim across.

Eventually, when I was back on deck, we were all given a patient each to look after, to try and make them more comfortable you know? I paired off with this bloke who had horrible burns on his hands and face, knees and feet. He had a bandage around his head and proceeded to tell me his story. We chatted most of the night, and he was really shaken up. He was telling me how they were all told to muster in the galley. The smoke in there was so bad he eventually said to himself,

I have got to get out of this myself. He told me he knew there was a corridor at the back of the galley that led to the outside. By now the whole rig was beginning to shake and move. He started along the corridor on his hands and knees because the smoke was so thick, the only place he could breathe was with his face on the deck. The metal floor was so hot he was leaving the skin of his hands and knees and feet behind. As he was crawling in the black smoke he said he thought he would never get to the end of the corridor, when all of a sudden the rig moved and the door at the end swung open to give him a glimpse of the outside world. He said that was his cue, he went as fast as he could go out of the door and straight over the side, he jumped without even thinking about it. I don't remember his name and have never seen him since.

The choppers were flying all the next day, taking these survivors ashore and to hospital. They changed all of the *Tharos* crew fairly quickly as well as some were pretty shaken up. I myself drank a little too much after the event, this resulted in a serious injury to my legs and kept me off work for months.

Grahame Murr

Only 62 crewmembers survived out of 229 on board that day; 167 perished.

Health and Safety avert your eyes

Before relating his side of the Piper Alpha story, Grahame was telling me a dit (Navalese for a funny story) about someone he had just been in sat with. This guy had previously been in sat in India. There is no safety out there. That may seem like a bold statement to make, but from all the lads that go there, usually when they are starting out, it would appear to be the case. You have to be your own safety officer and decide how far to go, before you say 'no, I'm going home.' These guys by all accounts were on a fairly decent boat and everything was fine, apart from maybe all the attention they had been receiving from the sharks.

It was hot and the water was so warm, even at 180 metres,

that they just dived in overalls. Nothing particularly wrong with that, but instead of doing six- or eight-hour lockouts, like we do over here, they could, and do, go on a lot longer. I have heard of there being only four men in a tiny sat system, but the client still requires 24-hour diving coverage. So, if you want a long and decent time off, you have to do at least twelve hours in the bell and the water. These bell runs frequently go on for eighteen hours. This lad was telling Grahame that on a particularly long run, they would clip sandwiches and cold drinks to the clump weight wire and it would then run down to the bell. The clump weight is a huge weight that hangs on two wires under the bell to stop the bell from spinning and twisting. The bellman would hear the 'delivery' hit the bell and would then take a deep breath and duck dive out of the bell to retrieve them. You see why I don't think the HSE would like this system? I can't see it catching on in the North Sea.

The bellman on this occasion left the bell just as the diver was on his way back. They didn't see each other. So imagine the diver's surprise when he arrives back at the bell, sticks his hat in to find the bellman ... gone! But that is nothing to the bellman's surprise and, yes, panic to find that the only entrance to safety, and another breath, is blocked by a diver.

The bellman apparently gave the diver in the trunking a sharp tug on the leg, as in, 'Get the f**k out of the trunking, or I'm going to die!' As indeed we all would. The diver, already in a state of shock and confusion, thought he had been attacked by a shark, or something had attacked his leg. He screamed, and tried his utmost to get into the safety of the bell and away from whatever was biting him. The now gagging bellman was determined to get in there first, as his needs were undoubtedly the greater. The supervisor would of course be woken from a slumber with his diver screaming blue murder, and not being able to get a response from his bellman. I think Grahame said the practice has now been terminated.

Sat rat

You have to be a bit individual, a bit unique, if you like, to do any amount of time in sat. The money can draw you in, but if you get to need it too much, you are in trouble, because then you can't say no. The taxman knows how much you are on, so you do more days in the bin to keep paying him, so your tax bill goes up. Two hundred days a year in sat is perfectly possible, and in 2007 it would earn you around 200 grand. Not difficult maths that, even for me. Of course you don't get to keep all that, but you will start out with good intentions to save, and put 40% away, etc – but then comes the big house, the kids, the car. It's easy to lose it all.

I've been in the bin with all sorts or characters, and there are a few wild ones out there. There's a guy I was with on one of my first courses in the Navy who's been a 200-days-a-year man almost since he left the mob in the early 80s, and he still hasn't really got ahead. When I worked with him last he would do a full sat, 28 days, then go on deck to either supervise or be standby diver for about two weeks, then go straight back in for 28! That's only because of the new-ish ruling that stops you doing back-to-back sats. What used to happen is he, or they, would come out, make a phone call home to someone who could still remember them, then go straight back in.

These are not the norm, but nor are they the exception. On every boat, and in every company, there is a group of guys who are the 'superstars', as they are called by their fellow sat rats. I've dived with lots of these men. Some were good, some were brilliant, and some just lived on their past reputation.

Some are so full of their own self-importance that they would find it hard to speak to us normal sat divers. One lad I did a sat with on the *Orelia* was so far up himself he hardly spoke to me or my other bell partner in the whole 28 days. That is quite an achievement when you live that close to two people.

There are that many divorced or thrice-married men out there it is amazing. They all have their own stories to tell, how they've made and lost a fortune over the years and how 'the bitch took everything whilst I was offshore!'

One lad I spoke to went home and got the usual frosty reception from the wife. He said he'd been getting that for a while so didn't think much about it. He said he went up to the bedroom after getting home and sat down to take off his shoes. Hanging out of the bed was one of his ties, so thinking it was just untidy he grabbed hold of it, but it was stuck. Following it back, he found it was tied to the bed post. He told me he untied it, and just sat there thinking. Then he checked the other end of the bed, and guess what? There was another of his ties tied to the bed. Believe it or not, there were ties on all the corners of the bed. He couldn't understand what had happened, so went to ask his wife if she could shed any light on the mystery. She proceeded to tell him all about her bondage sessions with her lover. Well, the poor man was so shocked, they had a bit of a row, and he said he did what all men do after an argument, he went down the pub. After a few beers, life didn't seem so bad and having been away for so long he went home with the idea of talking his wife into a bit of bondage. Well, if it was what she was into, why not, what was the worst that could happen? The worst that could happen was she could say no. She did. She apparently only did sordid and disgusting things like that with her boyfriend, not her husband!

There are many slightly mad characters out there and many of them great friends. Another Jock lad is now in his fifties and still doing it. He's been bankrupt three times to my knowledge, married for a day (they split up at the reception), run off the job for failing a drugs test, and knew all the hookers in Aberdeen by their *real* first names. I was in with him once and he would have me in stitches with his tales of woe. He was just coming out of his second bankruptcy, and was now allowed to get a mortgage again. So, whilst we were in, he bought a flat, out of the paper, like you or I would buy a table lamp or a book. Most people might consider going to see it first. Not him. 'Oh I know the area, that'll be fine.' He never gave a damn that all his money was gone again, and would tell me he would usually do 200 quid *a day* on clothes! One time, he decided to be good and chop his seven series BMW in for a five series. Now that is dedication to saving! Anyway, he part-exchanged his big beamer for the smaller one, and drove around in it for a matter of days – but decided it wasn't as nice as his old bigger car. So, seeing his old baby still on the garage forecourt, he went in and bought it back, losing the best part of three grand in the process.

The shit list

Every day draws us closer to death, the poor man's friend.

The hierarchy of the offshore world goes something like this:

(1) Ex-military or frustrated Scooby Doo, which is military parlance for any scuba diver. Then you generally go to civil engineering diving, which is inshore small engineering type stuff. We've all done it and it's horrible. You will find yourself in pitch-black dockyards, in the cooling tanks of a nuclear power station or halfway up some sewage outfall pipe. The money is garbage and so is the diving. If you don't go the civil route, you could try going to the far-flung reaches of the Earth and get work with virtually no qualifications or experience. Nearly everyone has started in one of these two ways, hence my Nigerian and other African

SO I DO A BIT OF DIVING......
I'VE GOT AN AIR COURSE.. SO WHAT!!
I DON'T NEED IT!

experiences. Other people go to India, a good way to take your life in your hands, some go out to the Far East, or the Middle East. One thing you will notice whilst travelling around the world looking for diving work is that hardly any of it is somewhere nice. Why is that? Why is it that oil is not in the Caribbean, Jamaica for instance, the Mediterranean or Miami? You will find plenty north of Scotland, in West Africa, or in nice places like Iraq or the Siberian parts of Russia. If you phone up and get a job too easily, say in Angola, beware, there is a reason for this, which will only become apparent when you get there. And then it's too late.

(2) Then you will usually scrape one or two air diving jobs somewhere decent like the North Sea. Whilst there, you will notice the 'sat rats' getting a lot more money for fewer days away. Eventually most people think, 'I could do that, lying in your bunk all day, having LSTs run around for you.'

So I DO A BIT OF INSPECTION.....
I PAY FOR A CSWIP...... WHO CARES......
I CAN STOP ANY TIME I LIKE!

(3) After a few trips or maybe even years as an air diver, one of the superintendents will have a word in your shell-like if he thinks you could cut the mustard. 'Get your sat ticket, sonny, and I'll definitely put you in the bin.' Watch out, they do lie! You then have to weigh up whether to believe him and go and blow your ten grand on a sat course.

So I HAVE A SAT COURSE, I DO A BIT
OF DIVING....... SO WHAT ....
I CAN GIVE IT UP ANY TIME I LIKE!!!

(4) You haven't cracked it even then. Your sat course could well be a backward step in that you have to go traipsing off abroad again to get your first sat. Eventually coming back it could well be a case of who you know again and whether your superintendent was lying to you. Either that, or he's moved to another company so can't help you anyway. If

he is still around, and you get your first sat, congratulations, that's where the money is, saturation in the North Sea. As long as your first sat is quickly followed by your second, that is, which will of course depend on how your first one went. With the money comes the best safety in the world, so once you've dived there, you rarely go anywhere else. How long you keep this up is of course entirely up to you. I have been in sat at the age of 45 and been the new boy, a young lad, the whippersnapper. There are many sat divers over 50. To have someone under 30 is really quite rare.

(5) After as many years as you can take, locked up in a chamber you can barely take three paces in, for a month at a time, with people you may well love or hate, you may decide to hang up your fins. If you do, and you've been in the game as long as most of us, it is the only thing that you know how to do. Which of course means spending more money, to become a supervisor.

(6) This again could be a backward step. You may have to go air supervising before you can go sat supervising. It is absolutely amazing how quickly a newly qualified supervisor can forget what it's like to be in the water. Within a month of supervising they will be bollocking 'you' for moaning about the raging tide, not getting out of the bell quick enough, getting lost in shit visibility, losing tools, etc, when only a matter of weeks earlier it would have been him doing exactly the same thing.

(7) From sat supervisor you might aspire to reach the dizzying heights of Night Superintendent, and then on to Supreme Being, otherwise known as Superintendent. The only way then is to sell your soul to Beelzebub and become Operations Manager. NEVER!!

North Sea sat

I got my first sat in the North Sea with a company called Svitzer. They were a Danish outfit with just the one ageing sat boat, the *Maersk Defender*, but it was a steady month on month off for most of the year. The first one you feel the heat a bit, as in the pressure is on for every minute you are in the water. This was a cheap boat, say 40–50 grand a day to hire. This was in the early 1990s. Nowadays a modern boat will cost you 100–150 thousand pounds a day plus! You may have about 150 men, and in reality their job is to get just two men on a single bell system to work.

You do rush everything, you have to. The client who is paying this money will have a representative on board all the

time making sure his pound goes as far as possible. As the bell is leaving the ship, you in the bell as 'diver one' will be getting your hat on. As soon as the bottom door of the bell is open, you have to drop out and be off to work. Time is money. This attitude is easing a bit as the powers that be realise that rushing is often the slower way of doing something. The rushed jobs invariably have to be done again. I have leapt out of the bell like a young gazelle, dashed over to the job, and then waited for five hours for the rig above me to operate one valve. 'Yep, it moved.' OK, that's it, back to the bell. Yes, you can fall asleep underwater in these situations. You find yourself a comfy spot, ask the supervisor to turn your hot water up a degree, then ZZZZZZ.

The hot water suit is a diver's godsend. The umbilical down to the bell and on to the diver carries an insulated pipe. Through this is pumped hot water, sometimes close to boiling at the surface. It will cool considerably on its long journey to say 220 metres (700 feet). As bellman, one of your jobs is to connect the diver's hot water pipe to a push fitting at his hip just before he drops through the bell's mini moon pool. This fitting has a simple quarter-turn valve on it: open it and all the water goes to you, close it and you ditch it into the sea. You, at the end of your 70 metre umbilical, can then regulate how much HW you have. The HW suits are nothing more than a neoprene set of overalls with sprinkler pipes inside that transport the water to the limbs and torso. It is open at the cuffs, ankles and neck and has a zip up the front. All the excess just spills out of these openings. Sat diving in the northern hemisphere would be impossible with out it. 'Number ones' is therefore not a problem in a hot water suit: it's gone before you can say aaaahh. Number twos, well that is another story. It is possible, and it involves a quiet five minutes to undo your bailout, unzip, squat and scoop. Need I say more? After years of sat and six hours at a time in the water, you will get caught short. It ain't pretty but that's the reality.

Other times they will say go back to the bell and you can't believe six hours is up because you've been so busy. You will then get into the bell, remove your hat and drink a litre or two of water down in one. Six hours of often very physical work without a drink is hard. Around three hours into the dive they will ask, 'Do you want to go back to the bell for a drink?' You are allowed to, but the unwritten rule is to say, 'No, I'm fine thanks.' Lying through your back teeth.

Other times you will just reach the job and something will go wrong, and you are straight back wondering what it is. My buddy Mick O'Leary had this happen in September 1996.

O'Leary's luck

He was working on the *Wellservicer*, a modern 12,000-ton, single, sometimes double-bell DSV in the North Sea. This was the state-of-the-art diving ship at the time – it has since been modernised and is still going now. She can have eighteen guys in sat, two bells, ROVs, the lot. She also has two 35-ton 'heave compensated' cranes that are a joy to work with. I've been on there, and the surface may be lowering a huge 65-ton pipeline end manifold (PLEM) down to you on the seabed, for instance. Contrary to popular opinion, the visibility in the North Sea can be brilliant, by which I mean blue water and for some summer months up to 100 metres. They would generally lower it well away from you and swing it to you, or nowadays even watch it with an ROV until it is near the seabed, before letting you anywhere near it. Like I've said, the pressure is always on to get the job done, so the weather isn't always perfect – in fact, it is rarely even approaching flat up north. My point is, you will see heavy stuff come down and it will be bouncing around all over the place. Don't forget, if the sea is rough, and you lift something from a high crane, the arm of the crane increases the arc and so worsens the momentum. With a big load such as this, you would have the two cranes attached and they will be working as one. As soon as you can see the load and it's maybe behaving wildly on the end of a 200-metre wire, they will 'engage heave comp' and as if by magic the weather effect has gone. The load will be almost rock-steady. The million-pound-plus computer systems on the cranes can pay out and heave in exactly to the tune of the ship and the uneven swell. How this works, I have no idea.

So, she is a complicated ship, and when complicated things go wrong, it will invariably take longer to fix, because you don't know where to start. One of Sod's laws is if it's all going to go wrong, it will go wrong in the worst possible situation. So what is the worst time, the worst place to be, for the whole well-thought-out process to collapse? What about at night, in the early part of a bell run, inside an anchor pattern?

The Balmoral is a huge 34,000-ton semi-sub drilling/production rig. When it starts drilling, or in this case actually producing oil, it will not want to move, not at any cost, so it will lay about eight massive anchors, and each link on these cables is about the size of a small car, weighing in at around a ton per link. If you come into contact with one of these cables, you will lose, especially if either you or the cable is moving.

It went somewhat wrong on 29 September that year for Mick. He had just left the bell and dropped to the bottom at a little over 150 metres (500 feet) and walked the 35 or so metres to the gravity base. These bases hold the pipelines in place that go from the wellhead, taking the oil up to the semi-sub.

He had just made it to the job and placed his hand on the gravity base when his world collapsed around him. His hat light went off, his comms went dead, his gas stopped being reclaimed and his hot water went off. The only thing he still had was gas. Nothing he'd done wrong, nothing anyone he knew had done wrong. I know I keep harping on about this but again there was nothing in the world he could do about the events that unfolded. He would never meet the man who installed the software that wasn't up to the job of running the boat. Or the man who designed it, or the man who should have spotted the flaw in the system. The 200 or so men on the *Wellservicer* at the time would just moan that their light or computers had gone off. Not if you're at the end of your umbilical and you lose everything. You are in a world of shit, and it is only going to get worse.

This is what Mick told me:

I had not left the bell long as diver 2 and the first I knew anything was wrong was when everything went black, and it is black that deep with no artificial light. I had just touched the GB and a perfectly normal day was turned upside down. I turned to look back along my umbilical and there was nothing. No bell lights, no ROV lights and no other diver's lights, my partner was also out here with me somewhere. It was deadly quiet with nothing in the way of instructions or updates coming through the comms. I grabbed my umbilical and started feeling my way along it to the only sanctuary there might be, the bell. On my way back the battery-operated emergency comms came on, so at least I could talk with the supervisor. Within seconds I knew we were in big trouble, I was at 500-odd foot with no hot water. At this depth, that is a situation that cannot go on for more than a minute or so.

It had all happened so quickly after I had locked out that the bell-man wasn't even ready for my return.

As bellman, when the two divers go out, you will set your bell for all possible eventualities. You will first pay out their umbilicals until told they are on the job. You will prepare for maybe having to go out and rescue someone, or the divers losing surface gas and you having to put them on bell gas, any number of things. When your divers are set and happily at work, you would then drop out a ladder and flood the bell up a bit so that anyone coming back could swim in quite a way, then climb the last bit.

> When I arrived back at the bell it wasn't lit with its usual mega flood lights – it was dark, inside and out. Another very disturbing thing was that I could tell it was moving horizontally through the water. That can only mean the ship has lost all power as well, no thrusters, no control. I didn't have the time or the light to see where the Balmoral's massive mooring chains were, but I knew they were close.
>
> The bell wasn't flooded and the ladder wasn't out, but I swam in and climbed into the bell without even slowing down. Twin bailouts on, a suit full of now cold water and covered in tools, no one was going to stop me getting in that bell. I was already freezing cold.

Instead of having a backup for the backup, which is the norm on a diving vessel of this size, all the backup power supplies and spare generators tripped at once, which can't, in theory, happen, but it had. The vessel and the dangling bell were now at the mercy of the wind and tide. Whichever was the stronger, that was the way she would drift.

When all is going well, the bellman will get one diver back at a time and neatly rack the 70-odd metres of unwieldy diver's umbilical in as small a coil as possible, but all was not going well.

> I don't know how I did it to this day but l positively leapt into the bell, took off my bailout bottles and my own hat and just threw it on the untidy pile of my umbilical. I then helped Glynn the bellman pull like mad on Duncan's umbilical. It was pretty eerie with just a hanging torch in there and one bloke missing. It was around this time we heard and felt an enormous crash that knocked us both off our feet. It was metal on metal. This should never happen in a bell. We had just made contact

with the biggest anchor chain you will ever see in you life. I knew then that if our two-inch bell lift wire had a fight with those links, we were going to lose.

The bell then started jumping over the links. Crashing its way along, one link after the next. What in effect was happening now was the bell, with us in it, was catching on the cable, acting as an anchor to try and stop the 12,000 ton *Wellservicer* moving through the water.

On the *Wellservicer*, in dive control, you can see where the bell wire goes down through the moon pool, and the wire was jumping and snatching around as it leapt over and along each and every link. The supervisors and standby divers would have seen all this going on and would have had the vision of getting back the bell wire and umbilical with nothing on the end of it.

All this time, in the bell, we could hear Pete Waller, the supervisor, trying to get a response out of Duncan. He was saying 'Duncan ... Duncan ... Speak to me Duncan ... Duncan ...'

Nothing! There was no response. At one point the bell tipped a long way over and begun filling up as something on the bell caught on the huge links. Glynn and I exchanged a brief look at each other. We had to get this bell door shut, now, but Duncan's umbilical was still hanging out through the bottom. I thought he'd been crushed or at least badly injured. He may have been dead already. Would we have to cut his umbilical with a hacksaw, which I could see out of the corner of my eye and was within easy reach, to save our own lives? The thought crossed my mind. Then the next thing that I thought was even scarier, I thought, 'Fuck it, if he goes, we all go!' With that Glynn and I redoubled our efforts to pull on Duncan's umbilical and get him back into the bell, dead or alive.

Eventually we saw that tantalising glimpse of a yellow diver's helmet. He was under the bell and still just moving but he was so cold and weak he couldn't help himself. He told me later that he just felt like going to sleep, which is the classic symptom of the onset of hypothermia. We dropped the ladder back in the water, which again put us in a very dodgy position, not being able to close the bottom door in the event of being severed from the ship, or the bell turning over. We just man-handled him into the bell.

We were by no means out of the woods yet, and we would need, and get, a huge stroke of luck to rescue us from this situation.

On board the *Welly* was a Sun Oil representative, Martin Dane, who had been in a similar situation in 1978 on board a DSV called the *Star Canopus.*

She'd had a DP (dynamic positioning – computer-controlled thrusters that keep the ship on station) runoff in a force 8 gale and crashed into the Beryl Alpha platform with a bell dangling underneath. It was a two-man bell run and the diver was successfully recovered into the bell and they managed to close the bottom door. The *Canopus* then gained some semblance of control with the use of her main engines. The ship then started recovering the bell, but when it got to the 30-metre level it became entangled in one of the Beryl's anchor cables, just as was happening here to Mick and his team. The lift wire and umbilical parted and the bell sank to the seabed. The bell was not located for around four hours, and when it was later recovered both the divers had died, from either hypothermia or drowning, according to the post mortem.

> Martin the rep, no doubt with the memory of what had happened in 78, knew exactly where the bell was in relation to where the anchors were, and took it upon himself to do something about it. He got on his hand-held radio and called up the Balmoral and told them to drop anchor number 8.

Now you can't really do that. Can you imagine the required amount of paperwork and permissions to be able to drop the anchor cable from a floating oil rig that is actually producing oil? In the normal working way of offshore life, it would take many meetings and many signatures and agreeing parties, before they would be able to take that action.

As luck would have it, the engineer on the Balmoral was in the winch room doing his hourly checks and did as he was asked. He shouldn't have, and Martin shouldn't have asked him to. Maybe it was the desperate tone in Martin's voice. Whatever it was, they broke protocol and did it.

We were of course unaware of this at the time as we were intent on getting Duncan in and the bottom door shut. We were still grinding and scraping our way up the huge cable links. I could tell we were getting shallower as well because the bell was getting warmer and misty and my ears were constantly popping.

As the colossal weight of the hundreds of links were slackened from the Balmoral, they for a while draped themselves over the top or our bell. The bell groaned and tipped up alarmingly to its steepest angle yet. We were now about waist-deep in water. Then, as quickly as it happened, the cable must have slipped off the top of the bell and sunk to the seabed and we righted ourselves.

We then eventually got Duncan in and the door shut and immediately blew the bell down deeper than the seabed, to over 160 metres (530 feet), so if we were severed from the ship we would still be sealed.

Roughly 15 minutes after it had all begun, power was restored, the lights in the bell came on and things were looking up. Pete Waller had been brilliant throughout, he was talking to us the whole time and that helped.

When we were eventually locked back on to the system and I got down to the wet pot I just ditched my hat liner and personal stuff into the corner and said 'Fuck that, I won't be doing that again.'

The thing that sticks with me most, is in that moment, when it was dark and eerie and quiet, not like how it should be, that is when you get that sensation that it's all over and you're about to die, you don't just give up. Self-preservation kicks in and you fight back.

At the end of the sat we went for a well-earned drink in one of the divers' watering holes in Aberdeen. A superintendent I know called John Segar walked in and said, 'Hello Mick, how you doing, what boat are you on?' I said the *Welly*. He said, 'I've just been on the Balmoral and I'll tell you what, the boys in the bell on there were lucky to get away with what they did!'

I said, 'Tell me about it, I was in the bell!' He then proceeded to tell me about the engineer who just happened to be by the winches and did as he was 'asked' and dropped the anchor cable.

If it wasn't weird enough bumping into John, no more than 10 minutes later Martin Dane walked in. I just introduced myself and said, 'Martin, I think I owe you a beer!'

Mick O'Leary

Oceaneering

Undoubtedly my happiest years in the diving industry were with Oceaneering aboard the DSV *Stephaniturm*. We had the best crew and divers anywhere. There were no superstars, no big-wigs, we all got on and we laughed. We laughed a lot.

The *Stephaniturm* herself had her brief spell of fame, when she embarked on probably the most dangerous sat dive ever, in the freezing Barents Sea north of Russia. She was the sat boat that recovered the millions of pounds' worth of gold from deep inside the wreck of HMS *Edinburgh* in 1981. The team, led and organised by Keith Jessop, recovered 431 gold bars worth then around £100,000 per bar, and only had to leave the last 34 bars on board because of the horrendous weather and injuries to divers. They encountered hurricane-force winds, scalding from the hot water system, ear infections and dislocated shoulders among other problems. They were at the very edge of what it was possible to dive to with the equipment they had. Their saturation chambers were stored at 750 feet (230 metres) and the divers worked at 800 feet (eight days' decompression back to the surface). One diver, an ex-CD called Scouse Cooper, even perforated an eardrum when in the bell because it was at times rising and falling ten metres in the heavy seas.

Never mind all that, how exciting is that for a job? Recovering Russian solid gold bars from an English WWII cruiser, on a no-cure, no-pay contract. Bars that were mysteriously loaded on board the warship in the dead of night on 25 April 1942. The ship's company had no idea what was going on when both watches were rudely woken by the arrival alongside of two barges bristling with armed Red Army soldiers. The duty watch then had to go onto the deck in a snow storm in Murmansk and haul very heavy ammunition cases up to the flight deck. Their suspicions were aroused even more when they somehow 'accidentally on purpose', if I know matelots, managed to drop one on the deck and it spilled its beautiful cargo for all to see.

Unfortunately these jobs don't come around very often, in fact once in a lifetime to be precise, and if you don't get on it, that's it, tough, there won't be another, and there hasn't been one since.

Christ! It's Shady

One of the supervisors I worked with was a God botherer by the name of Shady. We would have fascinating debates during the long night shift, lasting hours, about religion and Bible-related subjects. He would try and convert me to the church, and I would try and convert him to atheism. He let slip one day that he had punched his neighbour in the stomach whilst rowing with him.

'What happened to turning the other cheek?' I would ask. 'Which bits of the Bible do you follow, or do you just pick the bits you like?'

I'd read a good Patrick O'Brian once and said to Shady, 'Here, you should read this, it's a good book.'

'I've only got one book,' he said.

'Well here you go, you can have two now.'

'The Bible is the only book I need,' he said.

'Oh, I've read that, he gets killed in the end doesn't he?'

'Yes!' he said, 'but he came back to life again!'

'Oh,' I said, 'I haven't read that one, is that ... The Bible Two?'

Another subject was the whole 'How can God have built the Earth in seven days?' It has been proved (to me at least) that the earth evolved over about 4.6 billion years after the big bang. Our discussions covered such subjects as 'Why is there no mention of the dinosaurs in the Bible?' I even brought him back a Greenpeace T shirt with the life of the earth on the front. It went along the lines of ...

Planet Earth is 4,600 million years old

If we condense this inconceivable time-span into an understandable concept, we can liken Earth to a person of 46 years of age.

Nothing is known about the first seven years of this person's life. Whilst only scattered information exists about the middle span, we know that only at the age of 42 did the Earth begin to flower.

Dinosaurs and the great reptiles did not appear until one year ago, when the planet was 45. Mammals arrived only eight months ago. In the middle of last week man-like apes evolved into ape-like men, and at the weekend the last ice age enveloped the Earth.

Modern man has been around for four hours. During the last hour man discovered agriculture. The industrial revolution began a minute ago. During those 60 seconds of biological time, Modern Man has made a rubbish tip of Paradise.

We have caused the extinction of many thousands of animal species, ransacked the planet for fuel and now stand gloating over this meteoric rise, on the brink of the final mass extinction. We have almost destroyed this oasis of life in the solar system.

Not seven days, Shady! The other thing I recently found that I wrote for him was this:

In the beginning ...

On the First Day, God shouted, 'Let there be light!' And sure enough, as He flipped the switch, there it was, a ray of light on diver one's hat, so wide and so bright that everything upon which it shone was illuminated. Which was a lot then, as fishing with factory ships had yet to be invented.

On the Second Day, God tired of shit underwater visibility, and set about cleaning it up. As He swam the Ocean, creating the perfect vis, He became weary. God seemed to have trouble doing the miles, so looked down at his sandaled feet and recoiled with disgust. 'I'm wearing sandals!' He yelled, to no one in particular, 'All I own are sandals, and they're gross to wear and no good for swimming.' So God took drastic action. He looked at the first fish He had been creating, and copied his own work to make himself some Flippers. Later to be called Fins.

With the wave of a finger and the wink of an eye, God created the atmosphere, which made sunlight. God's sandals finally dried, and God again was comfortable when upon the land.

On the Third Day, God had another radical idea. 'I'll break up the only dry ground, Pangaea.' He had never been quite happy with its chunky design, the globe looked lopsided. He thought to himself, anyway, one Ocean was not a very inventive idea. Why not have loads, say ... five? Yes five was a good number – and what about some slightly smaller Oceans? Yes, and I shall call them Seas. Then divers will have many places to plunge. I'll do it, He thought, no one can stop me, because I haven't invented anyone yet. And just like that He did it, and He clapped His mighty hands together and wiped them clean for emphasis. 'There. Done. Finished,' He said. 'Can't take it back now.'

He looked where Pangaea once had once lain, and then He looked at it now in seven pieces strewn across the Oceans. A moment passed as God surveyed his handiwork, and God grew visibly contemplative. And then another instant passed, and God began to vex. He chewed His beard. He bit His lip. He furrowed His brow. He became restless. 'Oh, dear,' He said. 'I hope that wasn't a blunder.'

On the Fourth Day, God created the moon and the sun as a gift to the tides and currents around the world. That'll keep the beggars guessing, He thought. Even with tide tables, they'll never know what is going to happen one day after the next. And God laughed, and thunder echoed around the globe. Dark clouds gathered in only minutes, howling gales of wind appeared as if from nowhere, when all else suggested it would be a good day for diving.

On the Fifth Day, boredom plagued The Almighty, and He stocked the rivers, lands and oceans with animals and wondrous creatures, so that men and women (when He got round to inventing them) would want to venture below them and float upon them. They would wonder at the beauty He had created. The colours and variations in species, He decided, would be endless. Whenever a human thought he had seen them all, He would add another, yes, that is how it would be. He had decided it. 'I might even dive myself,' He said unto Himself. Then stopped Himself. Talking to oneself is not cool, He thought.

On the Sixth Day, God cast His eyes toward Earth – yes he might call it that. His first idea, 'Portsmouth', didn't quite have the right ring about it. Then God created people, because people at least will do stuff, like dive, to see what He, the Almighty, had created down there.

'Do stuff then!' He said. 'Go on.' And the divers didn't only dive, they quickly sinned. They sinned a lot, in every kind of way, some unnatural, and God knew it was unnatural, having also invented 'nature' once on his day off. Some things they did were even ungodly! Oh even God Himself was sometimes embarrassed with the things that they did. But he had to laugh. Well? If you can't laugh?

On the Seventh Day, God did not rest, as many scholars have long suggested. It was the Sabbath, so He took the morning off to take a dip and afterwards appeared to be knackered. It wasn't as easy as he thought it might be, this diving lark. He then dived again and again, until, by Jove, He seemed to be getting it. Until he got a bend.

Then he rested.

To dive or not to dive?

Compared to a lot of youngsters, I was lucky. Not because I had a privileged background or upbringing, far from it, but because from a young age I knew where I wanted to be, where I wanted to spend my working life. I'm not saying I knew all along I was going to dive, but I did know my fascination with the wet stuff was not the norm. When I was four or five my Nan was the first to comment on my infatuation with the sea. Apparently she said to my mum, 'Look at that boy, he just stares at the water for ever.'

It is the most abundant element on the planet, and I find it mesmerising. I still find myself staring at rivers or a tranquil sea and wondering what is just below. I don't know what I expect to find. I've yet to find my piece of treasure or *objet d'art*, but I'm always looking. I haven't given up. In fact my latest acquisition is an underwater metal detector. Well, you never know!

In preparation for writing this book I broke out all of my diving logbooks, knowing full well I might depress myself. I started adding up my hours in a saturation chamber. Over a fifteen-year sat diving career, I did around 900 days, or two and a half years, in chambers around the world. You can get less than that for armed robbery. That is 21,600 hours in a chamber you cannot walk more that two or three paces in, with usually seven other men who would, on occasion, smell and sound like feeding time at the monkey sanctuary. Take away say 100 days for decompression and bad weather. That leaves us with 19,200 hours or 800 working days. Say an average diving day of six hours, and that gives us 4,800 hours or 200 full 24-hour days actually in the water. Six and a half months either blowing bubbles or in the bell. Six and a half months wet. Now I'm by no means the most prolific diver; there are guys out there that either can't get enough diving, or money, and they would blow my hours out of the water. None of those hours, days, weeks and months even include the thousands of air and mixed-gas dives I've done. Not that I wish I had done more. Not at all, that is quite enough for me. In all that time, have I ever found a gold coin or a virgin wreck?

Wars have started and finished while I've been in sat and I've not even known about them. Television in sat is a relatively new phenomenon in the diving game and newspapers are an extravagance that get devoured, if they ever make it into the chambers.

I've found a fridge in the middle of the Irish Sea that I was told, whilst donning my gear, was 'definitely, 100% absolutely certainly a mine'. I've found Spitfire engines in Greece, a Jeep in the middle of the South Pacific, and fishermen and pilots still inside their craft, but I've not really found what I was looking for as a child. That bit of mystery is still there, maybe because I don't know what it looks like. I know I'm in the wrong industry. You are, after all, unlikely to find anything mysterious in the oil industry or hunting for mines.

From the age of fifteen at nautical boarding school onwards, I have spent most of my life on, in or under the sea, and I feel very privileged for that. For a couple of years when I wasn't working much, I did as much sailing as I could and got my yachtmaster's certificate. Then, with my mate Tim, we bought an old 45-foot wooden gaff ketch. We sailed her back from Denmark, which was a story in itself, and I lived on board for a couple of years. So you can't keep me away from it, even when I'm away from it. It drives my son Harvey mad that whenever we go somewhere, even around Portsmouth, we have to go via the sea. 'Why are we going this way, dad?' and I tell him, 'Because the tide went out last night, and I always have to check that it has come back in again.'

Have I enjoyed all of it? Well, no, not all of it. I've had some pretty close calls in my time. I've had a heavy metal plate fall on me on a wreck dive in Guernsey (thanks for reminding me, Ian), taking my mask off at 42 metres. I've had a 40-ton load land on my umbilical and bury it into the seabed so I couldn't get back to the bell. I've had two bends that I know of and friends say the pressures have had an effect on my psyche. I've nearly drowned. I've been frozen to hypothermic levels and lost consciousness in the process. Not to mention watching bullets coming my way, and being bombed for weeks on end. But I survived. Usually because I was with an oppo, a shipmate, a buddy, a chum. If they did nothing to actually save my life, they were there with me, always dependable, steady, their actions always professionally predictable. Men I would trust my life to, and frequently did.

I can tell you something for absolutely sure, though. Apart from one or two cases, you could not surround yourself with a better bunch of friends. These men are the salt of the earth. They are a bunch of piss-heads also, by and large. I know that may be tarring a lot of men with the same brush but, there you have it. They may drink too much, and fight, and can sometimes be brash and too loud, but that I believe is a result of what they do. A lot are really loners and prefer their own company. This may have a lot to do with the need for self-preservation in their day-to-day diving life.

They are also the most reliable, professional, easygoing, big-hearted, trustworthy, down-to-earth, friendly bunch of men in any industry, you will ever meet. A lot of groups may claim that, but I am right. It may be the training we all go through; it may be the small, close-knit feeling that develops; at the risk of sounding over-romantic, it may even be the affinity we all have with the sea. We love it, and respect it, because if you get blasé with it, you will lose your life. The proof is in the many epitaphs.

So to all those that I've known in the business, thank you for the laughs, and to all those that didn't quite make it this far, thank you, it was good while it lasted though, wasn't it?

Alright Deeps?

Deep sea diver, sports car driver
I've been deeper than you've ever been.
My first stop was a hundred metres
You wouldn't believe the things that I've seen.
Deep diving whales and a sleeping shark
People say 'Diving! That's no walk in the park!'

I've dived the deep blue
I've dived the black black.
I've dived deep air
I've dived deep sat.

A month at a time locked up in a chamber!
They have to pay well
To keep down your anger.
Aberdeen, Africa, India and the Middle East.
The time away, I'll miss the least.

Thirty years plus I've had in this business,
Thanks to plenty of friends,
And a patient misses.
What else could I do, it's all that I know?
The Porsche 911, it's on hire,
For show.

Afterword

By Commodore Michael C Clapp, CB, Royal Navy
Commander, Falklands Amphibious Task Group, 1982

Professional divers such as Tony Groom live 'on the edge'. As Tony makes clear, this is not the life for everyone – but the rewards in friendship and excitement make up for much stress and risk. As the old naval saying goes, 'If you can't take a joke, you shouldn't have joined.' In this yarn, he shows that he found plenty to laugh about. *Diver* is largely an autobiography, but the inclusion of many letters and comments from colleagues makes it a far more wide-ranging, illuminating and sympathetic account of the life of a diver.

Tony's and my paths crossed in 1982. On 1 April, I had returned from an amphibious recce in Denmark and northern Germany oblivious to what was happening in the South Atlantic. On the following morning, along with many others, my life was dramatically changed. The Argentines had invaded South Georgia and the Falkland Islands. The signal went on to say that I was to command the Amphibious Task Group and prepare to land 3 Commando Brigade Royal Marines. A further signal followed, telling me what assets I would have to carry out this task.

Some of the ships listed were already well known to me but, immediately, I noticed there were no minesweepers or minehunters included. I telephoned the Fleet Mine-Countermeasures Officer on Admiral Fieldhouse's, my Commander-in-Chief's, staff, and asked for this to be rectified. He replied that there was no intention of sending me such ships. They would not be needed and they would be too slow. Anyhow, minesweeping would give away the chosen landing site and be unhelpful. I tried, as calmly as my rising anger allowed, to find out what he expected me to do, committed as I would be to approaching the landing site 8,000 miles away, only to find it was mined. He was adamant. The C-in-C had not suggested sending any. I wondered if the C-in-C had actually been consulted. I doubted it.

In some desperation, I asked what Mine Clearance Divers did. I had heard of them but could not recall meeting one. Their reputation as undisciplined and probably mad went before them, but in war such men can be useful. I had spent fifteen years in the Fleet Air Arm, and many of my colleagues had a similar reputation, but I would go to any war with them at my back. Men who thrive on risk and excitement are invaluable. They are rarely foolish.

About an hour later, there was a knock on my door. Lieutenant Commander Brian Dutton, the commanding officer of Fleet Clearance Diving Team 1 (FCDT1) with his Fleet Chief Petty Officer (Diver) Mick Fellows came in. They had received a phone call and wondered if they might help. At first they seemed to think there was not a lot they could do to replace mine clearance ships. As they left, Mr Fellows put his head back around the door and said, 'Leave it to me, sir.' I did. It was the best thing that I had done so far. FCDT1 joined us at Ascension about two weeks later. FCDT3, under the command of Lieutenant 'Bernie' Bruen, followed them.

These two teams rose to the challenge magnificently. If they had not removed safely some eleven unexploded bombs from the Royal Fleet Auxiliary's Landing Ships Logistic (LSLs) and from Royal Naval escorts, the campaign would have taken a very different turn. It was proving quite risky enough but, as a result of their work, not one item of 3 Commando Brigade's ammunition, fuel, food and equipment was lost to enemy action before it was landed in San Carlos Water. Furthermore, the list of the Royal Navy escorts damaged beyond repair or lost would have been far greater. All this was often, as you will read, without prior training and under very frightening conditions.

When they had a rare spare moment, the two teams also

helped with the wounded and the prisoners of war. The debt owed to these men was recognised in the number of awards given to them. Man for man their number of awards exceeded any other unit's 'down south'. Quite extraordinarily, this has had scant recognition since the conflict was over. The Stanley War Memorial did not list them, and the first edition of the Official History made no mention of them. Thankfully, both omissions have been rectified in the past year.

Tony Groom's story will be recognised by the other divers in those alarming days in San Carlos Water. This tale fills a massive gap and is long overdue. I salute them all. But his story does not stop there. Tony has also given us a remarkable insight into the lives and courage of many civilian divers, based on his experience since he retired from the Royal Navy.

AMPHIBIOUS ASSAULT
Manoeuvre from the sea
From Gallipoli to the Gulf – a definitive analysis

Edited by TRISTAN LOVERING MBE

In this uniquely authoritative study, leading international military and academic experts analyse 37 amphibious operations, from the 'how not to do it' catastrophe of Gallipoli in 1915 to the Al Faw landings in Iraq in 2003. In between, there are chapters on the Second World War in Europe, North Africa, the Indian Ocean and the Pacific; and on Korea, Suez, Vietnam, the Falklands and the first Gulf War. British, American, German, Japanese and Soviet operations are all included. With over 500 pages of text,  300 photographs and 95 maps, this definitive analysis of amphibious warfare in the twentieth century and beyond will be invaluable to anyone with an interest in military history, as well as to those who, as military practitioners or historians, study it professionally.

'Simply the best book on the subject'
> Dr Eric Grove, Salford University

'An indispensable "lessons learned" portfolio ... a key source document ... for all informed students of twentieth century maritime warfare'
> Lawrence Phillips, *The Royal Navy Day by Day*

'How I wish it had been available and read by many before 1982!'
> Commodore Michael Clapp CB RN,
> Commander Amphibious Task Group Falklands

'Outstanding'
> Professor George W Baer, *US Naval War College, Monterey*

'... required reading for all politicians who feel the urge to launch amphibious forces against substantial enemies'
> Dr Philip Towle, Centre for International Studies, University of Cambridge

With a foreword by CORRELLI BARNETT

Royalties from this book will go to the Royal Marines 1939 War Fund, Charity No. 248733

Illustrated · ISBN 978-0-9550243-5-1 pbk
ISBN 978-0-9550243-6-8 pbk with slip case   £45.00 + £4.95 p&p

Discounts available on multiple orders

SKELETONS FOR SADNESS

A novel

EWEN SOUTHBY-TAILYOUR

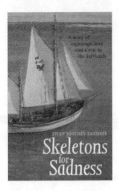

It is September 1980. Edward Casement, sailing with his crew towards Cape Horn and the Pacific in his ketch *Nomad*, calls in at the Falklands. Things do not go according to plan, and, having lost his crew, he ends up spending longer in the islands than he had intended, sailing on charter for the Governor in the company of an English nurse. In an atmosphere of growing intrigue, not all is as it seems, and then comes the Argentine invasion. A story of love, espionage, a yacht, and a war in the South Atlantic..

Illustrated • ISBN 978-1-906266-02-8 pbk   £9.95 + £1.05 p&p

SALVAGE – A personal odyssey

CAPTAIN IAN TEW

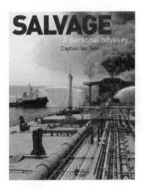

'No cure, no pay' is the rule. If a salvor is defeated by the elements, he receives nothing. Salvage is not a business for the faint-hearted. Ian Tew joined Selco of Singapore in 1974. As tug captain and salvage master, he roamed the world, from the coast of Cornwall to the Southern Ocean, from the Gulf of Suez to the South China Sea. Here he tells of the challenges of ten tough years – a barge adrift in a hurricane – a freighter aground on a reef – a tanker hit by a missile in the Gulf. This gripping account of drama at sea is a tribute to the seamanship, courage and resourcefulness of the salvor.

'The often heroic work, sterling seamanship and amazing professionalism of salvage vessel crews often goes unnoticed and unsung by the wider world ... a vivid and insightful account ...'

Andrew Linington, Head of Communications, Nautilus UK

Illustrated
ISBN 978-0-9550243-9-9 pbk   £19.95 + £1.05 p&p
ISBN 978-1-906266-00-4 hbk, signed limited edition   £24.95 + £1.05 p&p

SEAFARER BOOKS
Storytellers of the sea

www.seafarerbooks.com